Further Education or training?

Routledge Education Books

Advisory editor: John Eggleston
Professor of Education
University of Keele

Further Education or training?

A case study in the theory and practice of day-release education

Denis Gleeson and George Mardle
*Lecturers in Education, Department of
Education, University of Keele*

with the assistance of John McCourt
*Postgraduate Research Student, Department of
Education, University of Keele*

Routledge & Kegan Paul
London, Boston and Henley

First published in 1980
by Routledge & Kegan Paul Ltd
39 Store Street, London WC1E 7DD,
9 Park Street, Boston, Mass. 02108, USA and
Broadway House, Newtown Road,
Henley-on-Thames, Oxon RG9 1EN
Set in IBM Press Roman 10 on 11pt by
Hope Services
Abingdon, Oxon
and printed in Great Britain by
Redwood Burn Ltd
Trowbridge & Esher

British Library Cataloguing in Publication Data

Gleeson, David

Further Education or training? – (Routledge
education books).
1. Vocational education – Great Britain –
Case studies
2. Industry and education – Great Britain –
Case studies
I Title   II. Mardle, George   III. McCourt, John
374   LC1047.G7   79 41591

ISBN 0 7100 0447 8

Contents

Preface

This exploratory study seeks to understand the relationship between a college of further education and its local industrial environment. It examines the often contradictory relations which exist between the competing interests of 'education', 'training' and 'work', and which are commonly associated with the vocational preparation of craft apprentices.

Chapter 1 commences with an overview of developments within the FE sector, and seeks to introduce the reader to those features of the theory and practice of FE which constitute the background to our study, and against which our research 'problem' is located. Chapter 2 provides an ethnographic account of the history and development of Western College, and explores the character of the institution with reference to its staff, students and links with local industry. Chapter 3 takes the organisational analysis of Western College further. It examines the degree to which both the formal and the informal processes of decision-making within the college are influenced by the 'needs', present and future, of the industrial environment.

The link between industry and FE constitutes an important aspect of our study, and chapters 4 and 5 seek to understand the workings of two separate college departments in the light of that connection. Chapter 4 looks in depth at the Department of Mining, and attempts to understand both the formal and informal links between that Department and its corresponding industry. In particular, it examines the degree to which those 'links' influence the internal workings of the Department, and shape the 'identities' of both staff and students. In contrast, chapter 5 examines the ambiguous position of the Department of Liberal Studies at Western as a non-vocational Department within a college of FE geared to the technical preparation of apprentice students. In particular, it examines how Liberal Studies is perceived by technical personnel, and how the Department negotiates its position within the technical curriculum. The contrast between the Departments of Mining and Liberal Studies provides an interesting insight into the uneasy co-existence between the conflicting interests of 'Education' and 'Training' within the sphere of FE.

Chapter 6 focuses more specifically upon the issue of the 'fit' between college and industry. It analyses both the connections and disconnections which characterise the relationship, and proffers a particular theory of the relationship between FE and the social structure. Chapter 7 is intended to provide the reader with an account of our methodology and actions during the course of our fieldwork (September 1975 – summer 1977). Finally, some attempt is made to provide an alternative account of the conditions in which FE might be carried out.

It should be stated at the outset that our purpose in focusing upon one specific college of FE is twofold. First, it seems to us that the historic links between Western and a major industry, engineering, renders it 'a suitable case' through which to examine the relationship between 'education', 'training' and 'work'. And second, as a corollary to our first point, Western is representative of a relatively homogeneous institution through which to examine the processes of 'teaching' and 'learning' which constitute day-release education.

Acknowledgments

This study owes much to those employers, lecturers and apprentices who gave us their support and encouragement in 'the field'. We should like to thank them for allowing us to quote from their statements in the following pages. Thanks are also due to our University of Keele colleagues, John Eggleston, Geoff Powell, Phil Robinson and Iolo Roberts for their constructive criticisms of earlier drafts of this work. We are particularly indebted to Edwina Gleeson for her intelligent work on the manuscript and her editorial skills in ironing out innumerable stylistic problems. Finally, thanks go to Kathleen McKeown and Mary McBratney for typing the manuscript.

Interviewer: Can you tell me a bit about David Watson . . . how he's getting on at work . . .?
Employer: Who?
Interviewer: David Watson . . . he works for you . . . he's one of your apprentices. . . .
Employer: Can't say as I know him . . . an apprentice you say . . . name's familiar. . . .
Employer: (*into intercom to secretary*) Watson . . . David . . . he's an apprentice . . . what have we got on him . . .?
Secretary: He's on his third year . . . he's not in Wednesdays. . . .
Employer: Not in Wednesdays . . . Why's that . . .?
Secretary: He's on day release at 'Western', sir. . . .
Employer: I think I know him now . . . a ginger lad . . . I wondered where the little bugger got to on Wednesdays.

(Excerpt from an interview with the owner of a garage complex)

Chapter 1

Background to the study

Introduction

This study represents an attempt to understand what it is like for craft apprentices and their teachers to learn and teach within the FE sector. However, any empirical study of this nature must inevitably be assessed in terms of its ability to *generalise* from the *particular*, so that although we look primarily at the day-to-day workings of one particular college, our major objective is to reach a wider understanding of those issues which comprise the complex relationship between FE and the world of work.

Before proceeding to the empirical focus of this study, however, it would seem necessary to preface our investigations by some remarks of an introductory nature. Thus in this chapter we shall be concerned to outline three distinct but interrelated areas, which together constitute the background to our research interests. The first involves a brief overview of recent public commentary which has brought the sensitive relationship between education and employment to the forefront of public interest. In particular, we shall examine a number of arguments drawn from the 'human capital' approach, which stresses the need for planned investment in education as a prerequisite of economic progress. The second involves a brief exploration of what is *meant* by 'training' and what is *meant* by 'education' in this context. We shall argue that although those terms are fully explicated at the policy level, there exists considerable confusion over their practical application, which has serious consequences not only for the curriculum, but for the shape of developments within FE in general.

Our third area of interest concerns the extent to which developments in FE over recent years have corresponded to those principles of planned investment in education mentioned above. Moreover, since the education of craft apprentices represents only one dimension of FE practice, that brief overview of developments within the FE sector also serves to provide the reader with some perspective upon the status of apprentice-students within existing arrangements.

Investment and return

In recent years politicians, industrialists and educationalists have ex-pressed considerable anxiety about the failure of Britain's educational system to produce an adequately trained supply of technical personnel. In a proliferation of official exhortations, white, green and yellow, much has been said about the economic success of Britain's European partners who, it is held, have made economic progress because of their systematic investment in the training of craftsmen, technicians and technologists.

More recently James Callaghan, in his controversial Ruskin Speech (1976), repeated the view that insufficient emphasis had been placed upon science in schools and upon applied technological subjects.[1] In addition, he advocated a closer correspondence between educational objectives and the nation's manpower requirements. The argument runs that because the taxpayer pays for and invests in education, a degree of synchronisation between the educational system and the occupational structure is required, so that both the needs of the individual and of wider society might be met. Indeed, the recent 'Great Education Debate' centred largely upon that 'degree' of synchronisation. Should we, for example, continue to allow pupils complete freedom regarding occupational choice, since that free choice more often that not leads them into the arts, social sciences, humanities or dole queue? Or should we influence and guide their choice into areas where national demand is greatest? In support of the latter argument, it is suggested that there exists at present an alarming lack of correspondence between the processes of schooling and industry, and it is largely for this reason that the 'Great Debate' and subsequent curricular developments have tended to concentrate primarily upon the issues of supply and demand.

An important consquence of this overriding concern has been a con-certed attack upon schools and colleges which have been criticised for their over-emphasis upon academic knowledge at the expense of crucial practical and technical skills. In an otherwise free market, it has been suggested that the process of schooling actually interferes with the more nationally desirable occupational choices pupils might otherwise make.[2] Consequently there has been a call for more realistic counselling of school children and young workers, so that they might be made aware of the opportunities and choices available in FE and skilled manual work. Indeed, despite fundamental changes in the economic structure

2

which have rendered unemployment and the lack of occupational choice one of Britain's most serious social problems, politicians and industrialists alike remain confident that, in the long run, such problems may be overcome by extending the provision of Technical and Further Education.

Such optimism about the expected returns on planned investment in technical education reached a climax in the early 1960s with the 'White Heat of Technology' debate (Crosland, 1956, 1974; Benn, 1974). The concern then as now centred upon the sensitive relationship between technical education and economic progress. However today, despite recent pessimism about the failure of mass-education in general to influence social change (Jencks, 1972; Robinson, 1977; Tyler, 1977), faith in the power of scientific and applied technical education remains largely unshaken. Thus with recurring predictability government reports, research papers and academic texts have re-emphasised the functional necessity of synchronising the relations between FE, technical training and the occupational structure (Zuckerman, 1956; Carr, 1957; Henniker Heaton, 1964; Venables, 1967; Bristow, 1976).

In the 1950s and 1960s the articulation of such views could be found in the writings of sociologists and economists alike (Venables *et al.*, 1955; Cotgrove, 1958; Halsey *et al.*, 1960; Musgrave, 1967; Vaizey, 1967; Vaizey and Sheehan, 1968) whose ideas as in the case of Crowther (1959) influenced the wider areas of policy and legislation:

> Thousands of young people every year find, in Further Education, a path to the development of their individual personalities and to the realisation of their ambitions. If it did not exist, both they and the country would be spiritually and materially poorer . . . the association of work and study is, for many, a valuable educational method which can still produce results where nothing else could (Crowther Report, 1959).

For those pressing for the reform and extension of FE, the combined interests of the individual and society provided an excellent lever upon which to base their demand for change (Venables, 1967, 1974; Robinson, 1968, Cantor and Roberts, 1974; Bristow, 1976). It was argued that investment in technical education would benefit both; the young worker would receive his training, 'ticket' and just remuneration, while the employer would receive the necessary supply of trained labour; both 'returns' thus contributing to the general pool of national 'good'. Consequently, in the early 1960s, much criticism was expressed about blockages which prevented the extension of technical education to the majority of 16 to 19-year-olds. Research and policy documents, moreover, pointed to the need for reforms which might avoid the high levels of wastage in FE (Crowther, 1959; Lipshitz, 1972), as well as ensure a

3

more predictable supply of technically trained personnel (Bratchell, 1968; Haslegrave, 1969).

We shall argue, however, that the rationality which lies behind such common-sense thinking has its origins in broader theoretical assumptions within the 'human capital' approach (Cosin, 1972; Blaug, 1976; Westoby, 1974; Hussain, 1977). We shall return to a deeper discussion of the 'human capital' perspective in chapter 6, but for the moment it is enough to say that two interrelated assumptions govern such an approach to educational 'investment'. The first relates to a widespread belief that skill requirements in industrial societies are increasing in complexity due to technological change. From such a viewpoint, the need for unskilled labour declines as a corresponding demand for a more expert labour force increases. Thus education, within this technical-functional analysis (Collins, 1977), must not only furnish the economy with more highly trained manpower, but must also expand to meet the needs of an ever-increasing student population spending longer and longer periods at school or in FE (Dore, 1976; Karabel and Halsey, 1977). The second interrelated assumption which governs the Human Capital approach concerns certain liberal democratic and merito-cratic ideals which equate the pursuit of economic advancement with that of equality of opportunity, thereby acting as a legitimation of greater investment in education (Vaizey, 1967, 1975; Jencks, 1972; Tyler, 1977; Young and Whitty, 1977). In other words, it is argued that not only society in general, but also each individual, will benefit from planned investment in education, so that both public and personal interests are assumed to be synonymous (Williams, 1957; Crowther, 1959). We shall argue that this is not necessarily the case.

In our view, the Human Capital perspective has played an influential part in the continuing debate over the past twenty-five years on the aims and objectives of both education in general and FE in particular. What is not so clear, however, is the extent to which actual develop-ments within the FE sector have corresponded to the logic of that approach. Indeed, it is possible that such arguments have merely acted to legitimate *existing* forms of practice. We shall attempt to address that problem in our overview of recent developments within the FE sector, but what we wish to argue for the moment is that in the writings of Crowther (1959), Crosland (1956, 1974), Benn (1974) and Callaghan (1976), the concern for investment in technical education has consti-tuted a major political issue, and one repeatedly associated with econ-omic recovery. The call now, as then, is for an educational system able to respond to the changing needs of an advanced technology.

There exist, however, two alternative but interrelated critiques of the Human Capital approach. The first suggests that new technology fails to increase the range and level of skills available in the economy, and through the introduction of mechanised and automated plant, erodes industrial craft skills, thereby increasing the amount of semi-skilled and unskilled work available. We would argue, moreover, that although such work often remains officially designated 'skilled' by managements and unions alike, it has become, in reality, de-skilled (Liepmann, 1960; Braverman, 1974). One consequence of this process is *credentialism*, an inflationary effect set in motion by the vast upgrading of skills and qualifications in society which bear little actual relation to the work performed (Berg, 1973; Dore, 1976). The second viewpoint suggests that the pursuit of synchronisation between the educational system and the occupational structure is a utopian myth, which largely ignores the ways in which different forms of capital (economic, social and cultural) set limits on the types of employment available in the economy (Hussain, 1977, Bourdieu and Boltanski, 1978; Bourdieu, 1971). This viewpoint stresses the *ideological* dimension through which technical education is seen to reinforce existing inequalities within the occupational structure (Gorz, 1977; Althusser, 1971). Here, in contrast with its affectual 'function', education at the cognitive level is seen to be a relatively weak mechanism in the exchange relationship between education and jobs (Jencks, 1971; Bane and Jencks, 1977; Bowles and Gintis, 1976; Bourdieu, 1971; Tyler, 1977). While superficially schools or colleges may appear to be both continuous and heterogeneous in their development, they tend toward homogeneity in the totality of their practice (Holly, 1977). At one level, therefore, education is seen to reproduce the cognitive skills necessary to maintain the means of production, and at another, to sustain the affectual skills which underpin the social relations of production (Thompson, 1967; Althusser, 1971; Bourdieu, 1971).

Thus, both viewpoints emphasise the 'function' of control in education, whereby current developments are seen to obscure rather than clarify the connections between training, qualifications and jobs (Wilensky, 1964). We return to this issue in chapter 6 where we argue that the acquisition of the apprenticeship 'ticket' may not necessarily be associated with acquiring the practical skills of the trade.

To summarise, we have suggested so far that it is possible to identify two broadly contrasting views concerning the synchronisation between education and employment. On the one hand, there are those who argue for a closer relationship between technical education and the economy, wherein FE is seen to respond more coherently to societal needs and demands. On the other, there are those who argue that there exists too close a 'fit' already, so that existing institutional relations exert too tight a control on the individual in his day-to-day affairs. In the section which follows, we shall examine how such contrasting viewpoints have influenced the debate about the relationship between education and training.

FE and training

In view, then, of the ambiguity which surrounds the debate about the 'fit' between technical education and jobs, it seems surprising that we know little, at the empirical level, about the processes through which technical identities are fashioned in the sphere of FE, or what characterises the relationship between FE and industry. Indeed, we know even less about the sociological consequences for those who have 'chosen' craft work, and continued their studies through the alternative route of non-advanced FE.[3] To what extent, for example, does FE provide such students with a challenging and meaningful experience, through which they may make their way in the world (Crowther, 1959)? Or, to what extent does FE simply reinforce existing industrial processes, by merely channelling students into dead-end occupations (Brook, 1971; Gorringe, 1977)?

The discussion which surrounds such questions is inevitably controversial since much depends on how one defines the purpose of FE. Ostensibly, FE is not concerned with the more specific objectives of 'training', 'induction' or 'channelling'. Indeed, such objectives come under the responsibility of quite separate dimensions of political control, namely the Department of Employment (DEP) which, through its major agent the Manpower Services Commission (MSC), funds and controls training programmes carried out within government training schools, training centres and skill centres. FE, therefore, constitutes a separate area of technical provision, being administered and controlled by the Department of Education and Science (DES), and the local authorities. It would seem to us, however, that this separate control of 'education' and 'training' has not only led to much confusion about the use of such terms, but has also resulted in rather simplistic definitions of their meaning.[4] 'Training', for example, has come to be defined as a job-specific activity, concerned mainly with the transmission and acquisition of applied skills. FE, on the other hand, is seen to relate to those wider theoretical processes which underpin the broad application of skills. In other words, it is not necessarily tied to job objectives (Cantor and Roberts, 1974). However, these distinctions, which the Central Training Council (1966) and the Department of Employment (1972) perceives as 'differences of approach', would seem to bear little relation to what happens in practice (Ryrie and Weir, 1978). The assumption that 'education' is not 'training' and 'training' is not 'education' is clearly absurd (NATFHE, 1977; Stanton, 1978). Indeed, there is strong evidence to suggest that not only are such distinctions artificial (Venables, 1974; Cantor and Roberts, 1974), but also that considerable overlap exists between the work carried out within FE colleges and that carried out within training and skill centres (Hunter and Robertson,

1969; Singer and Macdonald, 1970; Venables, 1974; Kaneti-Barry, 1974).

In view, therefore, of the ambiguity which surrounds the terms 'education' and 'training', it would seem important to understand how their 'interests' become integrated within FE practice. In this study we seek to explore the consequences for practice of the ambiguity between the terms 'education' and 'training' by examining what it is like for craft apprentices and their teachers to learn and teach within FE. In particular, we examine the complex pattern of social relations which exists between young workers, college and industry. By focusing upon the organisational ethos of one particular college, we attempt to assess its influence upon the attitudes of apprentices towards both work and study. Thus we take a critical but constructive look at the ways in which apprentices, employers and teachers perceive the functions of FE, and at how their differing interpretations may shed light upon the ambiguous nature of practice within that area. One of our major concerns, however, is to challenge the view that apprentice-students represent no more than passive commodities processed by means of FE to meet the changing needs of the economic infrastructure. In addition, we seek to challenge the view that the FE system itself is solely defined by external forces beyond its influence or control (Tipton, 1973). We consider the anomaly that while the character of college itself may mirror the imperatives of local industry (particularly in its curriculum, organisation and pedagogical relations), the actual social construction of vocational knowledge is 'negotiated' rather than 'determined' by the *interaction* of forces operating between college and industry.[5]

We shall attempt to explain how FE has assisted the ideological dominance of industrial structures by presenting their modes of practice as 'natural' through the supposedly interlocking imperatives 'education', 'training' and the world of 'work'. A central feature of our analysis suggests that 'education' and 'training' are not necessarily guided by distinct ideologies, but constitute separate aspects of the *same* mechanism of control. In this respect Further Education may be seen to function by translating industrial imperatives into professional rhetoric. Thus the term FE becomes a misnomer which acts to legitimise the 'training' process through which young workers are instructed in the cognitive and affectual skills deemed appropriate to their position within the industrial hierarchy. We will suggest that not only does this process rationalise the *rites de passage* associated with the acquisition of the apprenticeship 'ticket', but that it also reconciles young workers to the realities of industrial life, including deferred gratification.

Before proceeding further it would seem important to point out that our study of craft apprentices in FE offers an account of a highly select and sponsored group within the British educational system. Contrary to

7

popular belief, the number of such students in FE constitutes a privileged minority of the 16–19 age group, of which total at least 53 per cent receive no further education at all. Indeed, the students in this study have emerged successfully from a highly competitive employment market, and are seen as the chosen few for whom skilled work and training is deemed feasible. They represent part of that small minority who achieve minimal qualifications at school and who have been able to turn those to advantage by gaining access to skilled work, FE and training. Yet, paradoxically, their status within FE not only remains marginal but continues to decline. Indeed, as we shall point out later, the craft lad is often perceived as 'troublesome' by his teachers, a type of student difficult to motivate and teach. Some perspective may be gained upon the status of craft apprentices by our examination in the section which follows of the changes which have recently taken place in FE in general.

Developments in FE

Innumerable problems, of course, arise in attempting to generalise from the particular about a system which like Topsy 'just growed' (Cantor and Roberts, 1974). Indeed, as we have observed so far, the nature of FE provision is extremely difficult to define. Its origins are numerous, and its organisation takes on various forms between different regional boundaries. The development of FE has not only been haphazard, but also difficult to pin down; the terms traditionally associated with it – 'craft', 'technician' and 'technological' – have come to possess various connotations at different times and in different places (Bristow, 1976). Moreover, a further complication arises due to the confusion of such terms with others drawn from tertiary education, since the processes such generalised terms seek to describe represent similar offshoots from the same historical stem (Erben, 1977).

What is confusing about the term FE is that it now encompasses most forms of educational provision, with the exception of schools and universities. However, under the umbrella concept of FE it is possible to discern two distinct sub-sectors of provision: the 'advanced' and the 'non-advanced' (DES, 1978). The advanced sector includes full or part-time provision in polytechnics or designated FE colleges which offer higher diploma, degree or degree-equivalent courses. The non-advanced sector includes full- or part-time provision in the colleges which offer general and vocational education up to the standard of GCE 'A' Level or its equivalent.[6] Yet, despite the changing status of Polytechnic and Teacher Education within the broad scope of FE, they share more in common with Higher Education. The paradox is that in practice the term FE has come to denote the nebulous but gaping middle ground which exists between school and Higher Education. Therefore, although the term may officially embrace Polytechnic and Teacher Education, it does so in name only. It is perhaps for such reasons that the provision for the 16–19 age-group has come to be referred to as the 'Cinderella' area of the educational system. Thus, any definitive attempt to explain the nature of FE becomes a highly problematic exercise. In addition, this issue is complicated further because, at the institutional level, one FE college is not necessarily like any other: its students, staff, curricula, administration, finance and so forth are dependent upon a variety of regional factors, not least of all those of local industry and employment. Hence Bristow (1976) remarks:

> It is, however, worth bearing in mind that Further Education is not entirely technical education, nor are further education colleges only 'technical' colleges. Further Education embraces colleges, schools and departments of art as well as the technical and technological aspects of education. It may also include diverse aspects of education and training such as nursery, training centres, sea training schools and agricultural colleges.

Unlike the growth of mass schooling, FE has taken a voluntaristic and individualistic path (Peters, 1967), its survival depending very much upon the patronage of industry and upon the ability of individual colleges to attract greater student numbers (Bratchell, 1968). Traditionally, the most persistent argument against comprehensive legislation on the question of FE is that FE should be the responsibility of employers, unions and workers. Indeed, it is widely held today that those seeking betterment, having failed to benefit from eleven years of compulsory schooling, should do so in their own time and with their own resources. In the past few decades, however, as technological processes have changed, and as the demand for skilled personnel has outgrown the 'training on the job' system, it has become increasingly apparent that there is a need for a more systematic form of technical education. Thus, in recent years, successive governments have attempted to encourage employers, through processes of inducement rather than legislation (grants, subsidies, tax relief etc.), to release for training a select and highly skilled section of young workers. While schools, therefore, have gradually moved away from a system of 'payment by results', the FE sector has come to inherit the legacy of that voluntaristic tradition – 'payment by numbers'. As a result, the emerging pattern of FE provision (size of college, establishment, resources, level of work and so on) has traditionally come to depend upon a points system[7] firmly anchored to the production forecasts of local industry. Consequently, the development of those forms of provision which fall within the compass of FE have until recently tended to be both parochial and chauvinistic, focusing mainly upon the technical training of young workers.

Although initially established to deal with the part-time and day-release training of young workers, the FE sector has changed considerably in the past decade to facilitate the incorporation of more diversified groups of students. While much of the bread and butter work of the college is still largely concerned with the vocational education of craft apprentices, the major growth has occurred in the areas of professional courses, GCE, full-time and in-service training, and, more recently, in the area of short-term courses for the unemployed. The rapid growth of the FE system, particularly in the 1960s, owed much to the changing nature of the post-war occupation structure, together with its expansion of the tertiary sector and subsequent decline in traditional nineteenth-century-based industries. The dual problems of de-skilling and growing unemployment posed a threat to the survival of many colleges which consequently sought new avenues of expansion. Thus, with the recognition of an increasing demand for FE coming from a growing 16–19 population within the white-collar sector, many colleges adapted in order to meet the demands of a new market (Tipton, 1973).

Indeed, the forces which impelled the expansion of FE in the 1960s would seem to correspond far more closely to shifts in the demographic and occupational structures than to the imperatives of current theories and policies directed towards the needs of an expanding economy. The recognition of a growing 16–19 population and the possibility of a wider tertiary sector, together with the entrepreneurial character of the colleges themselves, resulted in the development of new courses designed to pre-empt the new demand. Indeed, the diversification of the FE sector in the 1960s was caused more by a concern with survival than with the economic development of the nation. As a result, moreover, the colleges became less tied to the fortunes of local industry. Thus, while changes in the age and occupational structures did little to alter the points system within the colleges, they allowed them to trade on student numbers, a form of negotiation not previously available.

It is not perhaps surprising that many colleges welcomed the new possibilities afforded by such diversification, a term used by some to denote the extension of educational opportunities. Moreover, other writers interpreted such expansion as a crucial forerunner of the comprehensivisation of technical education. Hence Bristow (1976), echoing the sentiments of Peters (1967), Bratchell (1968), Crosland (1956 and 1974), Cantor and Roberts (1974), Venables (1967 and 1974) and so on, argues that FE offers a second chance or alternative route of social mobility which might enable young workers to find their way (Crowther, 1959) in the world:

For not only do we offer a second way, we also offer a second chance. It is not given to many of us in this life to wipe the slate clean and make a fresh start. Yet this is what the colleges offer to these young adults who have missed their footing or lost their sense of direction. Although we need to ensure students are suitably qualified to enter a course, once they are accepted that is it. It is up to them now (Bristow, 1976).

We would argue, however, that the terms equating economic growth, social justice and educational expansion ultimately came to represent little more than a convenient ideological icing for the expanding FE cake. In other words, we would suggest that despite considerable diversification of the FE sector in the past decade, its direction has been a highly pragmatic, selective and elitist one, which indicates little serious concern with investment in talent, not to mention the quest of social justice for the majority of 16 to 19-year-olds. It would seem to us that the ideological justification of the expansion of the FE sector, based as it was upon meritocratic conceptions of education, served ultimately to disguise the development of high-status 'academic' curricula at the upper end of the FE system. Thus, although some few reforms have percolated downwards, no comprehensive FE policy has been filtered off which might address Crowther's (1959) original concern for the mass of 16 to 19-year-olds who represent the 'wastage of the richest vein of untapped resources'.

Alternative views, however, have been expressed concerning the diversification of FE in the 1960s. It has been suggested that the restrictions of administrative, regional and employment conditions render the possibility of FE posing an alternative route more an illusion than reality. Hence Lee (1975) argues that unemployment alone

has hit hard at the heart of the voluntary system of part-time study *in employment*. It has revealed the glaring defects of the present structure, especially so in the less prosperous areas of the country. . . . How far does the system challenge, or instead go along, with the present obsolescence of the skill structure in a community? Secondly, what does the college do about the problems of disadvantaged youth, whether it be through unemployment, or type of employment or discrimination against colour or sex?

Any answer to the latter question must recognise the weakness of the colleges in the area of the disadvantaged. The problem remains, however, that FE has inherited the legacy of providing education to those already *in* employment. In addition, the archaic administrative structures of FE are ones which have been aptly described as 'very resistant to new ideas, and especially to ones challenging the dominance of the industrial viewpoint' (Lee 1975). Perhaps the most telling characterisation of the patchy path by which the diversification of FE has taken place concerns the pernicious connection between student numbers, level of work, and the points system.[7] As Tipton (1973) argues, the points system alone places the colleges in a perpetual state of uneasy innovation, since they are constantly called upon to re-define their courses for the purpose of attracting new customers. Consequently, it is not difficult to understand the motives underlying the diversification of the 1960s which led to the shelving of many low-level courses. Neither is it surprising that such external constraints acted to heighten competition between colleges, which led to the creation of more higher-status courses, and which in turn rendered the FE system less open and comprehensive than might at first appear.

Indeed, not only have many colleges shelved a large number of low-status courses, but they have also become even more reluctant to provide 'general education', either of a non-vocational or vocational nature, to non-examinees. This latter point has gained increasing significance in the past few years because of adverse changes in the employment market which have left many young workers, some with serious learning difficulties, unemployed or unemployable (Watts, 1978). It is this category of young people, which totals a rising 53 per cent of the 16–19 age-group, which receives next to no further education at all, and which has been repeatedly ignored by the expansionist movements of the 1960s and early 1970s. What would seem surprising is that very little is known about this sizeable group who have discontinued education altogether, except for the fact that at the time of writing a rising 500,000 of them are unemployed or unemployable. Of those presently employed, it is likely that a large number carry out unskilled or semi-skilled work where the opportunities for training or day-release are minimal. The figures in Table 1 indicate the problem to which we refer, and show two distinct groups within the 16–19 age bracket:[8]

1 those who have continued full- or part-time or evening education (of which a high proportion are following courses in school or FE). Here the wastage rates are very high;
2 those who have discontinued education completely (of whom an increasing proportion are unemployed or unemployable).

It would seem to us that such statistics deny the claim that FE provides a second chance for the mass working-class youth on access criteria alone. Indeed, the recent statistical depiction of 'who gets what' from the system has led some writers to reflect more critically upon the need to press for comprehensive legislation concerning the further education of all 16 to 19-year-olds (Warnock, 1978; Roberts, 1977; Mansell, 1977; NATFHE, 1977). It is interesting, therefore, that recent

TABLE 1

Sector	16–19s size of cohort	Course pattern		
Under FE regulations		Left school: in or seeking employment	53%	Without access to FE
	109,000 38% male 62% female	Evening only	10%	
	268,000 79% male 21% female	Part-time or block release	14%	29%
	191,000 44% male 56% female	Full-time in FE	5%	
Under school regulations	357,000	Full-time in school	18%	

youth employment figures have once again stimulated discussion about FE policy. However, the plight of the 16–19 age-group did not reach the forefront of the Great Education Debate (1977) and while in office the Labour Party did not act upon its manifesto promise to make FE a right for all. Despite the absence of comprehensive legislation, the DES has remained slow in responding positively to the challenge presented in the non-advanced sector, preferring to monitor the situation through its recently conceived Further Education Curriculum Review Unit (1976-7). Ironically, it has been the DEP, through its wide ranging responsibility for training and its flexible control of funds, that has intervened to finance new initiatives for the young unemployed. Indeed, through its principal agent, the Manpower Services Commission, the DEP has encroached upon DES territory by funding a wide range of FE related courses. The impact of the Holland Report (1977), a feasibility study of schemes for the young unemployed, has therefore been considerable, not least of all because it established principles upon which the MSC might finance new developments. Not only have the DEP and the MSC stolen initiative in this way from the DES by implementing innovations in FE, they have also brought to the forefront of discussion the paradox of competition between two agents of state control. Once again, the dichotomy between the interests of training and education

13

would seem important. Indeed, the injection of MSC funds into schemes specifically concerned with training has created consternation among those in FE who question the narrow conditions of sponsorship and their apparent disregard for wider educational objectives. On the other hand, while the Holland Report (1977) does claim to support the interests of both education and training, its working definition of the former is clearly bound to the vocational aspects of *communications*, namely the three Rs which have traditionally formed an integral part of training programmes. Despite this, the report insists that vocational courses should combine both elements, in the interests of the individual and society:

> During the course of 1976 over 800,000 young people between the ages of 16 and 18 registered as unemployed with either the Careers Services or the Employment Service Agency, and perhaps as many as 80,000 more experienced a spell of unemployment but did not register. . . . Behind the figures lie hardship and waste.[9] These young people are at a crucial stage of their development. . . . We hope that the programme we propose can provide as many opportunities as are likely to be needed. . . . It thus aims to demonstrate by deeds rather than words that society cares about them and through them, about its own future. Such a programme is not cheap, but, bearing in mind the costs of unemployment to society, it is very much cheaper than might at first be supposed. . . . Since resources are inevitably limited, society is faced with difficult choices. In such a situation we have little doubt than an investment in helping young people to acquire relevant skills and knowledge, abilities and attitudes will yield handsome returns and should rank high in the country's priorities (Holland Report, 1977).

It would seem to us that once again such language seeks to reconcile a number of conflicting and indeed disparate interests. As usual, the aims of education are confused with those of training and presented as meeting the needs, both personal and public, of the individual and society. Moreover, it is assumed that no evidence is necessary to justify this time-weary, and, in our view, mistaken equation. Furthermore, what is even more discouraging, as Roberts (1977) indicates, is the absence of any thorough-going examination of all the curricular implications involved. In particular, what should count as appropriate curricula for the unemployed or unemployable young worker (Watts, 1978), and, more importantly, what should constitute our overall objectives for the 16–19 age group as a whole (Dean and Choppin, 1977)?

It would be only too easy to point an accusing finger at the DEP and the MSC as the forces of intervention which have prevented governments, local authorities and indeed colleges themselves from adjusting the imbalance between education and training. However, nothing would be further from the case, particularly in view of the notable absence of any comprehensive policy for the 16-19s in general and the unemployed in particular. Indeed, it is not surprising that we may identify a growing gulf within FE between two distinct vocational strands: 'training' which is increasingly associated with low status students: craft apprentices, blacks, illiterates, the unemployed and so forth, and 'education' which has come to describe the courses provided for academic and higher status middle class students (Hordley and Lee, 1970).

Although our analysis so far has taken us some way from our initial concern with craft apprentices in FE, we have attempted through this brief overview of developments in FE, to provide the reader with some background against which the status of craft apprentices within existing FE arrangements may be assessed. Having indicated aspects of the ambiguity which surrounds the whole concept of FE we do not wish to dwell on questions of definition for too long, since the patchwork development of the FE area in general does not lend itself to the description of a systematic process. Neither is it within the scope of this study to provide a full historical documentation of the many and various strands of educational provision which fall within the compass of FE. Such information may be found elsewhere (Peters, 1967; Bratchell, 1968; Cantor and Roberts, 1974; Argles, 1964; Bristow, 1976; Venables, 1967, 1974).

To summarise, we have argued in this chapter that many of the contradictions which characterise the term FE are rooted in the equation of national and economic prosperity with the quest of social equality, and find expression in the subsequent confusion between what is meant by 'education' and what is meant by 'training'. Thus, it seems important at this stage to explain something more of the organisation and curriculum of FE, and in so doing to indicate the nature of its practice. The chapter which follows, therefore, contains the first part of our empirical study, in which we outline an ethnography of the history and location of Western College, and attempt to explore the complex pattern of social relations which mark the problematic relations between industry, college and the young worker.

Chapter 2

Western College: an ethnographic description

In this section, we shall be concerned to outline a brief ethnography of the subject of our study: Western College. For obvious reasons, it is not possible at this stage to attempt an all-embracing analysis of the theoretical implications of such a description. Therefore, we shall simply acquaint the reader with those features of the college in its day-to-day affairs which indicate its character and practice. For this purpose, the chapter will be divided into five interrelated parts exploring 'Historical background and development', 'The students', 'The teachers', 'Teaching relations' and 'College and industry'.

Historical background and development

The historical development of Western College may be traced to an administratively and organisationally complex foundation, drawn together from a series of disparate institutions to form one entity. Prior to its inception in 1967 as the Central College of Further Education in the west of the county, Western was among a number of city technical schools which acted as feeders to a larger, more prestigious technical college, later to achieve the status of Polytechnic. From the early twentieth century, vocational education in the area had been handled by these city technical schools, whose main departments were incorporated at the end of the 1960s into one new College of Further Education – Western.[1]

Following the expansionist wave inspired by the 1961 White Paper on technical education, the new building was erected in Barton on land acquired from the National Coal Board, and was to house the main teaching and administrative centre of the college, drawing together the diverse strands of the separate technical schools under the auspices of one institution. Originally it was intended that Western should provide

16

engineering and mining courses for the west of the area, while another new college yet to be built, Eastern, would cater for the needs of the other side. With such a strategy in mind, each department at Western anticipated ample space, good facilities and adequate resources which would eventually allow the college to rid itself of the antiquated buildings from which it originally emerged. Such expectations, however, were soon disappointed when a new Sixth Form College was built on the site of the projected Eastern College. As a result, Western was left with a far greater strain on its resources than originally intended.

Despite attempts to alleviate the pressure of demand on Western by extending the main college building, it was not possible to abandon the six antiquated annexes spread over a radius of some ten miles. Thus, increasingly many staff were forced to travel between the various buildings in order to perform their teaching duties. As a result, feelings of transience and isolation from the central core of college life intensified for those involved as their travelling commitments increased. In addition the annexes themselves, ugly monuments of some of the worst aspects of Victorian architecture, were found to be woefully inadequate in their provision of resources and comfort. Moreover, the continued use of such buildings, condemned by the authorities at the beginning of the century as unfit for human habitation or for use as 'normal' schools, reflect something of the traditional status accorded to the 'technical man'. Indeed, despite efforts in recent years to 'brighten up' the buildings with new colours, new desks, central heating and so on, the architectural legacy (high ceilings, school board classrooms, oblique windows, etc.) remains bleak and austere. Thus the accommodation of apprentices (many of them secondary school 'failures') in such drab and dreary conditions, often miles from the central college, heightens their feelings of estrangement. Such a learning environment tends to reinforce in students their self-image of academic failures, channelled inevitably into manual work, and thrown back again into the one place they had hoped to escape – school. It is an organisational problem about which most staff feel very strongly. Ian, a lecturer in Foundry Work, expresses the general consensus of opinion of those involved in the following manner:

'Both the staff and the students here feel as if they have been sent to the outposts . . . far removed from the central college. The conditions here are pretty appalling. . . . Those students come to college expecting something great . . . or at least to pick up a skill . . . and they are put in these broken down old buildings. . . . This has got to have an effect on them . . . it obviously reflects on them . . . who they are if you know what I mean. It's this constant knocking down of those craft lads . . . it can't do their confidence any good. . . . The fact that we travel between the annexes like nomads can't help either . . .

your teaching gets to be like "one night stands". . . . This can't help relationships between the staff and the students.'

The central building itself is situated in Barton, one of a cluster of towns which constitute a large and sprawling connurbation, whose principal industries include engineering, mining and ceramics. Nowhere can the image of technical education as 'the handmaiden of employment' be more patent than at Western. Indeed, the most striking feature of the college is the imminent proximity of a colliery together with its concomitant coal heap, literally only yards from the main building. An eastward glance reveals a large coal slag and pit wheel set against a background of high chimneys, factories, pylons and grey buildings.

Barton itself is a farrago of cramped terraces, blackened by the grime, pollution and bustle of one hundred and fifty years of industrial enterprise. Bristow (1976) attempts a vivid description of the popular conception of the archetypal college of FE – Slyme Green College. Slyme Green is depicted as the epitome of decay and deterioration which, Bristow asserts, is the common but misconceived image of the modern college of further education. He maintains that the archetypal conception of the FE college, as a multi-storeyed glasshouse set in a declining mid-industrial landscape, is not only an out-dated but a misleading image. We would suggest, however, that both the architectural characteristics of Western and its location, not unlike similar colleges in such areas, coincides far more closely with the 'Slyme Green' model than with any new image advanced by Bristow. Indeed, the main body of the college is in fact a multi-floored, predominantly glass edifice, whose interior projects an atmosphere of modern architectural delapidation – scuffed walls, broken door-handles and lockers, occasional smashed windows, kicked-in partitions, and so on. By and large, its internal appearance cannot be separated from the work by which it is sustained; that is, the lay-out of the classrooms, workshops, leisure areas and canteen faithfully reflect the factory conditions from which most students come.

The course work of the college is dealt with by five departments situated both in the main building and annexes: Electrical and Electronic Engineering, Mechanical and Automobile Engineering, Mining Engineering, Production and Fabrication Engineering, and General Studies. For the most part, college life is organised upon a part-time basis, there being only seven full-time courses referred to in the prospectus. There are, however, a number of courses of a block-release nature, where students perform their college commitments in three-weekly stints. Only one course, OND Mining Engineering, is organised on a sandwich basis.

Western operates in a very competitive catchment area, being closely bounded by two other local FE Colleges, a Sixth Form College, as well as a Polytechnic. Over the years, however, the college has acquired a reputation in the area for the provision of mining, engineering and production courses, which has enabled it to cast its net over a wider area. Thus, over the years, Western has acquired the characteristics of a regional college, drawing its students from both near and far. Competition with the neighbouring colleges for students has had an important bearing on the kind of work undertaken at Western. Indeed, because of the close proximity of the two local FE Colleges and the kinds of courses offered there, Western has had little option but to consolidate its long established reputation as *the* place to study craft engineering. Thus unlike many colleges in the 1960s Western did not diversify into such areas as GCE work, commerce, business studies and so on. On the contrary, the effort to ensure a secure intake of students resulted in the expansion of existing mining and engineering courses. It is a course of action best summarised by one of the heads of department:

'We've really become the specialists in Engineering despite the fact that one of the other two colleges offers courses in Engineering . . . but they've both diversified into other areas because their existing work couldn't sustain them . . . you name it they'll offer it . . . they offer a vast range of professional, GCE and in-service courses. . . . If you look at Smith College you'll now see a vast and expanding enterprise. . . . Not ten years ago it was one of the biggest and most specialised Building Colleges in the country . . . but with the recurring slumps in the Building Trade its numbers fell. . . . It had to diversify or go under. . . . To cut a long story short they are now in the exam business . . . offering any number of courses . . . the place is like a supermarket . . . its GCE department, for example, has taken on factory-like proportions . . . but it's survived. They've played the points system and escaped. . . . Our long association with craft work however . . . low status as it may be in the points system . . . has allowed us to develop steadily within our own terms of reference in engineering. . . . I think offering all these professional and GCE courses is a retrograde step . . . they call it diversification . . . but I do not feel that it offers the "ordinary" student anything . . . it doesn't offer them a skill or the principles of a general education . . . most of these places just encourage an elitist academic paper-chase . . . but nearly three quarters of the students who follow such courses do not get 5 "O" levels . . . and what percentage pass at "A" level?'

While such remarks appear critical of the direction in which expansion has proceeded elsewhere, they indicate a tacit agreement between the colleges which has ensured the continuation of their co-existence by the avoidance of course duplication. However, this agreement has placed Western in a position where it is strongly dependent upon local industry, since day-release apprentices make up the majority of its student intake. In addition, Western is located towards the bottom of the status hierarchy of local colleges, because of its provision of 'low-grade' craft courses and subservient relationship with the Polytechnic. Indeed, ten years after its foundation, such factors are still of considerable importance to the ontology of Western, which continues to transfer its ablest third- and fourth-year apprentice students to the Polytechnic through the creaming off process.

The route by which apprentice students find their way to Western in the first place, however, requires further consideration, since they represent a small percentage of 'fortunate' young workers in the area who have been able to avoid both the dole queue and the arduous, often dead-end, work associated with the two major employers. The circumstances in which young workers come to choose engineering as a form of employment is important both to our understanding of the concept 'occupational choice', and to our understanding of student attitudes towards work and college. In the section which follows, therefore, we shall pursue these issues in greater depth.

The students

For the majority of school leavers of the area, occupational choice is strongly influenced by the existence of two major industries which involve high levels of semi- and unskilled manual work. The relatively higher wages offered by those industries makes them extremely attractive to school leavers with few qualifications and little experience. The kind of work such young workers find themselves called upon to perform, however, is often dirty, arduous and generally unpleasant. Indeed, it is the latter factor which Gregory and Smyth (1971) represent as instrumental in the gradual decline of the popularity of the pottery industry. For unqualified early leavers in the area, however, occupational choice often amounts to little more than a '*choice*' between the two major employers. Nevertheless, because of the gradual disillusionment of young workers with these limited prospects, a 'privileged' few escape into the only other available industry which offers training – engineering. While not wishing to contradict the view which associates the choice of engineering with family background, we would wish to argue that the choice of such an occupation may often have little to do with the desire to become an engineer. In our experience, however, such an escapist form of social mobility for the fortunate few is not without its problems, not least of all because the decision to embark upon an engineering apprenticeship may not be based upon a *positive* choice. Indeed, such a decision would often appear to have its roots in the wish to attain some kind of security through those forms of training which are immediately available. Consequently, Western is attended by a large number of students who undertake particular courses simply because opportunities are restricted in other fields. Their commitment to the industry in which they are engaged, therefore, is often far from satisfactory. The following remarks express something of the background against which many students regard their career prospects in engineering:

Terry: I chose a career in engineering for various reasons. Mainly because I was interested in technical subjects at school and also because of my parents' persuasion. This was not so much a persuasion as a discouragement from taking a job in casting. I was discouraged from this because of the fatigue which it causes when you are older and also because prospects of promotion are not so easy to come by as it is not a skilled job.

Gerry: Like him I liked technical subjects at school . . . and I suppose I was quite handy at making things. It seems only natural to try and get into engineering since there aren't too many openings in the other industries. . . . At school I was told I could train to become an engineer in the Mines . . . but my dad works in the pit. . . . I didn't fancy it. . . . Really I'd like to have worked on aircraft . . . but anyway the Careers bloke sorted this job out for me, so I went along. . . .

Peter: The only reason why I took my present job is that it was the first I was offered, and was better than being on Social Security. Also, the firm offered me an apprenticeship which meant I was learning a trade so I thought I'd take it while looking for what I really want. My father is a miner . . . and he discouraged me from mining. I think he's glad I'm doing what I'm doing now.

Doug: I wanted to go into the Building Trade . . . like my father but he discouraged me. He said there's not much work about and there's too much travelling to where the jobs are. He said I'd get sick of it. Anyway he reckons the industry has got slack in its training of apprentices, and that apprentices are not given enough help and support. They're throwing up such rubbish these days that skill isn't wanted, just brute force, ignorance and standard equipment. I'll stick where I am for the present.

Ron: My parents encourage me to come to college so that I can get qualifications – so that I can get a job any time with good money and prospects. My father wants me to get qualifications so I can get a job because he didn't want to go to college when he was a lad and he wasted his time. He doesn't want me to make the same mistakes.

21

He says once you've got a skill you have got more choice. With unskilled or semi-skilled work there are no prospects. I'm not just talking about the money. I'm also taking about job satisfaction. I don't have to be an engineer all my life, I can move if I want into the office to become a manager or a draughtsman. If ever I try to get out of going to college, especially in the evening, my mum and dad get cross and upset so generally I come.

However, if the short-term problems associated with the initial stage of the transition from school to work do not appear too many or too great,[2] by the time students have reached the third or fourth year of their apprenticeships, the wider implications of their occupational choice are often only too painfully obvious (see Appendix 2). By that time, many colleagues may have either failed statutory examinations or simply dropped out of the training scheme. Those who remain are often extremely cynical about what they now see, with the knowledge of hindsight, as a false connection between training and skilled work. Such a position is summarised in the remarks which follow, made by a third-year craft apprentice who was 'compelled' to attend college:

'We have to come . . . last year I missed a fair bit of college in the afternoons and I had a letter saying unless this altered they'd terminate my employment. Well in the end they sent for me. There was a training officer, a union bloke and a managing director. I told them I was bored with college . . . that I was getting nothing out of it . . . they said you've got to go. . . . They said that going to college was part of my contract . . . that I'd get a certificate of training out of it. . . . But these are not real reasons though, are they? They're the kind of things your parents and teachers say – Get a trade. At school you think, Great, I'll get a skilled job, go to college and get qualified. It's only when you've been on the apprenticeship three years you realise how green you were . . . we make the tea, clear up, take orders, do dirty boring work and then go to college from 9 to 9 (a.m. – p.m.) and get talked at all day. The catch is that we'll all stay at it because our money goes up – that's the carrot. It's not just employers who tell you to go to college, but your school and your parents. They don't know anything . . . get a skill . . . a job with your hands they say . . . security and all that . . . it's cobblers really when the work is really boring.'

While one may be sceptical about some of the views expressed above, such an account serves to raise questions about the assumption that industrial craft work is necessarily to be equated with skilled work. It is often suggested that there are certain qualities intrinsic to craft work,

22

which relate to the worker's autonomy regarding the rate at which he produces the finished article. This assumption is usually linked with another; namely, that good industrial relations and work satisfaction are more likely to occur where the worker deals with the total product. It would seem to us, however, that underlying such assumptions rests a rather outdated conception of artisanship, which implies clear-cut demarcations between the work of craftsmen, operatives and labourers. Moreover, such a conception embraces the notion that a skill is passed on for the most part through a one-to-one relationship between craftsman and apprentice. In our view, however, mechanisation and automation have increasingly eroded such clear-cut distinctions, and have created a greater demand for workers who 'fit' things than for those who 'make' things. In the following discussion, fourth-year apprentices outline their experience of craft work:

Jo: I think I'll jack it in . . . craft work isn't really skilled, it's boring work . . . minding a machine, pressing buttons that kind of thing . . . or at a lathe or a machine churning out the same parts all the time . . . craftsmen don't make things any more . . . they become geared up to working on one machine. . . .

Alan: Craft just involves the practical side of things . . . working on the machines . . . it's the technician who has more of the theory side of things . . . for example . . . if machines go wrong or anything like that technicians are called in. Craft work is not like it used to be . . . it's become more routine . . . because of mechanisation . . . craft has generally become defined as machine operating.

David: After the first year or in some cases the second year the company hives you off into different jobs . . . they know how many fabricators, fitters, electricians, technicians that they want. . . . To have any real say in what skill you take up you've got to have at least 70 per cent scores in the jobs you do . . . the company assesses all your work. . . .

Geoff: What he's saying is that whilst all of us have gone into engineering . . . it's a very broad term . . . it's the employers who decide which branch we go in, not us. Here, we're all maintenance fitters . . . but we didn't all want to do that . . . I wanted to be an electrician . . . Mick wanted to be a technician. . . . In your first year they put you on every type of job to build up a picture of what you're good at . . . what you're like . . . then you can say what you want to be . . . and if it doesn't go along with how they see things well tough luck . . . for us I mean! It's what they want isn't it? Mind you I'm not that unhappy being a maintenance fitter . . . it gets boring sometimes but at least I'm not working in a shop, or doing an unskilled job . . . I'd rather be here than in mining or casting even if

23

I don't take home as much. If you don't want really boring labour, and you don't want to go down a hole, you've got to get into engineering.

However, as Geoff points out, getting into engineering may not be such a satisfactory move as might at first appear, since, once in, the kind of training scheme followed is determined mainly by the employer. In addition, many traditional craft skills in the engineering industry have become obsolete, while those which are still designated 'craft' have been rendered semi-skilled through the processes of specialisation and fragmentation.[3] Furthermore, as a result of increasing mechanisation and the introduction of productivity schemes like piece rates and bonus schemes, the demand for highly skilled work has become increasingly one-dimensional, so that the skilled worker is called upon to use only a small fraction of his aptitudes at a time. Such trends have resulted in widespread deskilling, which calls into question the whole role of FE, particularly with regard to its function in legitimating existing forms of apprenticeship systems. Young workers themselves are only too aware of this situation, and resent the fact that their status of apprentice adversely affects their pay and conditions of employment. The following remarks from two third-year apprentice students clearly indicate that the unsatisfactory nature of their position in this respect is not one simply imposed by their employers:

Dave: Well, when we're working we're making things that can be used on machines and in other parts of the factory . . . these things are necessary and are used. We do a lot of this work on our own . . . unsupervised like . . . it's illegal in fact but the supervisors and union don't say anything.

Arthur: If it wasn't for us they'd have to employ someone else to make those parts that are used . . . the things we make are fairly simple but as Dave says they're necessary. If we didn't make them they'd have to take on someone from outside and pay him a man's wages . . . someone's got to make things like lugs, studs, clamps and the like.

D.G.:   What about the union?

Arthur: What about it? The union doesn't care . . . and if they don't the managers won't will they. The blokes we work with are OK, but really we're all right if we shut up, take orders and make the tea . . . learn they call it. . . .

Dave: The apprentices mean nothing in our place . . . do your work and shut up. . . . Even when the union goes on strike we're not expected to go out . . . when they're out we still have to go to work . . . we're not expected to be involved in it . . . so I don't know much about it. I don't even know which union the blokes are in. I'm not interested.

24

In view, therefore, of what appears to many students as an all-round lack of support, it is not perhaps surprising that many apprentices develop a highly pragmatic and instrumental attitude towards both work and college. Thus the majority of young workers see college as having only one useful purpose, namely that of furnishing certificated proof of training in a particular trade – a conception of education which tolerates only those aspects which can be immediately translated into material benefits within a competitive industrial market. Moreover, the fact that apprentice students are excluded from decisions which affect the form and direction of their training, tends to heighten such instrumentality: hence Dave's remark: 'I don't know much about it . . . I'm not interested. . . .' In the long run, their criticisms of work become inseparable from their criticism of college as the following comments suggest:

Tony: We're just little teeth in a big machine . . . doing a little job.
. . . I expected when I left school to go to work . . . and be a respons-ible adult . . . to make something . . . to do something creative so that you can get a result from it. . . . I've been at work three years and I can't really show anything for it. . . .
Mick: We got the impression that we'd be going into a skilled job . . . and that we were going to do something worth doing. . . . It's a let down really . . . training? . . . that's a joke . . . taking orders more like.
Tony: We spend a lot of time looking at the clock . . . waiting to go home. We are here at college . . . or training somewhere else or at work. Never settled and never seeing any bit of the work finished. We don't see our own work finished. It's as if we're continually moving onto something else.
Mick: You're not expected to say anything . . . no one's interested . . . you're there to learn so shut up and get on with it. It's like this at work and at college. We're not expected to say anything. Learning is like having someone standing over you . . . 'You're a lad in training . . . so shut up and get on with it.'

While such remarks might appear exaggerated, we would wish to argue that they typify the feelings of many third-year apprentice students who, when persuaded to express their opinion about the system, tend to become extremely critical. Thus, although in the short term the transition from school to work may not be experienced as problematic, we would suggest that the longer-term implications are realised far more pertinently. Such experiences, however, must be understood against a history of socialisation processes taking place in an area of restricted career prospects, where school-leavers foresee few opportunities for personal betterment. Where employment conditions are tight and few apprenticeships are available, employers can afford to be extremely selective about whom they choose. Moreover, the present mounting unemployment figures and the scarcity of work, skilled or otherwise, reinforces the view that apprenticeship opportunities for 'the fortunate few' should not be taken lightly. Ultimately, however, the combined authority structures of work and college, together with the general acceptance of a *need* for discipline and hierarchy, result in social relations which, only too often, the apprentice experiences as oppressive.

It would be misleading to suggest that such a situation occurs because of a crude mechanistic correspondence between college and industry. On the other hand, however, the socialisation of apprentices into cognitive and affective skills is a highly structured process. For this reason, therefore, it would seem important to examine how such factors as 'the form of liaison between college and industry' and 'the nature of teacher/student relations' act to shape the organisational and social environment in which apprentices acquire their knowledge.

The teachers

It is often the case that technical teachers come from very similar backgrounds to their students, and consequently share with them a similar experience of the stresses and strains of the work process. However, as a result of further training and more numerous qualifications, often achieved through considerable personal effort, they tend to possess a clear-cut awareness of their own professional identity as trainers. The following comments from a technical teacher regarding his 'route' to his present position would seem to typify the experiences and attitudes of many recruits from industry to the sphere of FE

> *Teacher*: I did a sandwich course for the ONC . . . six months each year for three years. At the end of that, I went on to part-time day because in those days there were no full-time courses for HNC/D or anything like that. The opportunities weren't there at that time . . . a student today for example can go from ONC to the Polytechnic . . . things are certainly better today. After I got my HNC I was doing Developments work . . . but it's funny really, they said that I was too good to be in the workshop with my HNC . . . so I was encouraged into a drawing office. From there I went on to research and development work. . . .
>
> *D.G.*: How did you get involved in teaching?
>
> *Teacher*: I took night school on at the time . . . they needed people in my field and I leapt at the chance for the money. I was recently married and moved into a new house . . . my wife was expecting . . .

the usual story really . . . money was very short. I got a couple of
nights part-time teaching . . . I said to my wife at the time under no
circumstances will I ever do this job full-time . . . I hated it. . . . After
about seven years however I realised I wanted to do it full-time . . .
mainly because I started to enjoy teaching . . . I felt confident after
seven years part-time that I could be a good full-time technical
teacher. By the time I started teaching I was a chartered engineer. . . . Although I wanted to teach I still didn't see myself as a
teacher . . . I still don't . . . I rather see myself as a professional
engineer in teaching. . . . An engineer first and a teacher second! I
don't know why I think like this . . . it's probably to do with my
long . . . and sometimes hard and painful . . . tramp to become an
engineer. I was thirty-three when I became a chartered engineer and
decided to go into teaching full-time. So from when I started technical education at 13 . . . at 13 I left the senior boys' school and
spent two years at the junior technical school . . . and then on to
what were then called the city technical schools, and so on . . . I'd
spent twenty years getting my technical qualifications . . . I felt very
pleased and chuffed to become a chartered engineer . . . it was a hard
long slog . . . it is today, of course, but then it was much tougher
with mainly part-time night study. I suppose this is why I see myself
in that order . . . as an engineer first and a teacher second. I don't
feel any conflict about this because there's a difference between
teachers in schools and technical lecturers in FE . . . because we've
gone through the route that the students have gone through . . . I
think that makes you more at one with the students. You're more
sympathetic towards them, you know their problems . . . they also
know that you've been through it all and that they can learn from
you.

This feeling of communality with apprentice-students is a factor
which many technical teachers refer to. Hence another lecturer remarks:

I don't think a Craft lecturer is prejudiced about his students, he
knows what his students are, after all most of us were Craft
students, many of us didn't go to a grammar school, I didn't go to a
grammar school, I didn't go to university, I was an ordinary secondary school lad, and so, in that respect, we've got a lot of sympathy
with them.

The fact that many lecturers come from very similar backgrounds to
their students, and that they share similar experiences of both industry
and training, is clearly regarded by many technical teachers as invaluable
in understanding and getting on with students. By contrast, most lecturers in Liberal Studies are university educated, and consequently have

very different experiences of professional training. The latter factor is regarded by many of the technical staff as a prime reason why Liberal Studies teachers may face problems in the classroom.

'A General Studies bloke . . . they are generally speaking, more academically qualified than the Craft people and, I think, they perhaps unwittingly regard the Craft student as being inferior and they (the students) are very, very sensitive to this. . . .'

This awareness of an ability to empathise with craft students and to understand their attitudes, tends to make technical staff extremely critical of the liberal more academic approach adopted by teachers in the General Studies department. As a result, there tends to be a feeling of considerable scepticism among them regarding the contribution of that department, and its efforts to raise the level of cultural and social awareness among apprentice students. This scepticism is a clear illustration of the rivalry between *two distinct cultures* which are generated through the English educational system.[4]

At Western, the nature of technical socialisation predominates, and is highly significant both to the ways in which technical teachers perceive the job to be done, and to the forms of training which are necessarily associated with it. The attitude of technical teachers towards the job of teaching, therefore, is to be understood against such patterns of socialisation. Hence classroom authority may be seen to be founded upon the fact that most teachers are recruits from industry, who have been through the system, and who are therefore well placed to pass on the know-how to those who also want their 'ticket'. One effect of such instrumentality is that the process of training is presented as both neutral and inevitable, so that the authority structure of both work and college is accepted as beyond question or natural. A number of other factors, however, namely the sheer size of technical syllabuses and consequent restrictions on time, often make it extremely difficult for technical teachers to exploit that sense of communality with students which is seen as an important part of the teaching relationship.[5] In such circumstances many teachers have little option but to develop a highly pragmatic teaching style, which, contrary to the expressed spirit of empathy, objectifies the training process still further and acts to legitimate a highly narrative form of pedagogy.

Teaching relations

In both workshops and classroom, the process of learning appears to be a highly formal affair, in which teachers dictate or demonstrate particular principles or skills. Although discussion is neither readily forth-coming, nor often possible in the rush to complete syllabus, talk centres largely upon particular technical items, so that communication amounts to little more than verbal exchanges on matters of clarification. Inter-action, therefore, is highly specific and context bound, with little or no discussion of the social relations which characterise production, unless perhaps such issues as safety are touched upon. Indeed, because of high rates of failure and the sheer size of the syllabus to be covered, many teachers feel compelled to adopt highly narrative and often didactic teaching styles. The response of one technical teacher to certain obser-vations made of his teaching illustrates something of the nature of this problem:

> *Interviewer*: You seem to place a great emphasis upon giving stu-dents 'facts' . . . I mean providing information more or less by rote methods . . . students spend most of their time copying from the board, from dictated notes and from set texts and handouts. There's little discussion and rapport between yourselves and the students about these facts and any problems that arise. . . .
> *Teacher*: This is true to an extent . . . though you make it look worse than it is. I spend a good deal of my time explaining points to students, but there's little time for rapport and discussion as you put it. There may be time for this in Liberal Studies where, let's face it, . . . there's no set syllabus. But the technical teacher has got to im-part a vast amount of technical information and 'know how'. You've just got to get through it as quickly as possible . . . dictation, over-head projector, transparencies, blackboard . . . rote methods . . . call it what you like. . . . It's my job to give these students the necessary technical knowledge so that they can do their jobs. If you knew how cluttered up the syllabuses are you'd understand. What you say about my teaching methods may be true . . . but you'll find a lot of technical teachers in the same boat. . . . It's too easy for you to make these observations from the outside. . . . The overriding con-cern here is that you produce a competent craftsman or tradesman . . . able and qualified at the job he's taking on . . . no more, no less.

As we have suggested, one important effect of the pressures to which this teacher refers is that many technical teachers are compelled to adopt a highly formal and pragmatic style of teaching. However, while this situation may represent a particular response to the contradictions within which many teachers work, it also manifests further tensions within the learning context. Where students experience particular difficulties in assimilating materials which are disseminated at a very rapid rate, the learning context must be arranged so that their task is facilitated. Hence, the overall outcome is often that the expediency of the production line is adopted. It is not surprising, therefore, that the analogies students use to describe their experiences of college are often drawn not only from industry, but from highly mechanised industrial processes:

> *John*:   We just seem, to me, to be like sausage meat in a sausage machine . . . and getting sausages out at the other end all ready wrapped. They're just chucking us in here and, eventually, they'll process us. . . .'
>
> *Andy*:   We are treated like numbers. Employers want you to stand there and do that, go there and do that . . . they want you to do it as good as you can, quietly as you can, without fuss . . . without getting up anyone's nose, and then go away, at the end of the day, and return in the morning. College . . . isn't too different . . . we have to sit and listen . . . not speaking . . . it's just like work . . . we're just little teeth in a big machine . . . doing a little job.

The impersonality of the training process, to which such remarks refer, is not unnoticed by the majority of students. Indeed, it is often because of such conditions of learning that many become disillusioned and alienated.

Such formality is epitomised in the process of interaction where staff invariably refer to students as 'Mr' (there is scant time to recall Christian names), and where relationships are formed in the awareness that reports of attitudes, performance and attendance will be forwarded 'in confidence' to employers. Moreover, this problem is exacerbated by the transient and often fragmented nature of the contact between apprentice students, teachers and college authorities. The hot-house learning conditions of day release, for example, serve to accentuate the fragmented nature of pedagogical relations. Indeed, for both staff and students the college day is often long, tedious and exhausting, involving classroom and workshop practice until late in the evening. In addition, both the block and day-release systems ensure that students and lecturers meet only once a week, or in the case of block release, recurringly every three weeks. Thus lecturers can be involved in as many as twenty or thirty classes per week for whom their total weekly commitment amounts to only one hour. Consequently, most lecturers deal with a large and constantly changing body of students each academic year, and it is unlikely that they will meet many of that shifting population the following year. Tipton (1973) points to some of the tensions created by such fragmented relations:

> If one consequence of these short or fractured relationships is that there is small opportunity for the teacher to get to know his students,

another is that he is forced to deal with a large number of classes to fill his timetable. . . . An inordinate amount of physical and mental energy is required if the teacher is to enter into deep relationships with students when they come to him on this kind of scale.

An unintended consequence of such fractured relationships, therefore, is that the activity of learning tends to become formalised in response to a pragmatic and narrative mode of transmission. Invariably, such circumstances give rise to passive learning situations in which technical know-how takes an objectified commodity appearance, and social relations are characterised by an absence of dialogue and collaboration. The point we would wish to stress here is that such educational activity ultimately serves to legitimate the conditions of apprenticeship, and give rise to an objectified learning process which closely resembles the disciplined features of work. In other words, apprentice students come to college to 'work', and must not be encouraged to question their place within the relations of production, or to develop critical views of either employer or college.

It is clear that the background against which we have attempted to describe the nature of social relations at Western requires further investigation, particularly with regard to the organisational ethos of the college and how it is influenced by local industry. In the section which follows, therefore, some attempt is made to examine the connection between college and industry, and some of the curricular implications involved.

College and industry – some curricular implications

Throughout its history, Western has pursued close working relations with local industry, which by and large are perceived to be both mutually co-operative and supportive. Indeed, the college prides itself on its knowledge of the manpower requirements of local industry, so that its courses tend to be structured accordingly. It is a relationship best described by one of the technical heads of department:

'I think in general departments such as ours are closely involved in what is going on in industry. . . . We make it our business to know exactly what they are doing . . . as they know exactly what we're doing at the College . . . so we have very organised and structured courses. . . . It has taken seven or eight years to develop, but this is how close we are with both industry and 'the powers that be' in technical education.'

Such a position is endorsed in the following comments from a head of industrial training in a major nationalised industry serviced by the college:

> 'We have excellent relations with the college. . . . As you know, the main departments there keep in close contact with us. Only very recently some of them went around the factories with us . . . meeting staff and having a good look round. We're all on similar committees and we keep in contact about training requirements and the sorts of changes which are going on. There seems to be a team spirit at the college among the staff which is not always in existence in the other colleges we seem to deal with. The college is way ahead in leading others in the country in developing courses and supporting the changes in this industry. . . . I'm lucky in a way to be able to have such good relations with them. . . . The teachers provide interesting courses . . . they know how to treat the lads . . . they don't rub them up the wrong way and they try to provide courses which interest them.'

It would seem to us that this emphasis upon liaison or 'making it our business to know', illustrates the fact that Western identifies most strongly with the objectives of local industry, most particularly with regard to the need for a predictable supply of trained personnel. Thus, as a consequence, the college tends to reflect rather than challenge the immediacy of the demand from industry that young workers should be made more 'productive' in their work. Consequently, the conditions of learning in college, in terms of its organisation and physical layout, tend to mirror the working conditions from which most students come. Thus hard and fast rules concerning time-keeping, behaviour and access to resources, are rigorously applied in conditions which are often dirty, noisy and potentially dangerous. In addition, the extended nature of the educational day (9 a.m. to 9 p.m.), together with particular emphasis upon such issues as speed, accuracy and safety, ensures a disciplined and time-conscious atmosphere very similar to work. To this end, college authorities insist upon strict registration throughout the day, and warn students in the prospectus (without detracting from the ultimate power of the employer under whose control they remain), that reports concerning progress will be forwarded regularly to employers.

> A sessional report showing the number of possible and actual attendances, homework, classwork, laboratory, workshop and examination marks obtained for each class will be forwarded to the students, and in the case of block-release and part-time day-release students, a copy will be sent to their employer. This report should be received before the commencement of the next session and will include details of the course recommended for the next academic year, irrespective

of examination results. . . . Absentee and lateness reports will be forwarded to employers who release students during working hours.'

The rationale behind Western's concern for attendance and discipline, however, is more complex than might at first appear. Ultimately, it would seem to be an expression of the college's sensitivity to the directive of employers that apprentices are released for training only on the condition that they work. Because of this sensitivity, the college authorities have appointed a special liaison officer, among whose particular duties is that of maintaining close contact with employers. In the following comments he lays particular stress upon his role in toning down potential conflict.

'The continual areas of conflict . . . are the minor errors made with regard to the reporting . . . or non-reporting . . . of student absentee-ism. . . . Employers demand that absentees or late-comers are reported promptly. . . . This takes up to four or five days through the office. . . . Also, employers tend to be wary of Liberal Studies and are continually sceptical about what goes on in this area. . . . It's often the case that they do not have any information . . . part of my job is to inform them about what is happening . . . they take a little bit of persuading sometimes. . . . This explains why we have never been able to introduce a period of physical recreation into the day . . . employers will never hear of it. We also have to be very careful when we organise external visits, for example, which tell apprentices more about potential opportunities with other employers. They say that they don't employ their lads and send them to college to go and visit someone else's factory. . . . There is a continual need . . . and it's part of my job . . . like others who work here to establish links and provide information for employers . . . it tones down potential conflict.'

Another way in which Western minimises potential conflict with employers is through the image it projects of itself as a *pragmatic* training institution. Indeed the college exudes an atmosphere of expediency through its overt concern with tangible assets, which can be readily transformed into productive labour, and fitted into the industrial order of things. Consequently, the *material* conditions of work, in terms of the exploitation of resources and the conversion of education into economic benefits (through the *training* of young workers), take precedence over other more *abstract* aspects associated with the aims of a 'liberal' education. In this way employers are reassured that the courses followed by their employees represent the interests of industry. Indeed, it is because of its popularity with employers, who prefer it because of its minimum intrusion upon production, that the day-release scheme

33

predominates at Western. The following remarks from an owner of a large mechanical engineering firm would seem to confirm such a view:

A: We've always found that the work done at the college is very good . . . within two years of the apprenticeship we find that our trainees provide an important and useful back-up to the trained men that they work with . . . under supervision rather than, of course, working alone. . . .

Interviewer: Have you ever thought of training the mechanics within the works here . . . rather than, say, sending them to college?

A.: We could train them ourselves but it would mean employing an instructor . . . but there is not sufficient time for a qualified mechanic to spend the time necessary to train an apprentice . . . because while he's doing that he isn't earning any money for the firm. So in other words it's most important that a mechanic's daily tasks are chargeable to the customer. . . . The cheapest way obviously of training the lads is to send them to school or college. The equipment and training at the college is first class.

Interviewer: Does that mean FE actually pays you? . . .

A.: They're getting practical work for four days in the week . . . and at college on the fifth. . . . To train someone on the job is too expensive. You could take on a boy who just helps as he goes along, but he is not learning a skill and he's really only useful for us in terms of lending a general hand. But our apprentices can go to college for one day and work with sophisticated equipment, they have practical work and training and also the necessary elements of theory . . . maths for example. . . . No one could teach them that here.

Interviewer: Which form of release do you prefer, day or block?

A.: On day release we do at least get four days work out of them . . . even if it's only sweeping up, cleaning the tools or making the tea . . . whereas on the block system they're out of our hands for perhaps weeks on end.

Here the employer not only assesses the training provision at Western in terms of the direct benefits gained by his business, but also in terms of its minimal intrusion upon overall production. However, while his comments indicate the ways in which 'off the job' training can save money and resources, his remarks are clearly concerned with only the *material* features of the returns generated through technical training. What he neglects to consider is the fact that labour becomes more productive not only through the provision of cognitive skills, but also through the nurturing of certain affective features which are of a less immediately apparent nature. This latter factor, which may be regarded as a different kind of return, is referred to in the following conversation with a personnel director in a large local firm:

J.R.:   Training generates greater enthusiasm on the part of employees . . . it's challenging to the school leaver's enthusiasm. They at least see we care about their job and help them in their training. They tend to stay with the firm as a result . . . as well as knowing about the job they become more loyal and involved in the firm's work. We don't want high staff turnover. It's no good to us. . . . We aim for some kind of continuity through training . . . it also gives the school leavers a chance to get on . . . it gives them a career structure . . . something to aim at. They can see where they're going.

D.G.:   Is it worth sending half your labour force per week on day release though . . . I mean you're paying their wages . . . is that a financial gamble?

J.R.:   Training is a gamble . . . it's costly so there have got to be returns . . . we're paying people's wages while they're on day release. . . . But if we don't give staff training they don't know the job and very often drift off somewhere else . . . so with training we get two benefits. One, in the form of reliable and quite skilled support . . . continuity is obviously important . . . and secondly we keep them. . . . But as I say training on the job is difficult . . . because the work is more complicated than ever . . . and it requires a settled form of instruction. To send them off to college is a predictable and continuous form of training which we can't really give them . . . although they do, of course, get the practice here at work.

Both employers quoted above recognise that FE 'pays'. Indeed, not only does it provide a steady form of training which enhances production, but it also gains for employers generous tax concessions to offset outlay on investment in training. Thus, because of its 'off the job' and supportive nature, FE is seen by many employers as an attractive low-cost proposition. Such mutually advantageous realities have tended to set the tone for the kinds of relations which have arisen between FE and industry. However, it would seem to us that the nature of such a liaison can adversely affect college proceedings, not least of all in the way in which manpower requirement projections can actually dictate college courses. Such a close correspondence between work and college would seem to leave little room for innovation or change. This problem is particularly pertinent to Western where courses are designed primarily to meet both long- and short-term plans provided by local industry. Hence the curriculum tends to reflect either the abundance or dearth of career opportunities at any particular time. Thus it sometimes happens that students are refused permission by their employers to follow higher-grade courses because manpower projections currently show little demand for such skills.

In our view, such circumstances would seem to denote a rather

incestuous situation which has arisen because of too close a synchronisation between FE and industry. In other words, where industry can
dictate the number, form and stratification of courses in an educational
institution, the consequences for curricular innovation and change by
the college are bleak. Thus, contrary to the popular misconception, it
may be the case that industry, rather than college, stifles curricular
change and innovation. This is perhaps best illustrated with reference
to TEC, a college-based curriculum project moderated regionally
through the committees of the Technician Education Council.[6]

Although the bulk of courses at Western are of a craft nature (see
Appendix 1), in recent years the college has increased its commitment
to courses for technicians. Thus each department has become involved
in both redeveloping existing courses and designing new ones to meet
the broad aims of TEC. That is to say, they have sought to up-date and
rationalise the national provision of courses for technician students.
In principle, TEC offers exciting opportunities for technical colleges to
both develop their own curricula in liaison with local industry, as well
as to enlist the support of other agencies interested in supporting such
schemes. Indeed, a central feature of TEC is that the success of the
project depends largely upon the nature of the collaboration between
college and industry. However, at the level of practice, many lecturers
have found that while local industry has been prepared to co-operate
as in the past, it has often been reluctant to support ideas of an innovative nature. In the following comments, one Head of Department we
interviewed outlines this predicament:

'To some of my department this kind of innovation is entirely new
... but in fact it isn't really ... those of us around at the time of
City and Guilds III know the experience of having our ideas solicited
about what the curriculum should be ... only to be told later on
"thou shalt do this" by central authorities. The real problem is that
we have to satisfy two masters for TEC to be successful ... one is
the TEC hierarchy itself ... in approving units and so forth ... and
the other is in getting the active collaboration of industry in developing the curriculum. ... After all, that's what it's supposed to be
about. The real problem is that industry doesn't really know how to
define a technician ... let alone offer constructive ideas on his training needs. I'm afraid that after months of negotiations with industry
we haven't really gone very far forward. ... Industry seems anxious
to leave decisions to us ... yet they are non-committal about
whether they will support the new schemes. ... This makes my staff
very cynical ... and I must say I can't blame them. ...'

The observations quoted above identify two interrelated problems
experienced by many colleges regarding the viability of TEC: first, a

certain level of scepticism concerning the ability of TEC to support a truly local project; and second, the fear that the attitude of local industry might serve to frustrate the development of courses based upon largely innovative principles. Such widely held concerns, exacerbated by the Great Education Debate which has focused primarily upon the need to establish closer links with industry, are elaborated in the following remarks from a senior lecturer:

'I can only speak for this department and perhaps one or two others. ... There are really two points as I see it. ... In the first place ... contrary to all the public discussion of the Great Debate ... industry doesn't know what it wants or needs at this level ... we are placed in a vulnerable position because if we innovate in progressive directions ... over and above our main bread-and-butter courses, industry may not want what we have to offer. ... The point I'm making is that you can innovate till the cows come home, but if local industry wants bread and butter nothing can get off the ground. ... The second point I want to make ... and it emerges from my cynicism ... and it's the part none of us can see ... how will all this setting out of aims and objectives really help the teacher in the classroom. ... Sometimes I think it's all part of a vast exercise to shake us up ... to make us rethink our aims and objectives. ... Of course that's a good thing ... but TEC is supposed to be more than that. ... One gets the idea that TEC is another of these gimmicks ... it appears as if the teacher develops the curriculum ... but in fact he can't ... all he ends up doing is chasing his tail ... or re-naming parts. ... But I don't call that an innovation. It's given some colleges, of course, the chance to jump on the bandwagon ... a sort of one-upmanship in producing apparently new and wonderful aims and objectives ... but if you look closely at these schemes they are really brushed up rehashes of what they're already doing. It may well be that the behavioural objectives, etc., look good when set out in intricate format ... but when you get behind the detail it's got to be mostly revamped material.'

In our view, while such assessments of a scheme which has had little time to develop may appear premature, they serve to highlight a certain situation which has been referred to in the past as 'innovation without change' (Shipman, 1974). In addition, they call into question the advisability of introducing innovatory programmes into situations where either the companies involved have little real understanding of their own training requirements, or where demand is geared largely towards bread-and-butter needs. In such situations, the colleges find themselves taking all the initiatives and running all the risks. Such a position is not only contrary to the original aims of TEC, but places the college in danger of ending up unsupported both by local industry, as well as by the Council's validating committee. Thus, while the college may possess the potential to innovate and perhaps influence industrial processes, the existence of certain external constraints would seem to curb its opportunity to do so. However, it would be misleading to assume that as a consequence, the college adopts a passive role in its relations with industry.

In citing this particular example of the limitations which may be placed upon FE by local industry, we have attempted to show some of the ways in which certain normative conceptions of the technical curriculum may be maintained through the college/industry relationship. However, while on face value such an example serves to illustrate those features of social control which may be enforced upon an educational institution from outside, we would not wish to support those over-tidy patterns of relations between college and industry which are currently being described by those who adhere to the 'correspondence' theories of education (Bowles and Gintis, 1976). It is not our intention at this stage, however, to continue discussion of TEC or correspondence theories of education. Such matters will be taken up in later chapters. What is important to recognise from the preceding analysis is that FE enjoys an *active* relationship with industry and is not simply its hand-maiden.

In this chapter we have sought to provide some insight into those aspects of Western's background which have shaped its general development and relations with industry. It is intended that this brief account should provide the reader with some understanding of the institution, its participants and their problems. Our purpose here has been to acquaint the reader with those features of the college in its day-to-day affairs which indicate its character and practice. However, it is important at this stage to examine in greater detail the ways in which the organisational framework of Western is actually influenced by its active interchange with local industry. Thus we now turn to an examination of those internal features of Western's organisation which are as much concerned with resisting influences from outsiders as they are with accommodating them. In the chapter which follows, we seek to describe and evaluate those decision-making processes which characterise the college's attempts both to maintain professional autonomy, as well as to serve local industry. It will be argued that Western's organisational framework not only renders it highly flexible in achieving such objectives but also extremely adaptable in negotiating with outside agencies.

Chapter 3

Organisational framework

So far in this study, we have attempted a brief résumé of the major theoretical traditions which inform our understanding of FE as a system. In addition, we have attempted, through an ethnographic approach, to acquaint the reader with those features of the college in its day-to-day affairs which are of particular relevance to our research interests.

In this chapter, we turn to the development of an organisational analysis of Western College, so that we may reach a greater understanding of some of those important issues referred to in the preceding chapters.

Before embarking upon the empirical reality of Western as an institution, however, it would seem necessary to provide some indication of the nature of the organisational analysis to be pursued, as well as to locate that analysis within our overall theoretical framework.[1] In other words, we need to explain why it is necessary to examine the organisational context of FE, and to indicate what form such an examination will take.

Theoretical framework of analysis

There has been, in recent years, a growing tendency within the sociology of education to direct the analysis of educational issues away from the micro approach, which focuses primarily upon processes of interaction, towards a more rigorous conceptual examination of the structural conditions within which interaction takes place. However, while this emphasis upon the importance of structural explanations provides a timely redress to that trend of the early 1970s, which was largely concerned with the elucidation of specific features of interaction, it also presents a number of important methodological difficulties. Amongst these perhaps the most serious is that which finds expression in an over-riding concern to promote theory as the sole determinant of social reality. Indeed, in our view, it seems paradoxical that such a movement, far from enhancing the empirical reality of objects in a theoretical frame, has often resulted in little more than a disturbing reminder of an earlier movement within sociology, namely functionalism, which over-emphasised the power of the structure over the participant. In both cases, unpredictability is ultimately reduced at the expense of crucial insights into the interaction of participants in the conditions described.

That is not to say that there have not been a number of attempts to mount empirical studies which have sought to avoid the idealism of much *verstehen* analysis. Perhaps the most notable among these is that of Sharp and Green (1975), who attempted a study of progressive education in which social action was examined within specific structural parameters, which ultimately were seen to condition the kinds of alternatives available to participants. Hence they write:

> The perspective which we are advocating is one which attempts to situate teachers' world views and practices within the context of social and physical resources and constraints which they may or may not perceive, but which structure their situation and set limits to their freedom of action through the opportunities and facilities made available to them and the constraints and limitations imposed on them.

Here the idealism which characterised New Directions is replaced by an effort to understand the conscious actor within the context of certain material conditions.[2] As researchers, we would wish to express much sympathy with such a conception of theory. There remains, however, one serious difficulty which arises when we examine more closely the empirical aspects of Sharp and Green's study. Indeed, it would seem to us that the use of the phrase 'may *or* may not perceive' in relation to the actor's perception of social reality, betrays the fact that for Sharp and Green (1975) the accounts of participants are ultimately to be understood within the theorist's frame of reference and by the rules of interpretation he chooses to apply. In other words, where the actor's account coincides with the theorist's frame of reference, the actor is seen to be conscious, but where it does not, he is seen to be falsely so.

We would wish to argue that while such a method of locating individual perceptions within a wider structural frame allows the researcher to follow a rigorous theoretical conceptualisation, it ultimately treats the participant as a mere epiphenomenon of the conditions and contradictions of everyday life. Indeed, the forces of culture which permeate the lives of participants are inevitably perceived as totally mystificatory, or apparent only to the chosen few.

If the problem is posed in the work of Sharp and Green (1975), however, so, we would suggest, may the answer be found there. It would seem to us that the phrase 'social and physical resources and constraints' provides the basis of an essential mediatory mechanism whereby the contradictions of action may be located within a structural context. In other words, what we are suggesting is that these social and physical resources, together with the constraints associated with them at the empirical level, find expression to a large extent in the forms of institutional relationships which arise from them. It is this factor which is often neglected in many attempts to explain social life. This crucial mediation between empirical circumstances and the kinds of social relationships they give rise to, is too often relegated to a teleological irrelevance, or seen as a feature of something else which must be explained in some other way. Indeed, if the role of the superstructure and its relation to the economic base is to be understood,[3] then surely a reappraisal of the nature of organisation is required. It would seem to us that without such a reappraisal the extent to which we can explain practice becomes limited, and that theory, far from advancing our understanding of reality, retreats further into the realms of abstraction.

We recognise of course that there are many arguments against institutional or organisational forms of understanding, particularly in relation to educational processes. Indeed, many researchers have been understandably deterred by the heavy structural functionalist overtones of management ideology which characterise much of the work in the area of organisational theory. Moreover, this mistrust of organisational analysis has been augmented by the tendency of some theorists to over-reify the constraints of organisation, so that institutions like 'the school' are treated merely as 'people-processing' mechanisms. Consequently, the discussion of organisational features has often been reduced to a mere technical description of particular forms and functions, through which it is assumed participants move unproblematically.

Thus, considerations of educational institutions, particularly those in the sphere of FE, are very few. Indeed both Hoyle (1973) and Davies (1973) point to this under-researched area of educational analysis. In terms of FE specifically, the only studies of any empirical substance are those of Tipton (1973) and Venables (1967 and 1974).

It would seem to us that this lack of material at the empirical level, together with our particular theoretical objective to link biography and structure[4] at the institutional level, provide more than adequate grounds for the development of a rigorous organisational study. We are left with the problem, however, of clarifying which of the possible frames of reference available we intend to adopt, and it is to this problem that we now turn.

The choice of any particular form of analysis raises two immediate

41

and interrelated problems: the first concerns the relationship of any particular theoretical model to an overall concept of FE; and the second concerns the problem of extracting the most suitable analytical framework from the many and various forms of understanding currently in existence.[5]

At the substantive level, our prime objective is to examine how the theory of FE relates, or fails to relate, to its practice. In essence, we are seeking to ascertain what counts as educational provision within the sphere of FE. It is not our concern, however, to examine such a process as if it were a mere mechanical translation of some functional imperative. On the contrary, we are seeking to expose an active and highly complex set of social relations, which characterise the context within which those who are engaged in FE actively participate.

In seeking to examine these social relations, we shall pursue many of the important issues raised in our ethnographic account of Western College. Our central concern, however, arises from the desire to understand how those complex relationships which exist between industry, college-administrators, lecturers and students may be contexted within an organisational framework, so as to both locate and reflect certain crucial aspects of the conditions of practice. However, our problem does not rest there. We are also concerned to locate this organisational framework within our overall theoretical conceptualisation of the functions and features of FE.

The choice of any theoretical path poses a number of difficulties since each course necessarily presupposes a variety of preferences and assumptions. Our choice is made more difficult because at the methodological level we are not so much concerned with locating a neat *correspondence* between some taken-for-granted reality and our own particular frame of reference, but more with constructing a framework which will facilitate a *coherent* examination of our particular interests.

The amalgamation of our substantive and theoretical concerns gives rise to a model which seeks to understand the crucial linking mechanisms which exist at the institutional level, and which shape the social structure for those who participate. It is at the commonsense level, however, that the participants may be seen to respond to the material and social constraints of their lives. For such institutional parameters do not merely represent arbitrary social conditions through which actors move, but rather real material and social forms in a specific relationship with the infrastructure in which they work (Erben and Gleeson, 1977).

Our primary objective, therefore, is to ascertain how institutional life sets the 'agenda' for participants, not so much in terms of some all-determining constraint which the organisation places on member's activities, but as a scenario within which the activities of members can be understood. We do not wish to ignore the specific problems of biography and structure, but rather to locate their intersection in time and space.

With such an objective in mind, we have chosen to focus initially upon some of the more important points of analysis deriving from the work of March and Simon (1958) on decision-making theory. Consideration has been given elsewhere to its possible application to the analysis of educational institutions:[6] its importance here lies in its emphasis upon the power of the organisational form to act as a dominant frame of reference for the activities of participants within the institution. This power, however, is not to be understood in the deterministic sense of a total definition, but rather in terms of the context which sets the premises of action, thereby allowing a greater understanding of how and why people behave in particular ways. There are of course a number of problems arising from such a form of analysis, like that of its difficulty in dealing with the nature of coercive power within institutions. However, since our initial problem is to examine how theory relates to practice by focusing upon those real material and social constraints which influence the activities of participants, then such an analytical framework would seem a highly appropriate approach to adopt. Indeed, many of the constraints involved will become self-evident by simply examining the plausibility or otherwise of certain actions. Such an approach will in effect circumscribe not only what is possible, but also why alternatives are impossible. In short, we shall look at many of the ground rules governing action, and examine the basis of their existence.

The main objectives of this chapter therefore is to relate some of the tentative ideas discussed in the preceding chapters to an analysis of the organisational features of Western College. In particular, we shall be concerned to ascertain how the nature of those organisational features *influence* rather than determine the actions and perceptions of those involved. We have already outlined many of the general characteristics of the history of Western College in the preceding chapters. Thus we shall start our organisational analysis by simply considering some of the administrative and academic structures of the college as they appear to the outsider.

The college structure

The college governing body, consisting of twelve representatives from the LEA, seven from local industry, and four from the college (the Principal, two staff and one student), heads the bureaucratic hierarchy. It is to this governing committee that the principal is directly responsible, although we shall qualify the nature of that responsibility later. Within the college itself, there are two distinct but related lines of organisation. First, the *academic* structure around which teaching commitments are organised, and second, the *committee* structure which operates at various levels to advise the principal and staff about such issues as course formats, academic policy and so on. We may also distinguish a third line of organisation which operates to service the day-to-day running of the college.[7] However, while this third feature must not be underestimated *vis-à-vis* the smooth running of college affairs, it does not enter our immediate concerns. Initially, we propose to examine the two major forms of organisation mentioned above.

The college academic structure: departmental divisions

Since a broad general description of the departmental structure of the college has been given in the preceding chapter, we shall not dwell at length upon such factors of information here. It suffices to say that each department has a head and at least one senior lecturer. The remainder of the staff are located on scales I and II of the Burnham Technical Scale.

The importance of the departmental structure of Western cannot be overestimated. Indeed, it may be seen to dominate a large number of the conversations we held with members of staff, as well as to provide the basis upon which staff identify with the college itself. We hope to show later that the departmental structure of Western is at the very heart of all institutionalised conflict. It is interesting to note at this point that throughout the duration of our field-work we met no member of staff, with the exception of the Principal and his immediate subordinates, who identified with the college as a whole as opposed to his particular department. In other words, college life is characterised by a kind of reciprocal departmental independence. One lecturer we spoke to described the situation in the following way:

'We're one of the biggest and busiest departments . . . but because we are not based in the main college . . . but down the road a few hundred yards . . . I think we are viewed as a separate entity from the rest of college life. . . . We don't often meet lecturers from other departments. I haven't a clue really about how any of the departments here interrelate.'

In effect, the social division of labour appears to reify into a positive and dominant ethos for the individual. As we have indicated in the ethnography and as the above quotation would seem to confirm, this situation is reinforced by the simple division of the college into annexes and outposts. Staff, of course, are well aware of the problem as the following comments from a technical lecturer would appear to indicate:

'It seems to me that the staff in each department see themselves and their department as completely separate entities . . . you know . . . as separate from Western itself. . . . But this leads to many problems . . . the main one being that duplication goes on at a ridiculous level . . . it's a waste of resources in fact. People in different departments . . . for instance . . . are teaching similar subjects and areas. It just doesn't happen by accident . . . the left hand doesn't know what the right hand is doing. The Principal has tried to do something about this . . . but without much success . . . you see there are departmental divisions which go deeper . . . into industry for instance. Mining is Mining and Electrical Engineering is Electrical Engineering. . . . You get an immediate cut-off. . . . In my fourteen years here I think this is a major drawback . . . and I think I shall continue to feel this way in the future.'

Yet if members of staff are aware of such problems, they are not necessarily anxious to dismantle such departmental barriers as the latter remarks would seem to confirm. Indeed such divisions are not without their advantages. In the following comments, the Vice-Principal while expressing an awareness of the *diversiveness* of the college departmental structure, is also recommending it as an efficient form of management:

'You have got to have a departmental management structure. It's an ideal situation of management, it's good line management if you like *but* what you've got to instil into people is that we are a college and the thing is that departments have got to co-operate and co-ordinate.'

It is the departmental structure, therefore, which provides the major form of identification for most college staff. Indeed, the continual emphasis upon departmental identities not only fashions the general running of college affairs, but also creates an atmosphere of insularity both with regard to the kinds of perceptions members of staff have of each other's departments, as well as with regard to the kinds of relationships, both formal and otherwise, which arise within such circumstances. The following comment from another member of staff indicates the kind of mutual scepticism which tends to characterise interdepartmental relations:

'We tend not to meet other members of departments. When you are moving around annexes all the time you don't have the time to sit down and talk about what's going on in the place as a whole. You might spend fifteen minutes nattering about a particular class . . . it tends to be on that level.'

The insularity which tends to influence the social relations of Western would seem to arise from both the organisational form of the college, as well as from the kinds of personal identities which arise within such circumstances. The latter, initially born of common experience within a particular industrial and geographical location, are heightened by the sheer physical and social separation of departments within the college as a whole. Moreover, this inter-departmental insularity, as a predominant feature of the organisational form of the college, operates in the sense March and Simon (1958) indicate to frame the perceptions of individuals with regard to the general events and activities of college life. An example of this insularity may be sighted when one considers the attitudes of lecturers teaching the *same* subject, but in *different* departments. Many courses include mathematics, for instance, but we came across no example of a lecturer who saw himself as a mathematician as opposed to a member of say the Motor Vehicle or Fabrication Departments. Similarly, those who organised workshop sessions tended to identify with the department rather than with a general trade or skill.

Furthermore, this identification of members of staff with particular departments, largely created by the form of industrial socialisation experienced by many lecturers, not only presents a very positive but at times an over-reified conception of its own importance. It would seem to us that a more objective assessment of its importance might be reached by simply examining its effect upon the day-to-day running of college affairs.

We have already indicated that within the immediate environment of Western there exists much competition between local colleges of FE. The survival of Western itself is largely due to the consolidation of its reputation as *the* college in which to study engineering. Indeed, the very development of Western College and the names of the departments it comprises testifies to this important aspect of its history. Thus pressure from outside, mediated through the policy decisions of the Principal, may be seen to be translated internally within the college. In other words, the competition which characterises the immediate educational environment of Western, inevitably finds explicit expression within the college itself. Quite simply, if the survival of the college depends upon student numbers, then the survival of individual departments also depends upon student numbers. However, this inter-departmental competition is not confined to the question of numbers alone. Indeed, it became increasingly obvious during the course of our field-work that the internal struggle also found expression in terms of access to the scarce physical resources of both plant and capital allowance.

Ultimately, therefore, inter-departmental competition involves not only the need to survive, but also to remain healthy in terms of both student numbers, staffing posts and the amount of available resources. Thus it is not perhaps surprising that it also provides the source of much underlying institutionalised conflict, since the actions of all departments are inevitably viewed in terms of their success or failure in acquiring more resources or holding on to those already acquired. One member of staff we interviewed described the situation in the following way:

'To be frank it reflects a desire for empire building at the expense of educational issues. . . . This attitude influences the implementation of college policy . . . it prevents departments working together . . . you need co-operation rather than indifference in a place like this. . . . We're spread out in a number of annexes and so forth. . . . The — department for instance has a divisive insularity which makes its members parochial and this prevents rationalising curriculum across the board. . . . The whole of education is bedevilled by head counting. Educational objectives become obscured in the fight for points. . . . It makes the relations between departments competitive . . . people are continually trying to upgrade their department.'

In our view, the atmosphere of heated competition described above is not only detrimental to relationships within college, but more importantly detrimental to the very *raison d'être* of Western as an educational institution. As the following remarks suggest, the system inevitably becomes a scapegoat for everything:

'The departments here are all empire builders, holding on to their staff . . . the *system* encourages this of course . . . but you can see that it's not conducive to co-operation, planning, or the redistribution of college resources.'

Perhaps more to the point, if the fault is not seen to be with the system, then it is seen to lie with those individuals who comprise it. Thus the degree of the success or failure of any particular department to gain access to scant resources tends to be accredited to or blamed upon certain individuals. Hence a successful Head of Department is described as 'strong, dynamic and innovatory', while one who is perceived as unsuccessful is described as 'weak, lethargic and lacking in initiative'.

It would seem that the 'numbers game', as it is referred to by many

47

members of staff, provides a constant basis for tension and conflict at Western. Yet to confine our analysis to one aspect, no matter how important, of departmental relations, is to ignore more complex processes which derive directly from the relationship of FE to its environment, and more particularly to the immediate industrial infrastructure. However, while the status of individual departments is clearly linked to such issues as the manpower requirements of their corresponding industries, it would be misleading to suggest that those links with local industry actually determine the internal workings of college affairs. Indeed, the relationship between Western and its local industrial environment is far more subtle. Its complexity is perhaps best understood by considering who is taught what, and how that is decided, in relation to external influences.

External influences upon the academic structure

It was suggested earlier that one of the most important characteristics of the FE system is its voluntaristic nature. Indeed, since FE has no compulsory student population, its entire intake depends upon the success of enrolment incentives. Thus it is not surprising that the unavoidable 'selling' of college courses has sometimes evoked the criticism that FE is merely the handmaiden of industry. However, it would seem to us that such a criticism betrays the acceptance of an over-simplified correspondence theory between the needs of industry and the supply of trained personnel through FE. The most obvious problem with this assumption is that when we examine the practice of FE, we find it presents a rather haphazard response to industrial needs. Moreover, the contribution of employers to the recent Great Debate would seem to confirm our observation that FE responds in no direct sense to the dictates of local industry.

Thus if industry neither theoretically nor empirically determines the nature of college courses, we must identify the alternative influences in play and ascertain how they operate.

Government, for example, and more specifically local government, has a hand in the definition of policy guidelines. However, with regard to FE, statements of policy have usually taken the form of circulars and appendices as opposed to full-scale policy declarations. The central framework of policy regarding the FE sector, therefore, has changed very little since the original guidelines stated in the 1944 Education Act. Education Authorities also place certain statutory requirements upon the internal organisation of schools and colleges. In addition the various examination boards and professional bodies wield influence through the award of qualifications and certificates. And last, but certainly not least, both national and local industry issue projections of manpower requirements for the consideration of college governing committees. Moreover, it could be argued that the manning levels set by the various trade unions also present a contributory influence upon ·the internal organisation of educational institutions.

We would not wish to argue of course that the various agencies referred to above actually *determine* the nature of the curriculum, but see them rather as presenting a set of justificatory ideologies against which the structuring of courses and hence the balance of power within college is negotiated. However, what we want to draw attention to is the fact that such ideologies of justification often act to hide those essential material conditions which unite them, namely the *dependence* of the college upon external agencies to provide both students and material plant. Thus, while the ideology of autonomous developments might prevail, it is frequently circumscribed by the conditions set upon the avenues of choice available to college authorities.

The consequences of this overall ideology which we have described as masking the underlying tension between competing interests within Western, may be most clearly sighted by examining how the college sets about attracting students. In a more general sense, however, we have already discussed how this overall ideology found expression during the expansionist period of FE in the need to equate programmes of national economic advancement through education with certain principles of social justice. *We wish to present this apparent merging of interests, acted out through the development of policies at a local level, as the basic premise upon which colleges of FE organise their programmes of activity.*

Thus, in our view, enrolment incentives which present FE as personally beneficial to both the prospective student and his employer, may be interpreted as masking a complex interplay of demand factors well beyond the control of those individuals. The most obvious example of this process may be found in the language of the college prospectus which suggests that everyone, student or employer, who enters or contributes to the institution, will benefit in some directly personal way. In other words it is assumed that FE is necessarily a 'good' thing both for the student and those who employ him. Consider, for example, the following extracts:

The Principal and Governing Body are most anxious that the excellent facilities available for further education in the College and its annexes are known by all those wishing to continue their education after leaving school. The maximum use and benefit must be obtained from the resources made available by the Education Authority and it is hoped that all concerned will take advantage of these facilities.

49

It is hoped that all concerned will take advantage of the facilities offered and not hesitate to contact the liaison officer who will be pleased to give all the assistance he can.

At first glance such statements represent no more than intentions of goodwill upon the part of the college in its attempt to attract students. Yet the very recurrence of such terms as 'use', 'benefit' and 'advantage' cannot be isolated from the complex exchange of external influences which operate in the wider structure of society, well beyond the control of those immediately concerned, i.e. students, college, employers. Thus not only are these terms circumscribed by rapid change in technological requirements, they are also subject to opportunity for implementation in an ever-fluctuating market. In other words, it would seem to us that while the language of the prospectus clearly promises the individual greater control over his destiny, it also masks the underlying controls which may impinge upon him through the wider interests of industry and government.

Indeed, the power of those external controls only begins to become apparent when one considers the nature of 'failure' in FE.[8] The usual explanations of individual failure tend to lay blame upon the student's lack of 'psychological' motivation in undertaking the course. Very rarely is it considered necessary to examine the forms of relationships and conditions within which students work, or the degree to which curricular knowledge may be operationalised. Thus in our view, the language of mutual benefit which characterises the college prospectus not only masks the interplay of external demands imposed by government and industry, but condenses them into a common theme, which appears to be primarily concerned with 'advantages' which may be gained by the individual as a result of FE. In other words, when viewed in this light, the college prospectus presents little more than a general image of justification for certain external and competing interests which may be brought to bear upon the recipient of FE.

A further area of external influence may be sighted when one considers the atmosphere of competition which exists between Western and other neighbouring colleges. Indeed, Western may be said to have adapted to pressures arising from competition from neighbouring colleges through the process of diversification. In other words, courses at Western, their range and structure, may be seen to be largely dependent not only upon demands imposed by local industry but also upon the kinds of courses available in neighbouring institutions. Thus the relationship of the college to the 'outside' comprises a number of different levels, from the most direct to the most indirect. Let us examine, for example, the kind of pragmatic negotiation which goes on at the most obvious level. In the following comments a senior member of the college hierarchy is discussing the certificate of FE, and may be seen to legitimate a policy decision concerning that certificate by reference to the needs of local industry:

'The certificate is a course designed for young people leaving school who have no real idea where they are going . . . or what they want to do. The idea behind such a vocationally related course . . . a course which is of not too high an academic level . . . is that it provides some insight into the needs of industry. . . . It provides a general knowledge and background. This course has been developed because we, along with the Area Board, foresaw a demand for it some years ago.'

Clearly, the comments quoted above are a direct response to the kinds of employment opportunities which may be available to students at a later date. Such remarks, however, appear quite guarded when compared with comments taken from a later discussion on course development:

'But then you get the other development of courses. You get Heads of Department in discussion with Industry . . . a particular firm may, for example, say they've got trouble with foundry work and suggest that we run courses on foundry work . . . this is what's happened here. We've just developed a full-time foundry training course for moulders and tool-makers which has taken some years of negotiation with the Head of Department and industry. So courses emerge by Heads of Department knowing their industry . . . knowing what it wants and meeting their needs through discussion.'

Quite simply, local industry needs foundry men, and the college needs students. Thus organising training for foundry workers provides an answer for both parties. The result of such negotiation, therefore, is a total response to the market situation, in which the demand and supply of labour become one. The college has little option but to respond in this way, although it could be argued that the development of particular courses is not necessarily instigated by local industrial needs, but rather concerned with the wider objective of increasing the general stock of trained personnel. Such an argument, however, not only assumes perfect competition for labour and a highly mobile work force, but also treats the process of technological change as an unproblematic phenomenon.

The social relationship, therefore, between Western and local employers is one of negotiation, but because of the kinds of control employers can bring to bear upon the 'life-blood' of the college, it is not a relationship of *equal* negotiation. Thus in our view, much of the discussion, liaison and negotiation between college authorities and local employers about course development is little more than an exercise of

51

legitimation which provides a gloss for the interplay of competing interests which ultimately shape FE. The following extract from a discussion about course development with a Head of Department at Western would seem to confirm such a view:

> 'But we are not stupid enough to think that our needs come before those of industry. They don't. They complement each other; once a lad's qualified he's needed, and we should lose all sympathy if we started banging on the table and saying that we wanted T3, and this, that, and the other, on block release. (a) There is no guarantee we should get it and (b) we should lose the sympathy of the people on whom we depend for sending these students.' (See appendix 1.)

It is not surprising, therefore, that the aims of Western as an educational institution appear almost synonymous with those of local industry. Whether all those who participate in the institution share those aims, however, is another matter.

A number of consequences may be seen to arise directly from the relationship between Western and outside agencies, notably industry. The most obvious of these concerns the curriculum and how it is organised. However, while at the level of actual negotiation we may locate a consensus of opinion about the aims and objectives of FE, on further examination this consensus would seem to be underpinned by a somewhat contradictory set of principles.

This contradiction appears to arise from the competing demands imposed upon the college by government. While local industry demands that the college should supply a specifically trained work force to meet certain local industrial needs, government is concerned that the college should contribute towards the national pool of trained labour, so as to provide a well qualified and mobile work force.[9] It could perhaps be argued that such interests ultimately coincide. It is our contention, however, that they do not. Indeed, in our view such an argument emanates from a wider contradiction highlighted in chapter 1, namely that of the tension between the competing interests of education and training.

An area of the curriculum in which we may sight this contradiction in operation most clearly is the area of Liberal Studies. While government directives have laid emphasis upon the need for broadly-based courses of an educational nature, the idea that students released for training in the firm's time should spend a whole lesson discussing politics, sex or religion, is often the target of considerable criticism. Yet while Liberal Studies is the most obvious scapegoat for such opposition, in our view it represents only the tip of the iceberg concerning the whole problem of who ultimately controls FE. One employer we spoke to put it this way:

'As far as I am concerned so long as the college provides the employer with his fundamental needs everything is all right, after all
it's the employer who's paying for it. I don't object to them broadening the vision of the lads. They're pretty limited after all. But
the overriding necessity is for the employer to get back a return on
the time, effort and energy he has paid out on sending the lads to
college.'

Inevitably, Western resolves the conflict between contradictory pressures in the only way which will ensure its survival. In effect, it pays
lip-service to government policy by rationalising courses in terms of
educational objectives, while at the same time directing those courses
towards the *training* of apprentice-students in the specific skills required
by local industry.[10]

In the chapters which follow we shall look more closely at the consequences for the curriculum of this liaison between Western and local
industry. For the present, however, we are concerned primarily with its
influence upon the college's internal structure. If contradictory pressures
may be seen to arise from sources outside the college (i.e. government
and industry), it is within the institution that they are acted out. The
most obvious expression of such pressures may be found not only in
the competition between departments, but in the explicit vertical
division of the college.

As we have seen, Western responds to the demands of local industry.
Thus a strong demand from a particular industry for specifically trained
workers places its corresponding college department in a favourable
position to attract student numbers. In more subtle ways, industry can
project the required number of workers at particular levels of skills
which will be required at a later date. Thus, as we suggested in the
ethnographic section, industry not only influences the content of the
curriculum, but also its stratification (see our discussion on differentiation in Appendix 2).

Within such a competitive atmosphere, most departments devise
strategies for survival. Indeed, as we suggested earlier, the success or
failure of a particular department often becomes personalised, so that
the heads of department inevitably 'carry the can' or 'wear the laurels'.
Moreover, as the college must be flexible and diversify in order to
survive, those who are most successful in the competition will enjoy
greatest access to scant resources. There remains, however, an alternative
strategy of survival, namely that of being involved in the decision-making
processes of the college. Whether or not those processes actually contribute to the resolution of the problems which arise at Western is open
to question. It is, however, to an examination of those processes that
we now turn.

The committee structure

We have suggested so far that the atmosphere of heated competition which tends to characterise the day-to-day affairs of Western College finds its roots to a large extent in sources beyond the control of those immediately involved. Yet in the day-to-day running of the college, decisions have to be made and courses of action found, which will allow participants to manage the on-going nature of organisational life. At Western the process of decision-making presents an avenue of negotiation within the college through which outside pressures can be managed by the participants. Furthermore, it provides the context in which particular decisions can be legitimated to those whose job it is to operationalise them.[11]

Any attempt, however, to examine such a process raises a whole range of both methodological and substantive problems, and since some of these may have significant consequences for our research, it is important to give some indication of them here.

The most immediate difficulty that the researcher confronts in any institution is actually gaining access to the meetings at which decisions are supposed to be made. Indeed, such gatherings are usually inaccessible even to those whose lives they most affect. Consequently, our analysis here is based to a large extent upon the accounts of those who participate in such proceedings, rather than upon direct observation. It would seem to us, however, that this indirect access to decision-making processes ultimately allows us some insight into the interpretation placed upon that process by those most closely involved. Indeed, through discussion with participants we gained some understanding of the way in which individuals or groups act in order to promote their own interests.

Moreover, the unspecific nature of much that passes for decision-making presents a difficulty in itself. Indeed the game-like quality of much institutional life, even at its most overt level, makes it difficult for the researcher to distinguish between official and unofficial forms of decision-making. The process of coalition-forming itself is extremely difficult for the outsider to recognise. Indeed, the informal discussion of members over coffee, the small gathering after a larger meeting, even the 'sounding of opinion' among junior staff, may or may not be part of the process. However, it is often the case that such informal proceedings actually influence a particular decision and its implementation in a far more concrete way than several hours of hard bargaining in some formal committee structure.

A further area of difficulty concerns the social relations of those who participate in decision-making, particularly in view of the hierarchical nature of the college which cannot fail to influence the perceptions and actions of participants. It is very easy for a person at the top of the hierarchy to say that he values the opinions of his colleagues, particularly those of the team below him. But whether he takes notice of those opinions, or whether they are given freely and without bias, is quite another matter. Indeed, a 'sounding of opinion' often constitutes little more than an exercise of legitimation, which satisfies the potential frustrations of all concerned, but makes little difference to what is actually decided.

It is problems such as these, which represent just a sample of those which confront the researcher in his attempt to understand processes of decision-making. Nevertheless, we gained considerable insights from our observations, direct and otherwise, of the committee structure of the college and its relationship with the 'outside'.

The internal function of the committee structure

At the most elementary level, committee meetings at Western have no formal executive power, except that they are attended by heads of departments. That is to say that the various committees have no apparent autonomy and act in an advisory manner. This conception of the committee structure as a sounding board for ideas is endorsed wholeheartedly by most members of the college administration as the following remarks indicate:

'I know it's undemocratic but the vote doesn't always give you the answer. You've got to discuss the problems but in the end the committee may not have a solution. Its as simple as that, but if they [meaning the committee] haven't got a solution someone has to take the decision for him [meaning the Principal]. So I believe in a committee being advisable. Though I believe in discussion I also believe in one man saying "I've got the responsibility of taking the decision based on what I've heard from all my committee." That's the way I feel good committees work.'

In view, however, of the elaborate committee structure at Western it seems surprising that such proceedings have no real teeth. Clearly in a situation where particular decisions have to be implemented, some degree of consultation is required. Moreover, meetings of members of staff to discuss courses of action promotes a general feeling of consensus about an agreed set of principles. The following comments from one committee member we spoke to indicate the role of the committee in this respect:

'I'm a strong believer in committees, but committees that work, not committees that sit around talking. You need committees with a strong chairman, who is also a good listener. I'm a strong believer in leadership because I am a team player as well; so I believe in team-work but I also believe in a good captain. Because I think you get the views of different people with different experiences and these are valuable when you're making decisions on things. Your own views are limited by your own experience and knowledge.'

The committee structure, therefore, plays an important part in mini-mising potential conflict by promoting the idea that everybody is an important member of a team. This view is held not only by those at the top of the hierarchy, but by most members of the college administration right down to junior members of large departments who have experi-enced some form of committee involvement. The following remarks from one lecturer we spoke to express the general consensus of opinion among college staff concerning the role of the committee in decision-making processes:

'The Principal and Vice-Principal when they started here . . . and they've been here a few years now . . . expressed the opinion that the college should be run from the bottom upwards, and not from the top down. They believe that lecturers should, to some extent, through the committees, indicate the kinds of directions that the college should take. They have also stated that the committees are very important to this issue of direction. . . . Being fairly new to the teaching game I think the idea is sound and I fully support these ideas on this. The committees as yet however haven't got much teeth, as they've only been going a couple of years. In this department . . . with its work patterns so flexible . . . and work loads constantly changing . . . it isn't always possible to attend the meetings . . . though I do try to follow things up and find out what's going on.'

Such comments indicate a degree of faith in the committee structure itself which is endorsed by most members of staff. In our view, how-ever, what is more interesting about such remarks is the way in which that faith is expressed. Where Heads of Department look upon involve-ment in committee work as promoting the idea of being part of a team, lecturers see the committee structure as a way of allowing those at the bottom of the college hierarchy to influence decisions made at the top. Although both groups refer to different but equally idealised versions of the process, both recognise the existence of underlying power rela-tionships and therefore the limitations which are imposed on practice. The committee structure, however, constitutes a means whereby poten-tial conflict can be minimised, and a unified public image presents to external agencies.

It is this latter point which in our view is of particular significance here, and in order to understand this consensus about the need to present an image of the college as a unified body, we must again reflect upon those external factors which impinge upon decision-making processes within the college.

We have already discussed the ways in which internal relations at Western are circumscribed by forces beyond the college itself. In particular, we focused upon the relationship between the supply and demand of students, and the consequences of that relationship for the nature and format of the curriculum. In addition, we examined the sources of pressure, both within and without the college, which give rise to an atmosphere of competition between departments. Such internal conflict, however, would seem to be in direct contradiction with the public image of the college as a unified educational institution offering courses of benefit to both student and employer. Indeed, in view of the external controls exerted upon the life-blood of the college, namely student numbers, it is not surprising that the college administration seeks to present a unified front. Moreover, it would seem to us that in this respect the committee structure performs a crucial task. In effect, it acts as a levelling mechanism whereby the internal contradictions and problems created by external forces are resolved. However, while the committee provides a means whereby internal tensions can be fought out and channelled, in no way does it endow its members with sufficient power to create divisions within the structure itself.

Our examination of the committee structure at Western, however, cannot rest here. For in an institution where committees fulfil an essentially advisory function,[12] some form of power inevitably resides in the informal avenues of influence available to participants.

By informal avenues of influence we mean the formation of coalitions which may develop on an *ad hoc* basis, and which serve to foster the notion of alternative courses of action within the more formal decision-making process. In this way, particular groups may reach temporary agreement with others in order to promote longer-term and often quite separate interests.[13] Within such a framework, the power of argument becomes the major force of influence available to participants. However, such a conception of the internal processes of the institution suggests a far too simplistic view of the committee structure at Western. Moreover, it ignores the existence of a further level of committee intervention which has considerable bearing upon the internal processes of decision-making within the college.

Indeed, the governing body ensures that the ordinances of the college are observed. The members of the governing committee itself are almost without exception nominees from either the LEA or local industry. In our view, the membership of the committee constitutes a manifestation of the conflicting dimensions of FE, namely those interested in the 'training' of skilled labour (industry), and those interested in its 'education' (LEA). We would not of course wish to present such conflicting interests as being in any way clear-cut or simple. However, although we can only conjecture whether the various governors have any autonomy from the bodies they represent, in our view, it seems unlikely that they could be at odds with the interests of those parties. Thus, the interests of the various sections of the governing body constitute a framework within which decisions are made. For those competing interests can not only exert influence upon such mundane matters as the purchase of an expensive piece of equipment, but can also predict the future demand for particular skills, and, more importantly, decide whether the college should organise courses to meet that future demand.

We would not wish to present a *total* correspondence between the decisions of the college administration and the interests of those external agencies represented by the governing body. Such a conclusion would be inaccurate as alternative courses of action *do* exist. However, we would argue that the viability of those alternatives are limited by the demands articulated by the various factions of the governing body. Thus, what counts as 'knowledge', 'training' and 'provision' become items for discussion within the format of the governing body. Moreover, their definitions of those terms inevitably constitute the taken-for-granted premises, in accordance with which internal committees offer advice. In such a way, therefore, internal decisions become aligned with external expectations, and are perceived as *naturally* meeting the needs of *all* concerned. Individual departments, as we will attempt to demonstrate in the chapters which follow, have little choice but to operate within the boundaries set by that structure. Thus although departmental involvement in the decision-making process is essential for self-protection, individual departments remain relatively powerless in the face of wider areas of control.

At the centre of this whole process is the Principal. Designated as the executive officer of the college, it is he who ultimately articulates decisions. His role is clearly influenced by the governing body, but in no way can he be seen as a mere functionary of their demands. Neither can his actions be condemned as dictatorial by the college administration, since he must rely upon both its consent and commitment in order to operationalise decisions. Indeed, as we suggested earlier (see p. 56), the principal has considerable regard for the opinions of his staff, but ultimately those opinions must be condensed into executive decisions which will satisfy both internal *and* external agencies.

In such circumstances, it is obvious that the Principal cannot wholly satisfy the demands of *all* concerned, and therefore he has no alternative but to compromise and satisfice.[14] He achieves this compromise by the way in which he juggles the current market forces (government dictates, industrial needs, etc.) into premises for action. Thus he represents the centre of a network of information which must incorporate external pressures into internal courses of action. For example, a number of Heads of Department indicated that what counted as course expansion depended less upon criteria of an educational nature than upon the particular needs at any given time of the nation's industries. Thus courses which might attract greater student numbers *could* be seen as less acceptable than those fostering specific links with particular economic or industrial developments. The Principal, therefore, is limited by those very manifestations of material constraints which affect his administration as a whole. Moreover, his control resides in the degree to which he is able to translate the satisfaction of particular demands into sets of powerful rationalisations with which his subordinates can concur.

To summarise, we have attempted in this chapter to reach a general understanding of the organisational framework which governs Western College and its work. We have argued that its vertical division into departments not only presents a major frame of identification for its staff, but lies at the heart of all institutional competition and conflict. However, such conflict is minimised by the need of the college administration to present a unified public image to those external agencies which ensure its continued existence. In addition, we have attempted a brief explanation of the processes of decision-making which characterise the conduct of college affairs.

Of necessity, and particularly in relation to the ambiguous area of decision-making, we have advanced general rather than specific principles of operation. However, our analysis of the organisational arrangements of Western College represents a background to our discussion in the chapters which follow of the specific workings of the departments of Mining and Liberal Studies. We shall attempt to demonstrate how both departments and individuals may adopt widely varying strategies which will allow them to operate more effectively within the wider organisational framework.

Chapter 4

The Department of Mining

In the previous chapter, we examined at a general level the organisational framework of Western College. In particular, we attempted to highlight some of the more dominant organisational features of the college, and to consider the ways in which they affect participants. In this chapter, we shall be concerned to investigate one specific department, its *raison d'être* and function, within the broader organisational network of college affairs.

We have chosen to concentrate in this chapter upon the Department of Mining. Our choice of that department as a particular focus of interest may be explained quite simply. First, our study is primarily concerned with the disjuncture between the competing interests of education and training. In chapter 1 we sought to outline the disjuncture as a major problematic of our research. We are concerned, moreover, to understand the broader implications for practice of that disjuncture within the sphere of FE. Thus we have chosen to focus in this chapter upon a specific department within Western College which relates in a highly explicit manner to the vocational needs of the industry that it serves. In the chapter which follows, we shall contrast our initial examination of the Department of Mining with a study of a second department within the college, the Department of Liberal Studies, which is concerned in no direct sense with the training needs of industry, and which operates in theory to meet the general educational needs of apprentice students.

A second important reason for our choice of the Mining and Liberal Studies Departments as particular areas of interest became apparent during the course of our field-work. As we indicated in the previous chapter, where the organisational life of any institution is characterised by considerable competition between departments, those departments must operate a number of strategies in order to ensure their survival. In our analysis of the organisational framework of Western College, we

60

isolated two interrelated but separate strands of 'negotiation': the academic structure and the committee structure. In our view, the Mining and Liberal Studies Departments provide clear examples of those differential processes of negotiation in operation.

Our immediate concern in this chapter, however, is to provide an account of the rise of Mining Studies as a 'legitimate' area of study within the college. More specifically we shall be concerned to understand that process of legitimation in terms of the complex historical development of the Mining Industry itself. In addition, we shall focus upon the internal workings of the department in terms of its structure and organisation. To this end, we shall attempt to understand the departmental ethos which permeates all its internal workings, and give rise to its cohesion as a unit. In our view, this departmental ethos has important consequences for both teachers and students in terms of their identification with and involvement in college affairs. Finally, we shall examine how the relationship between college staff and a monopoly employer can not only affect inter-departmental relations, but shape the learning experience and social identity of students.

The socio-historical development of the Department of Mining at Western

In our organisational study of Western College, we laid emphasis upon the atmosphere of competition between departments in terms of access to such resources as space, time and plant. More importantly, we indicated that a major source of that competition was the need for each department to sustain a healthy student population in order to survive. Moreover, since the size of the student population at Western depends to a large extent upon the willingness of employers to release apprentices for day-release training, we suggested that local industry could wield considerable control over college affairs. Indeed, not only does local industry have considerable control over what is taught, but it also provides the means whereby particular departments negotiate their curricula and courses. In other words, we suggested that many decisions made by the college administration are influenced to a large extent by the manpower requirements, present and future, of local employers.

This form of negotiation regarding curricula and courses, dependent to a large extent upon forces external to the college, is central to our understanding of the Mining Department at Western. For, as we will attempt to explain, both the development of the department within the college and the kinds of relations it pursues with other college bodies, can only be understood in the light of the complex history of the Mining Industry itself.

The Department of Mining

No account of the rise and fall of the Mining Industry in Britain would be complete without a thorough-going examination of its role in our economic infrastructure. For obvious reasons, however, we cannot delve into the wider implications of that role in this study, although they have considerable bearing upon our specific analysis. Suffice it to say that the history of the British Mining Industry is characterised by a series of enormous upheavals which have had considerable repercussions for most of our social institutions, not least among those Education.

Perhaps the most important consequence for education of trends within the Mining Industry is due to the changing demand for miners over the past twenty years. Indeed, technological changes in the late 1950s and early 1960s led to the closure of many pits on the grounds of supposedly uneconomic methods of recovery. As a consequence there was a considerable drop-out of manpower from the industry together with a low take-up of apprenticeships. Such events within the Mining Industry itself were echoed within the technical colleges. At Western, during this recession, the Mining Department struggled for recognition. Indeed, prior to the completion of the new building, the Mining Department was located very much towards the bottom of the departmental hierarchy at Western. A glance at the 1960–1 college prospectus shows very few courses related to Mining, of which the main two are a pre-entry National Diploma Course and another described as a Mining Introductory Craft Course. Because of the declining numbers of mining students and the consequent cut-back of courses, the department was placed in a very weak position during those years. Indeed, many mining staff were seen as under-utilised and redeployed into other departments to teach mathematics or technology to students from other industries. Although this process of redeployment seemed a logical course of action in such circumstances, it gave the upper hand in terms of patronage to other more thriving departments within the college, which, if ever the situation was to be reversed, would prove to have long-standing repercussions.

Since the mid 1960s, increasing demands for energy have given rise to far-reaching expansion within the Mining Industry. Consequently, the college department, having suffered a number of lean years, was to experience corresponding expansion. Courses, which had been cut or which had only been half-filled, could now be filled twice over. By 1966, when the current head of department was appointed, the college as a whole was experiencing a wave of expansion. Within the Mining Department, a whole range of day-release, block-release and full-time courses were being developed. By 1970, the department had succeeded in developing its own Ordinary National Diploma in Mining.[1] Consequently, the department experienced a rapid expansion of staff, together with considerably improved access to available resources. Thus by the mid 1970s the Department of Mining at Western had been transformed into one of the College's most powerful departments. However, as we will explain later, the lean years of cut-backs and redeployment could not be easily forgotten.

As we suggested in the previous chapter, a department undergoing expansion also gains greater access to scarce resources because of its increased points rating. Consequently, those in a less powerful position vis-à-vis points must accept a reduced share in the distribution of resources. With the rapid expansion of the Mining Department, other less prosperous departments within the college began to look to the miners for a reciprocation of the help previously given them in their years of recession. However, the miners clearly did not see the earlier patronage of other departments in terms of help and felt under no obligation to reciprocate. Thus the Mining Department gradually acquired a reputation as being a law unto itself, and this image of insularity was reinforced by what other departments saw as an attitude of empire building on the part of the miners to the detriment of other interests. How this situation arose is difficult to explain, unless one sees it in terms of the inter-departmental struggle for survival, and it seems that we cannot underestimate the importance of that Machiavellian aspect of inter-departmental relations at Western.

Indeed, as we indicated in our organisational analysis of the college, the very fragmentation of departments renders the fight for survival inevitable. More importantly, that struggle exerts a powerful influence over the ways in which participants operate the college decision-making processes, no matter what other factors are in play. However, the competition between departments at Western is by no means the only key to our understanding of particular departments. Indeed, of equal importance with regard to the Department of Mining is the degree of solidarity which permeates the Mining Industry as a whole and which finds expression within its corresponding department at Western.

It would not be an exaggeration to say that throughout its history, the Mining Industry has shown a degree of unity and solidarity in its communities far beyond that usually associated with the working class. A perspective upon this solidarity may be gained by briefly considering the 'quality' of life underground. Where workers dice with death each day, eight hours and more away from fresh air, and suffer the possibility of long- and short-term problems of accident and disease, it is not surprising that they are united by a common bond. This sense of unity has manifested itself in many forms, of which the most explicit is the strong commitment to unionism which has frequently played an important role in situations of national controversy. The spirit of communality which has epitomised the Mining Industry throughout its history is perhaps best expressed in the book *Coal is Our Life* (Dennis, Henriques

63

and Slaughter, 1969). Indeed, such factors as those recorded there provide a crucial background to our understanding of mining workers.

When a miner is recruited from industry into the sphere of FE, therefore, it is not perhaps surprising that he brings with him his strong industrial identity. Indeed, it is virtually impossible to teach Mining Engineering unless one has had considerable experience within the industry itself. Thus, not only do lecturers in the Mining Department tend to take the manifestations of solidarity among their students for granted, but they also tend to share the vast majority of their attitudes. One member of the Mining Department we spoke to put it this way:

'There are one or two who are not of the Mining Industry . . . and they do have difficulties in the department. They have difficulty in getting used to our ways, because our ways are a bit unorthodox relative to other departments.'

Furthermore, this perception of their professional identity as 'miners above all else' does not go unnoticed by colleagues in other departments, who have been heard to say: 'There's a joke in this place that the miners can do anything . . . only miners can teach miners.'

Whether in fact it is the case that 'only miners can teach miners', or whether indeed only those who have actually worked in the Mining Industry can understand the 'needs' of mining students, is open to question. It seems to us, however, that such views are merely the surface expression of far more deep-seated factors. One member of the Mining Department we spoke to described the situation in the following way:

'Other departments in the college don't like the mining people. I think there's a resentment of the Mining Industry as a whole. I don't know whether it's the middle classes' resentment or not but I do certainly feel that there is antagonism toward the Mining Department as a whole.'

Clearly, the lecturer quoted above sees the situation in terms of social class. However, in our view, the situation of the Mining Department at Western is shaped by factors well beyond the 'them and us' context. Indeed, we would wish to argue that the identity of lecturers in the Mining Department is so much at one with workers in their industry of origin that their 'function' as technical teachers is seen very much as of secondary importance. Moreover, this feeling of solidarity with mining workers, above and beyond their relationships with other college staff, tends to create both an insular and militant image of the department. Indeed, this image of the Mining Department as a 'law unto itself' tends to colour perceptions both within and without the departments, so that where other staff may be critical of what they consider to be 'empire building' on the part of the miners, the miners themselves perceived this attitude as part of the general resentment harboured against their department.

It would seem to us that this uneasy climate not only sets the tone for relations between the Mining Department and other college bodies, but also provides an important background to our understanding of the internal organisation of the department, which we will now consider in greater detail.

Departmental organisation

Including the Head of Department, the Mining Department at Western comprises twenty-six members. The department itself may be seen to be divided both horizontally and vertically: vertically, in that the department comprises four senior lecturers and a number of other senior staff on the Lecturer II scale; and horizontally in the sense that the department is divided in terms of subject specialisms which include the following: Mining, Mining Mechanical, Mining Electrical and Mining Surveying. It is interesting to note at this point that these internal divisions echo to a considerable extent the isolation of the Mining Department as a whole from other college departments. Indeed, it became apparent during the course of our field-work that those involved in the various specialisms within the department identified very strongly with their corresponding specialised areas within the industry, a factor which served to heighten the atmosphere of aloofness which was seen by other college staff as a predominant characteristic of the department.

We have already indicated that a central factor in our understanding of the department as a whole concerns its solidarity with mining workers. Indeed, this feeling of solidarity with workers in their industry of origin provided a constant background to all the conversations and interviews we held with members of the department. Thus, they sometimes found it difficult to support the idea that arbitrary issues like promotion interests might influence the chain of organisation within the department. Indeed, it would seem that this intrinsic solidarity among mining workers somehow gives rise to an independence of mind which cuts across the various hierarchically differentiated positions within the department, so that ultimately we came to the conclusion that in our study of the Mining Department we were dealing with a different kind of value system from that shared by other college departments. Moreover, it became apparent that this value system has its roots in the very essence of the Mining Industry itself.

An important feature of this value system which is peculiar to the mining staff at Western is their emphasis upon democracy. In a large number of the interviews we held with members of the department the

65

word 'democratic' regularly occurred. Indeed, there is ample evidence both from our observations and interview material which suggests that the mining staff saw themselves as being more 'open' than other college departments. Perhaps the most obvious expression of this 'openness' lies in the fact that the Head of Department holds regularly monthly meetings of *all* the mining staff. Moreover, the distribution of resources among the various specialised areas in the department is openly discussed. In addition, there is a high level of informal contact among the mining staff, possibly over coffee or in the common room of the annexe where most of their work is carried out. Such factors give rise to an atmosphere of apparent open development, which is supported by the perceptions of all those involved. However, it would seem to us that in this atmosphere of democracy lies a paradox which is not immediately apparent, and which raises questions concerning its exact nature.

We have suggested so far that the mining staff at Western share a value system which differs from that of other college departments, and which gives rise to a certain independence of mind which cuts across the various hierarchical distinctions within the department. Thus one might suppose that a stereotyped form of leadership, particularly that of an authoritarian kind, would be doomed to failure in an organisational sense. However, in our view, where individuals believe that they have some access to processes of decision-making, it is often the case that a hidden form of social control is in operation. In other words, apparently democratic procedures can often exert considerable control over those involved. Moreover, when we examine the apparent democracy of the Mining Department at Western we uncover an explicit paradox in which that democracy becomes no more than a misleading expression of an underlying acquiescense to the authority of the Head of Department.

This paradox which would seem to characterise the organisational structure of the Mining Department initially came to light when we looked more closely at that aspect of democracy which asserts that disagreement among members is possible and can serve to challenge the ruling orthodoxy. To use Berger's (1971) terminology, such an assertion claims that members, such as those in the Mining Department at Western, have access to an alternative plausibility structure, so that issues relating to the department and its organisation are really open to negotiation. The problem in this case, however, is that such an alternative structure of plausibility is totally inconsistent with the notion of solidarity, and therefore with the very essence of the industry itself.

Indeed, mining by its very nature is a highly organised and disciplined occupation. Where workers operate in situations of continual danger, a very rigid hierarchy becomes necessary so that accidents may be avoided. Thus it is not surprising that a central feature of the value system of mining workers is an acceptance of authority. Thus, while at the administrative level of departmental affairs some semblance of democracy may be apparent, at the level of job competence and in the work situation, considerable deference to authority exists.

This deference, however, is by no means immediately apparent. Indeed, to both other college staff and the research worker himself, the department presents a tough and unified front. To this end, the mining staff tend to transmit an aura of professionalism, which arises from a highly pragmatic, 'no nonsense' attitude towards the job in hand. In the conversation which follows, one of the lecturers we spoke to attempts to rationalise the importance of practical experience for the teaching of mining students:

> 'Having served an apprenticeship on the Coal Board you've more or less been through the same apprenticeship that these lads are now on. Therefore, you're more likely to understand their problems and their needs, their weaknesses and their strengths. I think this is a good thing. You can talk to them in a way that they can understand ... you understand them, and they know it. You've worked in a pit ... you've [untranscribable] ... that cable ... you've been on the coal-face. The students come here with a practical turn of mind ... they want answers to practical questions. The fact that you've worked in the mines means you can answer questions from a more practical point of view. Rather than giving them the theory of why it should happen ... you use your practice to explain the theory.'

Here the emphasis is upon 'doing a good job' in a situation where teacher and taught share a common professional bond, and where the instrumental transference of a set of practical skills to a group of students that the lecturer 'understands', is the prime objective. Indeed, the relationship between lecturer and students depends almost entirely upon shared industrial experience. On closer examination, however, it becomes apparent that within the very recognition of that shared experience, there exists an explicit acceptance of and deference to the industrial value structure which gives rise to that sense of communality. Indeed, this unquestioning acceptance of the underlying value system not only finds expression in the way in which lecturers perceive their role in the department, but in the way in which they act out that role in their teaching. Moreover, the self-image projected by lecturers in their teaching is legitimated by the evidence of their 'success' in mining, since not only have they succeeded in becoming lecturers in the subject, but they have also succeeded in maintaining a close grasp of the realities of practice through their past industrial experience.

Thus, within the department there exists no means whereby the orthodoxy of the industry might be challenged. For to challenge the value system of the industry would be to admit a failure to understand the realities of practice, and, more importantly, to express an inability to understand the needs of mining students. The paradox we would wish to draw attention to here stems from a contradiction that arises for lecturers in the Mining Department at Western. If they observe, consciously or unconsciously, the norms of conformity, they will be allowed, perhaps for the first time in their lives, an autonomous role within the boundaries set by those norms of conformity. In other words, the paradox which tends to characterise the social relations of Mining staff at Western has its roots in the dimensions of autonomy lecturers enjoy *vis-à-vis* their teaching role, as well as in an implicit deference to the authority structure of the department. Indeed, it is as if the workings and nature of the Mining Industry itself have been adopted in their entirety by the department. Moreover, such a value system, together with the organisational workings it gives rise to, is not only supportive of the way in which the Mining staff define their role in teaching, but also of their taken-for-granted understanding of life at the coal-face.

Furthermore, such a situation which suggests both reciprocal respect and self-interest, allows the Head of Department enormous power in his management of the department. Not only can he present an image of the department as a cohesive working unit, but he can also control the internal departmental workings without recourse to any form of sanctions. Moreover, the efficiency of his actions is reinforced by the security of knowing that a constant supply of students is available. Indeed, he has no need to court alliances, even with those who feel that their earlier support of the Mining Department has not been reciprocated.

Thus, both internally and externally, the Department of Mining at Western may be seen to be in a very strong position. Consequently it is not perhaps surprising that other less prosperous college departments often resent and sometimes openly question that strength. However, since the strength of the Mining Department arises largely from both the solidarity and insularity of its staff *vis-à-vis* other college bodies, it is important to examine the underlying factors which shape the organisational identity of its members. In the section which follows, we shall consider in greater depth the nature of teacher involvement in the organisational structure of the department, and the subsequent implications for practice.

Teacher involvement and identity

One cannot begin to understand the nature of organisational or departmental life unless one considers the level of commitment members feel

towards the organisation itself. In other words, while the overall structure clearly sets the conditions of practice, it is the degree of involvement in that overall structure which ultimately determines how members
will operate. Thus it is necessary to isolate those particular factors
which shape the organisational identity of those involved.

We have suggested so far that the social relations of the mining
staff at Western are characterised by a high level of solidarity, which
shapes their attitudes towards other college bodies. Moreover, that
solidarity has its roots in the Mining Industry itself, and in the previous
industrial experience of the Mining staff. Almost without exception,
lecturers in the Mining Department had spent a considerable number of
years in the industry before entering the teaching profession. Indeed,
in order to embark upon a teaching career the lecturer is expected to
possess at least a colliery manager's ticket, which means that he will not
only have spent five years working in a pit, but that three of those five
years will have been spent at the coal-face.[2]

However, we cannot simply assume that this initial industrial socialisation necessarily gives rise to any strong normative commitment to the
Mining Industry. Indeed, it could be argued that the very transfer from
mining into teaching suggests the opposite. Moreover, when we asked a
cross-section of the department why they had come into teaching, their
answers largely concurred with Tipton's (1973) observation that 'there
was very little about these answers [i.e. her empirical data] to suggest
that the college was staffed by individuals who had left industry or
other jobs to teach in FE because of a strong sense of missionary zeal'.
In other words, few members of the Mining Department expressed a
strong commitment to either mining *or* teaching. The following comments illustrate the kinds of reasons lecturers in the Mining Department
gave for leaving the industry and entering teaching:

'I came into teaching through a general disillusionment with the Coal
board'
or
'I thought I'd give it a try'
or
'With heavy contraction in the industry I entered teaching for a
breather'
or
'Well, it was a combination of events really. I always wanted to
lecture. I was very interested in the engineering job that I'd got but
a certain amount of frustration crept in with the closing of collieries.
You know the promotion prospects decreased. So it was a combination of both things'
or

'Well let's put it like this, I was for a long time a scout leader and I
have always been interested in working with youth and I was never
really very happy working in the industry and so I saw my voca-
tion, if it is not too strong a word, in teaching in FE.'

Such comments present strong grounds for concurring with Tipton's
conclusion that 'negativity' provides a major reason for the transfer
from industry into teaching. On the other hand, we would wish to argue
that 'negativity' is not the only reason. Some lecturers we spoke to saw
the move into teaching as a form of promotion. Indeed, in times of
industrial recession, an alternative avenue of opportunity proved highly
attractive, particularly when teaching salaries on the higher scales were
seen to outstrip those of higher managerial staff at the coal board.

In our view, the various rationalisations expressed by the Mining staff
at Western concerning their recruitment into the teaching profession,
are underpinned by the rationale of instrumentality. Thus whether the
move into teaching is undertaken for either positive or negative reasons,
it is ultimately only an extension of previous industrial experience.
Moreover, this view is reinforced at the level of entry, since there is no
obligation for miners entering teaching to undertake a teacher-training
course. Indeed, less than a third of the mining staff at Western had
received any form of pedagogical training.[3] Yet having opted to enter
the sphere of FE, many of the lecturers we spoke to found themselves
faced with a problem they had not anticipated. Indeed, having been
recruited for their practical expertise, many lecturers found that the
longer they stayed away from their industry of origin, the more difficult it became to justify their role as lecturer in Mining Studies. One
member of staff summed the situation up in the following way:

'One thing about this job which really surprised me was to realise
how, once in it, how difficult it is to get out of it again! You come
from industry and education is pleased to welcome you, because you
bring fresh experience and up-to-date knowledge with you. But
when someone has been in this job for a few years there is a real
tendency to get out of date . . . not just technologically . . . but I
would also say out of date about changing relationships and patterns
in industry. There are some examples of it here . . . some of them
don't realise how things have changed since they left the industry.'

The comments quoted above express the underlying tension which
tends to characterise the role of Mining staff at Western. While their
position as teachers of Mining Studies depends to a considerable extent
upon their previous industrial experience, they are no longer ostensibly
within the Mining Industry, a factor which was essential to their recruitment into teaching in the first place. However, they cannot simply

redefine their past experience in terms of their new role. On the contrary, their definition of their new role as 'teacher' will be shaped to a large extent by their previous industrial experience. However, while that expertise, which provided the basis for their move into teaching, is gradually eroded because they are no longer practically involved in their industry of origin, no new *raison d'être* emerges to replace it from their present occupation, except an *ad hoc* desire to become a proficient lecturer. In the following comments, one member of department we spoke to describes his efforts to develop an efficient teaching style:

'Basically, I just went back to the methods by which I was taught when I was a student at technical college. You combine this by listening and watching other people in the way they go about it.'

Clearly, the lecturer quoted above relies entirely upon his understanding of 'teaching' acquired as a student, and upon the implicit cues he receives from others. Moreover, he is not atypical of many recruits from industry into teaching, as the following comments indicate:

'I was taking HNC myself at the Technical College. . . . I also worked there as a technician, full-time, so I was very much concerned with preparation of practicals and courses for nearly three years. This gave me sufficient background to be able to tackle my present teaching job.'

In our view, this reliance upon teaching styles that one may have observed as a student creates a self-perpetuating cycle, in which pedagogical relations experienced as an industrial trainee become a measure of one's competence as a teacher. The following comments typify the ways in which recruits from industry measure their success at teachers:

'So long as I feel that I'm getting the goods across I don't mind . . . I feel as if I've been fairly successful . . . it's difficult to measure . . . most of my groups are passing their exams and I don't have any trouble with them. Basically, I feel confident that I know my stuff and I've got the experience to put it over. . . . Anyway, you can always get support and advice from others in the department who are, or have been, experiencing similar worries and problems.'

With such an informal process of teacher socialisation, lecturers tend to develop a corresponding ideology of legitimation regarding their new occupational identity. Indeed, this professional aura, as we suggested earlier, has its own particular rhetoric of practice which take the place to a large extent of the educational rhetoric usually associated with formally trained members of the teaching profession. Consider, for example, the following remarks taken from a discussion on teacher-training among members of the Mining staff at Western:

'It is very important that new teachers have a sound grounding in
industry before they come into the job. It's a matter of background.
You can't really understand how our students tick unless you've
followed their experience. Teacher Trainers should recognise this,
but they don't. You only have to look at the problems that graduates
teaching Liberal Studies have, when teaching our lads. Someone,
straight from school to university and back to college, is bound to
have problems . . . not so much with the basic skill work . . . most
of our lads are well able to read and write properly anyway . . . but
more on the relationship side of things.'

Clearly, the lecturer quoted above considers that because he has
undergone similar industrial experiences to those of his students, he
knows what is required both in terms of his students' needs, and in
terms of the kinds of teaching relations which will best facilitate the
transference of certain skills. What he does not perhaps recognise is that
in his primary concern with transmitting a set of cognitive skills which
are necessary in order to operate at the practical level, he is also com-
municating through this overt concern with industrial reality, the social
context which bounds the practical application of those skills. In other
words, in transmitting a set of cognitive categories, he is also reproducing
the whole gambit of relations which surround the industrial situation in
which those cognitive skills will be applied.

Thus in terms of this professional aura or rhetoric of practice, teaching
becomes *more* than a matter of transmitting a range of cognitive skills
which are to become accepted as necessary technical accomplishments.
Such a conception of teaching not only accepts the technical curriculum
as unproblematic, but also those particular *attitudes* which are deemed
a necessary accompaniment to the required cognitive skills. Indeed, many
lecturers measure their competence as teachers in terms of their success
in legitimating the whole industrial process from which they came.

In this way the identity of teachers recruited from industry tends to
be *instrumental* in its conception of education, and *industrial* in its
focus upon practice. Yet as we indicated earlier, such an identity not
only finds expression in the classroom, but shapes the whole conception of college life, particularly in terms of relationships within and
without the department. In short, a marriage of convenience takes place
between industry and education which structures the total work experience. Thus it is inevitable that certain attitudes towards work, usually
associated with the industrial sector, are carried over into teaching, so
that *time*, for example, becomes a very important issue. Indeed, any
work outside the normal lecturing load is seen as overtime. Moreover,
administrative figures tend to be perceived as management, so that
lecturers, within this conception of the job, become workers.

Furthermore, the development of such an occupational identity, legitimated in terms of the rhetoric of practice, gives rise to the kinds of reciprocal relations between members of the department that we described earlier. In addition, the informal nature of this process of teacher socialisation not only makes it very difficult for the researcher to identify, but renders any form of criticism concerning its legitimacy virtually impossible. Indeed to criticise such a process would be to challenge the common sense of those involved. Moreover, that common sense is firmly rooted within industrial reality. Thus it would seem important to examine the nature of the relationship between industry and the practice of college staff, and in the section which follows we shall seek to understand that relationship.

Industry and departmental practice

Perhaps the most obvious starting-point for such an examination is to indicate the importance of the National Coal Board, as a monopoly employer, in providing the department with its student population. However, it would be incorrect to imply that because of its monopoly position the Coal Board can exercise overt control over the workings of the department. Indeed, the relationship between the Mining Department and the Coal Board comprises a variety of implicit and explicit links, which suggest to us that the relationship as a whole is not one of total harmony.

Let us consider first of all the primary link between the department and the Coal Board: because 90 per cent of mining courses are of a block-release nature, it is necessary that there should be a high level of integration and agreement between Coal Board officials and members of the Mining Department concerning the programmes for which they are jointly responsible. In the following comments, the Head of Department describes the nature of his mutual co-operation at an initial level:

> 'I think in general mining departments are closely involved. We work closely with industry. Our first-year Craft course is an integrated course that we run in alternate months both in the college and at the Coal Board training centre. We know exactly what they are doing at the Coal Board training centre. They know exactly what we are doing at the college. So it is a very highly organised, phased course.'

The linking of courses at this explicit administrative level, however, gives rise to less formal relations between departmental and Coal Board staff. Indeed most members of the department carry on some form of relationship, informal or otherwise, with Coal Board officials or managerial staff in the local mines. The closeness of these links at an informal level may be illustrated by the following comments:

'Communications between us and the employers are very good. This may be because before coming here I was a deputy engineer at a local mine. Since coming here I've kept up all my associations with the area and with the area staff. I only have to pick up the phone and ring a senior member of the colliery about a student, and I know exactly who I'm speaking to. We've overcome the distance problem by keeping up our contacts overall . . . we visit the collieries regularly and invite colliery staff back here. . . . In this way we keep the channels of communication open.'

In our view, the closeness of the relationship between departmental and Coal Board staff suggested by the comments quoted above is far beyond that usually associated with relations between industry and college staff. Indeed, on further examination, such links prove to be deep and lengthy, often stretching back to the time when departmental and Coal Board staff were colleagues or even students together. Moreover, such a long-standing and close relationship inevitably gives rise to a reciprocal flow of information regarding the demand and supply of necessary labour, which would lead us to believe that mining apprentices are explicitly trained to meet the specific manpower requirement projections provided by the Coal Board.

This conclusion, however, fails to take into account the problematic raised earlier with regard to the *marginal* status of Mining lecturers in relation to their industry of origin. As we suggested earlier, the Mining staff at Western are no longer ostensibly *within* industry. Thus although the links may be strong, they are not necessarily definitive. Consequently, fractures and tensions occur which suggest that demands made by the Coal Board are not simply accepted by college staff as of right, but that some form of negotiation takes place.

Let us consider for example exactly what the Coal Board expects of the college department. At the most immediate level, the Coal Board expects that its apprentices should be *appropriately* trained. However, it is this word *appropriate* which gives rise to a degree of contention between employers and the Mining staff. Indeed, it proved extremely difficult to get either Coal Board officials or departmental members to define exactly what is meant by appropriate training. What they were prepared to explain, off the record as it were, was their mutual difficulty in arriving at some form of agreement in this matter. Indeed, one senior member of the department we spoke to told us that the most common complaint he received from pit managers was that students were too *broadly trained*, and not specifically prepared for immediate industrial requirements. Thus, far from there being a conspiracy of interests between Coal Board and college staff, we concluded that there was a considerable degree of conflict regarding who should ultimately control the content of mining curricula. For while the Coal Board may wield material control over the student population, the relative autonomy of the college department from that material base in terms of its internal workings means that control is ultimately exercised through far more subtle mechanisms.

Thus, while the Coal Board may provide the college with specific manpower requirement projections, it cannot dictate entirely the number and level of courses. Such a decision is made internally by the college administration. In other words, where industry clearly sets the level of expectancy concerning the kinds and levels of skills that are required, it is the college department which decides how far that level of expectancy will be met. However, the more pressure that can be exerted by the Coal Board through its various formal and informal links with the department, the more likely it is that industrial demands will be fulfilled. The autonomy of college staff, however, cannot be breached, for it is they who must ultimately decide, even where there is little room for negotiation.

An important consequence of this process of negotiation is that the college becomes a scapegoat in circumstances of technological change. Because industrial demands are not *absolute*, the college is publicly responsible for the provision of appropriately trained personnel. Thus where the demand for certain skills alters because of technological change, the college bears the responsibility for meeting that new demand. In other words, it is in the interest of the Coal Board, in terms of public accountability, that their demands on the college should remain implicit. In this way, when problems arise concerning inappropriately or wrongly trained personnel, the college rather than the Coal Board will be seen to be at fault. It is interesting to note at this point that a central issue in the recent Great Debate centred upon the failure of schools and colleges to provide industry with appropriately trained manpower.

The relationship between the college department and the Coal Board, as a monopoly employer, therefore, may ultimately be seen to be a process of *limited* negotiation in which the material power of industry is legitimated through formal and informal links with college staff. We would however wish to stress that this relationship is neither inflexible nor definitive. Indeed, emphases both in industry and college curricula are constantly shifting. Moreover, the nature of the student population itself is far from static. Consider for example the following remarks about the quality of students taken from an interview with a senior member of the department.

'I've been here for the past six years . . . and in that time there's been a great improvement in the standard of student intake in the Mining Industry. Six years ago the craft intake was largely either people without any other job prospects . . . the unemployed or those who'd been sacked. . . . The Mining Industry at that time was taking in the failures. Teaching such people was very hard . . . they often lacked commitment and ability. Now, with changes and improvements in the industry, we and the industry can be more choosey. We are getting students with qualifications now – able people who are taking an interest in the industry and their work. There have been great improvements. The students are certainly much easier to teach.'

It would seem to us that where the status of entry to college courses is rising, and where the skills imparted through such courses increasingly fail to meet changes in both technology and the division of labour, a far more serious problem arises. Indeed, where there is a serious mismatch between college curricula and changing technological requirements, the whole *raison d'être* of FE falls open to question. However, whether college courses adequately prepare students for their future industrial roles or not, FE is seen to perform a crucial task for industry through the selection and examination process. In other words, a subtle manipulation of entry qualifications at all levels can bring about the necessary matching of skills to industrial requirements. Such a process, of course, rests on the assumption that industry does in fact require increasingly skilled personnel. It is possible, however, that some less immediately apparent process of selection is in operation than that of simply matching skilled personnel to their appropriate job levels. In the section which follows we shall attempt to investigate this possibility more thoroughly.

Student identity

A student embarking upon a career in mining may spend up to six years on various mining courses. However, since it is the case that the skills acquired through such training may at any time be outdated because of technological change, it is interesting to examine why the Coal Board lends such explicit support to the work of the college department. We have indicated that one possible reason for this unqualified support is that through its relations with the college, the Coal Board is enabled to shed some of its problems, particularly those caused by technological change. In this section, we shall examine a further important contribution made by the college department to the industry that it serves: namely, its role in the structuring of student identity both at the cognitive and affective levels.

We have already emphasised the informal nature of teacher socialisation which has considerable consequences for the ways in which recruits from industry perceive and perform their teaching duties. Indeed, we suggested that where teachers are recruited on the basis of their industrial expertise, it is inevitable that they will focus on the instrumental aspects of the job in terms of transmitting a range of skills and habits which are uncritically accepted as necessary industrial accomplishments. It would seem to us, however, that this taken-for-granted conception of the job of teaching is simply a gloss for a far more complex process of student selection in terms of providing them with the appropriate skills, expectations and work habits. Moreover, this process of selection not only provides the means of differentiating students into the levels of skills required by industry, but allows the teachers themselves to justify their own activities in the classroom. Such activities, moreover, play a large part in shaping appropriate student identities. Consider, for example, the following comments taken from an interview about teaching methods:

'Technicians, of course, are a little different because they're streamed out in the early days. You can get them to work independently. I don't believe, however, that you can do this with a C4 student. Perhaps only in very exceptional cases. Where you set tasks for the students I think they have got to have the will to learn. It's only very occasionally that you get students like this. There are say 20 per cent out of a full year of Craft students who probably want to learn, and therefore to set laboratory tasks or use the project method of learning is very, very difficult. I find that you've got to operate on a lecture and demonstration basis and then use demonstration to set up a sort of challenge for these people.' (See Appendices 1 and 2.)

Clearly, the lecturer quoted above has a precise picture of the capabilities of his students. In his opinion, the technicians and only 20 per cent of the craft apprentices really want to learn. Those who are unwilling students need practical instruction and demonstrations of skills. It would seem to us that such precise criteria concerning the aptitudes of students not only separates off the various skills, but also puts into operation the various social relationships students will enter into at work. Those who will be team leaders, or promoted off the shop floor into management, i.e. technicians and top craft apprentices, can be set tasks and trusted to carry them out. On the other hand, lower craft students will need direction and supervision in the same way as their future industrial roles will be supervised.

Some of the lecturers we interviewed took this process of student differentiation to the extreme of arguing that there should be no overlapping of craft and technician courses:

'In fact, it's true to say, I think, particularly with the Craft courses, that we take them here to C4 which at the moment is the Coal Mines

77

Certificate and after that, of course, the better lads will move into a
Technician stream. Whether this is right or wrong I don't know. My
own opinion is that I think it's wrong, because if we stream a lad
into a craft course I think that's what he should be at the end of his
line when he's got a C4 Certificate. I think this was the original idea
of the Craft course, that we get them a Craft Certificate and that's
the extent of his learning ability. We find this in most cases to be
true and I only feel that if this is not the case then we've slipped up
somewhere in our streaming.' (See Appendices 1 and 2.)

This line of argument, however, was not common to the majority of the
department, although they clearly accepted that some less extreme
form of student differentiation was required in the classification of
Craft and Technician.[4]

It is interesting to note at this point that although the process of
student selection or typification remains unchanged, the required entry
qualifications for the various courses have altered considerably. Consider, for example, the following remarks on the changing status of
craft students:

'I only go up the technician level . . . I don't really have much to do
with the OND. In the craft level the abilities of the students has
changed . . . I find a greater need now to use more flexible teaching
methods . . . that is because the type of student has now changed.
They're not that bright, but they are a great improvement on the old
days. The students have certainly got more about them . . . they
think they've got more status and therefore got more spunk . . . if
that's the right word to use.' (See Appendix 2.)

In other words, 'better' students are now opting for craft courses,
despite the fact that the college administration still uses the same categories of evaluation when sorting students into the various course levels.
Perhaps it is not just that the students have more 'spunk', but that they
have a greater understanding of the process of selection they are being
subjected to.

This process of sponsorship, however, whereby students are directed
to the courses deemed appropriate to their future industrial status, is
not simply a process of labelling. Indeed, the college is supported in this
respect by certain material constraints which make it very difficult for
students to opt out of the sponsorship system. The close links between
industry and college enable the college administration to apply monetary
sanctions on those who fail to attend. This process is best explained in
the following remarks:

'Sometimes we get the odd bad apple who is not highly motivated
but is coming to college because his employers say he must. They

have to complete this educational year, otherwise they won't for instance get the minimum qualification (Class 2) which will entitle them to particular classes of work on a statutory basis. So the bulk of the students know that they've got to do this; either they're motivated or they accept the discipline involved and just get on with it. But there's the odd apple in the barrel who really resents it and then of course we do have problems. Luckily we do have some hefty sanctions we can put on to them. We can stop them 'time', which is an awful lof of money nowadays; for example when you think that our students are earning something like £15 a day salary, they can lose half a day . . . they've lost £7.50 which is a sizeable amount; so we do have this as a constraint although this doesn't seem to bother some of them.'

In our view, the remarks quoted above lay bare the complex and highly material relationship between industry and college. Indeed, it is clear that despite the subtle processes of sponsorship and levels of negotiation between college and Coal Board staff, there exists an inescapable and material basis of liaison which compels students to attend. In this way, the college department avoids the problem of student absenteeism which would threaten the continuation of courses. Moreover, the Coal Board is assured that their apprentices will not only attend, but learn the appropriate 'ways' of industry. Such 'ways', however, have more to do with the acquiring of certain values and attitudes, than they have with learning specific industrial skills.

The labelling process is the mechanism whereby such values and attitudes are transmitted. In the course of such a process, certain skills are undoubtedly acquired, but the industrial situation itself is so unpredictable that those skills can be made redundant at any time. In our view, the major reason why the Coal Board, as a monopoly employer, lends such strong support to the work of the college, is that the college offers a 'foolproof' way of socialising apprentices into the appropriate industrial attitudes. Thus, according to their perceived level of aptitude, students will acquire the necessary work habits which will enable them to work as a group, or at the coal-face, or, for those who are seen as suitable, in a managerial position. However, the more successful the college becomes in enacting this process of differentiation, the more likely it is that conflicts and tensions, such as those indicated earlier in relation to student scepticism, will increasingly rise.

In this chapter, we have attempted to examine the nature of the Mining Department at Western in terms of its organisation and social relations. In particular, we have sought to understand the complex processes of socialisation whereby both staff and students acquire their identities in the sphere of FE. We have argued that such processes are neither absolute nor definitive, but are characterised by a variety of tensions and contradictions. We have suggested, moreover, that such processes of socialisation are often masked by an articulate ideology which is rooted in industry and finds expression in a rhetoric of practice. However, while such a rhetoric operates to legitimise the professional mandate and subsequent practice of those involved, it also operates to hide the growing gap between the skills imparted through college courses and those required by a changing technology. Thus, in our view, the major contribution of the college department to the industry that it serves is its role in transmitting appropriate industrial attitudes, and therefore in legitimating the social relations of the work-place. By way of contrast, the chapter which follows examines the role of Liberal Studies within the technical curriculum at Western. However, to what extent that non-vocational dimension of the curriculum challenges the legitimacy of the work-place or is accommodated by college practice, remains to be seen.

Chapter 5

The Department of
Liberal Studies

Any study of FE would be incomplete without some examination of the role of Liberal Studies within the vocational curriculum. The controversial status of that area of the curriculum has for long been associated with the criticism that its progressive teaching styles lack structure, and are an unnecessary intrusion into apprenticeship training schemes.

In this chapter our departmental emphasis shifts to focus specifically upon the function of Liberal Studies within a technical college such as Western. In particular, we shall examine Liberal Studies in the light of the uneasy relationship which exists between the competing interests of general education and vocational training. It would seem to us that that conflict finds its clearest expression within the activities of that department. Before turning to the empirical manifestation of that problem at Western, however, it is important to provide the reader with some brief insight into the developments which led up to the inception of Liberal Studies within the technical curriculum.

In the early 1960s directives to unite the concepts of 'education' and 'training' within the sphere of FE were met quite pragmatically with the injection of Liberal Studies into an already oversubscribed technical curriculum. Driven like a wedge into largely predefined and established technical traditions, that apparently nebulous area was supposed to provide the missing link, 'education'. Liberal Studies is now an established part of all FE and technical courses. Its title indicates the so-called non-vocational aspect of technical education, which was originally known quite simply as the liberal element. With the creation of its formal title, however, the liberal element was to acquire a more substantive identity as a distinct and separate subject.

Prior to the inception of Liberal Studies within the technical curriculum, the National Institute of Adult Education had espoused the view that factory methods of production had become too rigid, providing 'few human satisfactions and calling for less individual talents' (1955).

81

The Department of Liberal Studies

The introduction of Liberal Studies as a compulsory aspect of technical education, it was hoped, would provide a means of countering that trend. The idea of liberalising the technical curriculum, however, was far from newly conceived, indeed, the idea is a continuation of two late-nineteenth-century movements. The first of these stems from the efforts of Owenite Socialists to reform society, and to take account of the factory worker both in society as a whole, as well as in his place of work. The second has its roots in Fabian idealism, and stems largely from the Liberal tradition of John Stuart Mill. The character of that movement is perhaps best articulated in the writings of the Webbs:

> the formation of a noble character, the increase of intellectual faculty, stimulus of sense of beauty, sense of conduct, even sense of humour, are all ends that we shall regard as sanctioning action (Beatrice Webb, 1948).

> we must take even more care to improve the social organism of which we form part, than to perfect our own individual developments. Or, rather, the perfect and fitting development of each individual is not necessarily the utmost and highest cultivation of his own personality, but the filling, in the best possible way of his humble function in the great social machine (Sidney Webb, 1948).

It is not within the scope of this study to dwell at length upon the historical foundations of the concept Liberal Studies. Indeed, Matthew Arnold's concern with the moral and intellectual plight of the working masses is of considerable significance here.[1] However, since detailed documentation of the philosophies of those nineteenth-century educationalists may be found elsewhere, suffice it to say for our immediate purposes that unmistakable traces of their concerns prevail in the aims ascribed to Liberal Studies, particularly in official accounts. Willis Jackson's (1964) interpretation of Liberal Studies provides a clear example:

> it behoves us at least to open their [young workers'] minds to the sociological consequences of their work, and to ensure that they are properly prepared to fulfil the widening human as well as scientific and technical responsibilities that lie ahead of them.

Similar ideals abound in government White Papers and Reports, and are supported by a growing awareness that Sidney Webb's 'great social machine' has increased in complexity and continues to change.

The major official directives concerning the need for the inclusion of a general educational element within the technical curriculum may be found in the White Papers of 1956 and 1961. Both express strong criticism of the 'irrevocable specialisation' and 'narrowness' associated with the training of particular tradesmen. The Education Act of 1944, more-over, laid considerable emphasis upon the need for 'a well-balanced system of education', and following the act, a host of documents and papers, official and otherwise throughout the 1950s and 1960s, expressed severe criticism of what was seen to be the 'over-specialisation' of apprenticeship training schemes.

Perhaps the most significant document of that era which became widely known as Circular 323 was published in 1957. Here, not sur-prisingly, the call was for an immediate broadening of the technical curriculum, with the introduction of more diverse subjects which would meet the needs of the 'whole man'. Very briefly, Circular 323 recommended a wider treatment of technical subjects in an attempt to ally the vocational with the non-vocational. In the same year, the City and Guilds introduced Liberal Studies into one of their pro-grammes, and two years later, in 1959, that subject was to constitute a compulsory element in most of their courses.

The campaign to promote Liberal Studies in FE was given a further boost some years later, when the White Paper of 1961 recommended that Crowther's concern for expansion in the technical curriculum should be extended to the neglected areas of English and General Studies. By the mid 1960s, however, the focus of the Liberal Studies debate had shifted from definitions of the subject to how it could best contribute to the technical curriculum. Great pressure was brought to bear on what C. P. Snow (1959) has described as the English educational system's 'fanatical belief in educational specialisation'.[2] Attempts to bridge the gap between the 'two cultures'[2] were put into motion by a number of opposing groups, whose shared concern was in what they saw as the growing danger of specialisation, and the inevitable expansion of Sidney Webb's 'great social machine'. In 1956 one government report suggested that 'The main purpose of technical education . . . must be to teach boys and girls to be adaptable.' By 1969, however, official reports had become far more forceful, advocating the need to 'broaden attitudes to occupation and environment . . . to heighten the sense of responsibil-ity in young workers . . . to engender independence of thought and develop the ability to communicate' (Haslegrave, 1969). (See Appendix 3.)

Despite the forcefulness of such liberal argument, however, and despite the pressure brought to bear on technical colleges by such bodies as the Association for Liberal Education, Liberal Studies was simply injected into an apprenticeship training system which had changed very little in the past 150 years. Thus its lack of immediate relevance inevit-ably exposed it to the criticism that it lacked structure and served no useful purpose. It would seem to us that this unseemly injection of Liberal Studies into long-established technical processes has not only heightened the problem of the concept Liberal Studies within the technical curriculum, but has adversely affected both its development and practice within the sphere of FE.

Ostensibly, Liberal Studies entered the technical curriculum in response to the growing criticism levelled against a system of education characterised by overspecialisation and the limited notions of training. It would seem to us, however, that the criteria for its inclusion are inextricably linked with the long-established vocational aims of technical education. It is our contention, therefore, that the criteria for the inclusion of Liberal Studies in the technical curriculum, far from representing a new direction in FE, were ultimately very much a continuation of an established tradition.

A Report published by the National Institute of Adult Education (NIAE) in 1955 found that the majority of technical colleges opposed the introduction of Liberal Studies. The greater part of that opposition was expressed by existing technical staff, supported to a large extent by employers. Initially, improvements in the area were the result of the work of HMIs, and later the Association for Liberal education became an important influence. In the early years, the Department of Education demonstrated considerable commitment to the inclusion of Liberal Studies, so that most criticism was expressed by other interested parties on the grounds of irrelevant subject-matter. However, although such bodies as the Haslegrave Committee (1969) recognised a need for 'general and personal development' as an important aim in technical education, they were ultimately more concerned with the economic benefits of that movement than with its intrinsic worth. Through the development of the 'whole man', it was suggested, Liberal Studies could influence the 'effectiveness with which he (the apprentice) does his work'. The Haslegrave Committee emphasised the importance of technological advances, within an increasingly sophisticated society. Their reasoning, however, was based upon a rationality guided by the needs of technology, and that overriding concern was to have significant consequences for the whole concept of Liberal Studies. Not only did the technological rationality establish the parameters of Liberal Studies in terms of the requirements of a technological society, but it also sought to unite the objectives of both liberal and technical education: that is to say, the shared objective of both forms of knowledge was inextricably linked with the socio-economic organisation of society. Moreover, both formal and informal sanctions upon the Liberal Studies teacher left him with little option but to accept such a definition of his subject. Generally speaking, his task was bound up with establishing for the apprentice some perspective upon his place in the economy and in the community as a whole. In our view, such a definition of the contribution of Liberal Studies fails to allow for any form of dialogue regarding the contradiction and conflict traditionally associated with that role. Quite simply, the interests of the apprentice are superseded by those of society and its economic imperatives.

The technical curriculum has traditionally formed part of a process which Althusser (1971) has described as reproducing the 'conditions of production': that is to say, both labour and social organisation of that labour. Ostensibly, the liberal element would appear to offer some opportunity for a critical examination of the conditions of production. In our view, however, the rationality which has guided the inception of Liberal Studies within the technical curriculum has negated any critical potential such a curricular area might have afforded. Indeed, it would seem to us that Liberal Studies plays a very important part in reinforcing and perpetuating existing technological and social conditions. Handbooks on Liberal Studies teaching lay emphasis upon such topic areas as Earning and Spending, Town Planning, Local Social History and Government, and Standards of Living. Such themes recur with inevitable predictability throughout the texts of Catchpole (1971), Blackman (1962, 1964, 1967), Seymour and Acres (1974) and others. Their main preoccupations substantiate Harding's (1969) conclusion that a large percentage of Liberal Studies is not Liberal Studies at all, but a form of Social Studies devoted to reconciling the student to himself and to his fellows within an established society.

The most salient point, however, about the contribution of Liberal Studies concerns what should constitute its subject-matter. Educationalists, college administrators and teachers have all failed to agree upon the Liberal Studies brief. Hence Harding (1969) opens her debate on 'The Content and Method of Liberal Studies' by stating that 'There is no basic agreement on what ought to be taught in Liberal Studies.'

Such a situation is partially due to the very broad aims Liberal Studies teachers are required to address. Moreover, in our view, this marked lack of any formal syllabus has been the main cause of the illusion of freedom which surrounds Liberal Studies. It is still the case that colleges offering Liberal Studies courses validated by the City and Guilds Instite are free to determine the content of those courses within their own establishments. Thus it is not perhaps surprising that in recent years growing criticisms of the apparent autonomy of the Liberal Studies teacher have developed into a campaign to structure Liberal Studies. That is to say, support for those who wish to provide syllabuses and other teaching guidelines in order to define the place of Liberal Studies within the boundaries of the technical curriculum, has grown in strength. Indeed, this is an issue which both Haslegrave and the later Technician's Education Council were keen to address.

In our view, the freedom that the Liberal Studies teacher supposedly enjoys, constitutes a problem which requires considerable examination, despite the fact that its taken-for-granted existence has been the object of considerable contention for some years. It is to that problem that we now turn, and in the sections which follow, we shall examine the social context of Liberal Studies knowledge and practice at Western.

Background

Since its inception at Western in 1971, the Department of Liberal Studies has been the object of two distinct but interrelated lines of criticism. First, there are those who believe that the department enjoys far too much autonomy regarding curricular decisions, and that it should be made more accountable to the technical departments that it services; and second, there are those who believe that since Liberal Studies is of little relevance to the technical aims of the college, and because resources are scarce, the Department should be abandoned altogether. Moreover, the implications of such criticism, often supported by both employers and apprentices, have had far-reaching consequences for the way in which the department presents itself. One way in which the department had defended itself has been to silence its critics by taking greater notice of them, so that Liberal Studies within the college has become more vocationally orientated. This line of defence has enabled the department to negotiate an unholy alliance with its more vociferous critics, so that not only has the department managed to survive, but it has also remained surprisingly healthy in circumstances which are often antagonistic.

In this chapter, we shall seek to understand both the servicing role of the Liberal Studies department at Western, and the imperatives which have led to its development. We shall attempt to elucidate the ways in which Liberal Studies knowledge not only becomes part of the technical curriculum, but also the ways in which it can actually become incorporated into the vocational aims of the college. It will be suggested that this process of accommodation arises directly from what we have previously referred to as the technical ethos of the college. Indeed, we have suggested so far that the primary objective of Western as an educational institution is to train young workers for their appropriate place in industry, and to equip them with the corresponding cognitive and affectual skills. Thus it is not perhaps surprising that the Department of Liberal Studies is also expected to subscribe to such an aim. However, since in practice the vocational aims of the technical departments are far from clear-cut, it is also the case that within the Liberal Studies Department itself a number of conflicting interpretations co-exist regarding the contribution of that department to the technical and vocational objectives of the college as a whole.

In the pages which follow, we shall focus specifically upon such divergences of opinion. In particular, we shall examine how the department seeks to resolve such conflict, so as to both present a unified public image and enact a common policy among its members. The latter necessarily requires some examination of the ways in which technical teachers perceive the aims of Liberal Studies within an apprenticeship training system described by Cotgrove (1958) as 'rooted in a suspicion of theoretical studies and a preference for the practical man trained through practical experience'.

Thus we shall begin by considering the advent of Liberal Studies at Western, and its subsequent development as a department within the college. We shall attempt to familiarise the reader with the departmental set-up by outlining such factors as its size, pattern of staffing, and possible access to available resources. More particularly we shall focus upon the structural limitations imposed upon members of the department: that is to say, we shall examine the constraining factors of organisation, both formal and otherwise, which influence their work. It will be argued that such limitations represent a crucial yardstick by which the Liberal Studies teacher both defines his role and organises his classroom practice. Finally, we shall seek to dispel the myth that the Liberal Studies teacher is free to teach what he pleases, or indeed that what he teaches is necessarily either liberal or progressive.

Socio-historical development of Liberal Studies at Western

It is not perhaps surprising that the department of Liberal Studies is a comparatively late arrival at Western. The old City Technical Schools had responded to Circular 323 (1957) by dividing the Liberal Studies element among the existing technical staff. Even with the completion of the new building in 1969 which was to become Western, there was no formal provision for the curricular area of Liberal Studies. Indeed, three years were to elapse, after the opening of the main college, before Liberal Studies finally acquired a positive identity and became an established department. Moreover, because of the competition for space, timetable hours and resources, the creation of that department gave rise to considerable controversy.

As we suggested in the preceding chapters, the primary concern of colleges of FE and their departments has been with survival and growth in a highly competitive market. Thus the technical departments, founder members of the college, greeted the newly added Liberal Studies Department with some hostility. Perhaps not surprisingly, existing departments were very sensitive to the possible loss of space, time and equipment, with all the implications for status which that involved, to the newcomer whose claim to departmental status they viewed with considerable scepticism. In such a context, the very legitimacy of the Department of Liberal Studies, and its place in the technical curriculum, was subject to close scrutiny. To be accepted within a college such as Western, a new department must exhibit a strong claim as a necessary and useful contributor, without threatening the existence of other departments. However, in the eyes of many existing technical staff, the Liberal Studies Department was unable to do this. In their view, not only was Liberal Studies irrelevant to the technical curriculum, but it simply fed off the students from other departments, without attracting any of its own. Despite this, Liberal Studies was allocated jealously guarded hours and space, largely culled from those of established departments. As a result, the new addition found itself in a position of considerable difficulty, being closely monitored and constantly required to justify its activities. A senior member of the department we interviewed pinpointed the source of the conflict as being rooted in the points system. While the growth of each department at Western remains anchored to the number of points acquired through increased student numbers and courses, he envisages little chance of improving relations between Liberal Studies and technical staff:

> 'there are staff looking at Liberal Studies closely . . . looking for arguments . . . to demonstrate that the students are wasting their time, not working . . . or learning irrelevant topics . . . looking for arguments to present to their Heads of Department.'

Not only are the activities of Liberal Studies teachers closely monitored by the technical staff, but their working conditions are often less favourable than those of colleagues in other departments. Although the department is based on the top floor of the main college building, Liberal Studies teachers may be required to perform their duties in any of the annexes throughout the area. The Liberal Studies staff room in the main block is an expression of the department's status. The quarters, to say the least, are cramped, and when fully occupied, overcrowded. Similarly, the Head of Department is accommodated in a very small office, which contrasts markedly with the often spacious and carpeted quarters of other departmental heads. Such differences are indicative of the differential levels of status enjoyed by the various departments. They are grounded, moreover, in the comparatively recent introduction of Liberal Studies as an appendage to those departments whose work attracts students, and who are therefore seen as useful contributors to the well-being of the college as a whole. Needless to say, when privations are required, it is in the Liberal Studies Department that they are first implemented.

Thus while the technical staff undoubtedly require sophisticated and often expensive equipment, it is also the case that very few of them have cause for complaint about their working conditions. On the other hand, Liberal Studies teachers must expect to perform their teaching duties in spartan conditions, with few technical aids. Moreover, while most technical departments are permanently established in a particular annexe, Liberal Studies staff must expect to be highly mobile. This latter difficulty does not go unnoticed by other college staff. Indeed, one mining lecturer we spoke to expressed considerable sympathy for his colleagues in the Liberal Studies Department:

> 'the [Liberal Studies] staff have got a job on. . . . They're moved about from annexe to annexe, quite unnecessarily in my opinion . . . very few of the staff seem to belong anywhere . . . nomads, wandering around, doing a lecture here, a lecture there, this must have its effect on them.'

Furthermore, the 'nomadic' identity of the Liberal Studies teacher does little to enhance the importance of his subject to the student. Indeed, faced with the initial problem of lack of student interest in this curricular area, the Liberal Studies teacher's task is often aggravated by the conditions in which he is required to do his work. Such conditions not only reflect the low status of Liberal Studies within the technical curriculum but also the attitude of the college hierarchy towards that subject area. In our view, unwilling students are unlikely to become less so when the attitude of the college administration is so obviously lacking in support. Timetabled in inappropriate places, labs or workshops, at inconvenient times, immediately after lunch (the 'beer shift') or late in the evening, Liberal Studies is obviously low in the organisational priorities of the college. Moreover, it was the feeling of some Liberal Studies teachers that if the college administration were to organise a more integrated approach to the subject, and to provide better accommodation and facilities, many of the initial problems of motivation might be overcome.

The problem of motivation and communication

Lack of student interest and motivation in conditions such as those described above represent a major problem both for teachers of Liberal Studies and for their students. Apprentices, released for day-release training, attend colleges like Western to learn about their trade, and like their employers, are often suspicious of the 'liberal' and the 'theoretical'. Liberal Studies teachers are usually only too aware of this problem since it dominates their relationship with their students. Moreover, this initial difficulty often causes them to question the relevance of their subject-matter, and indeed their own abilities. The following comments from a Liberal Studies lecturer of some seven years' standing epitomises the feeling of dispiritedness which some Liberal Studies teachers experience about their work:

Teacher: It's a restriction. Teaching Liberal studies can be enjoyable ... but let's be honest about it ... it can be a pain in the neck if you're teaching it all the time. I don't think this is ideal over a full timetable. In an ideal situation you'd have teachers teaching their subject in conjunction with Liberal Studies ... Liberal Studies taking up about one-third of the time. I feel we've not been very quick to establish other courses in this department which might offer us a variety of teaching situations.
Interviewer: When you say 'pain in the neck' – presumably this sums up your attitude to your present job?
Teacher: Well, it's a strain to be quite honest. ... I'm dealing with ... for the most part likeable lads ... who, I've got to be honest, ... tolerate us rather than come here off their own bat. There is an added problem. The general attitude ... or policy, shall I say ... in FE, is that the higher the grade of pay the more the job's worth to you in terms of salary grade ... career ... etc. ... but it all seems back to front to me. We're the lowest status teachers. The hardest job we have to do is try to achieve ... through Liberal Studies ... some response from very limited students who are in many cases illiterate. To me teaching an Ordinary National group is more rewarding and easier ... than say having to slog with disinterested craft students ... who perhaps don't want to be here. One of our major problems is teaching students who are neither strongly committed to being at college for the day ... or if they are ... they certainly aren't committed to General Studies. You get dispirited teaching disinterested students ... it's as simple as that.

It is for reasons such as these that many Liberal Studies teachers advocate the introduction of a more comprehensive approach towards the technical curriculum, so that their skills may be employed at a variety of levels which would have more immediate relevance to the various groups of students. At Western, however, such a comprehensive approach does not exist, and indeed one lecturer we interviewed who had managed to introduce an 'O' Level sociology course, clearly stated a preference for the 'academic' student:

'I think it's the way you look around at the class and they tend to be paying attention. I've been doing this "O" Level class for four weeks and there's a different atmosphere in the class than in Liberal Studies ... where many of them seem to be uninterested in anything. ... I mean, maybe it's just moral indignation . . . or maybe it's that I expect them to perform in ways that they don't want to and because of this, I take this superior stance. I mean, in their position I would probably be just the same.'

While comments such as these might be interpreted as exposing the speaker's taken-for-granted expectations and assumptions about his students, they also indicate an oppressive reality in which the work of the Liberal Studies teacher is constantly rejected by disinterested young men. In our view, however, this lack of contact between the Liberal Studies teacher and his students is neither a personal nor a classroom problem. Indeed, our observations of classroom interaction at Western in general suggest that many students adopt a highly instrumental attitude towards both their Technical and Liberal Studies:

'well, you take so much in in a day, but, after that, you can't, it's very difficult. What time do we finish? Eight o'clock? I think the last lesson, well it isn't a waste of time, but it's approaching a waste of time, well, we're falling asleep. Everybody is fed up by five o'clock to be honest.'

Employers, however, continue to favour the day-release scheme and the advantages it offers them. Thus many apprentice students merely 'put up with' their system of training, knowing that it will bring them the necessary tradesmen's certificate, which in turn will lead to a possible increase in status and income. In a situation such as this, Liberal Studies often becomes for the sceptical student a way of alleviating the pressures of day-release. Besides being non-vocational, and in their view dispensable, it does not conform to their concept of 'work'. Indeed, the latter is grounded in frames of reference far removed from those of the Liberal Studies context, as the following comments indicate:

Teacher: What's a manual worker, as opposed to a non-manual worker? . . . A manual worker?
Len: Labourer.
Teacher: Not necessarily.
Paul: A fellow that works with his hands.
Teacher: Yea. . . . I mean that's the basic distinction. . . . I'm not sure how valid a distinction it is, this distinction between those that work with their hands and those that work with their brains. Now I don't believe it's a valid one, I think you have got to work with your brains as well as your hands. . . . What you do, you've got to read drawings and so on, you have to follow instructions. On the other hand, someone like myself would be classed as a non-manual worker, although I have to write on the board, fill in registers and do things like that.

John: That's easy!
Teacher: An easy job you say?
Frank: Do we have to write all this out?
Teacher: Not necessarily.
Frank: Well, it's easy then!

Such comments reflect the way in which many craft apprentices perceive the nature of 'real' work, as opposed to mental activity which in their view is 'easy'. Thus, because of the absence of compulsion and physical exertion normally associated with their working day, many such students find it difficult to apply the concept of 'hard work' to more 'academic' forms of study. As one student we interviewed pointed out: 'It's a doss. . . . Liberal Studies is a real waste of time. . . . I'd rather we got rid of it . . . have the last lesson at six o'clock and go home at seven.'

While students may also be critical of the technical curriculum, they do however recognise that it is for real. Not only is it indispensable to the acquisition of their 'ticket', but it is also the means whereby they will acquire certain rights with regard to promotion and increased wages. Moreover, the atmosphere of Western itself, what we have previously described as its technical ethos, reinforces such notions of work and hierarchy. Consequently, the apprentice-student will usually tolerate only those subjects which have direct relevance to his trade. In such a context, it is not perhaps surprising that Liberal Studies with its emphasis on the 'social', 'talk' and 'expression', is often viewed by both students and technical staff alike with considerable suspicion.

Liberal Studies, therefore, within a technical college such as Western, is not only seen to be of marginal relevance, but its content is often seen to be in direct conflict with the conceptions of 'work' held by both students and technical staff. Thus for the apprentices the Liberal Studies lecturer has no immediately recognisable specialism by which the conventional student/teacher relationship can be established. Without this, his legitimacy inevitably falls open to question, not only by students, but by employers and colleagues in other departments. On the other hand, the technical staff have a specific task to perform, which is to impart a defined body of knowledge and skills which will have direct relevance to the apprentice in his daily work. The technical lecturer draws both his authority and credibility from his expertise in a given trade. Moreover such a work-oriented identity inevitably causes him to ask critical questions not only about the subject-matter of Liberal Studies and its relevance to the students he is training, but also about the apparent autonomy that Liberal Studies lecturers appear to enjoy.

The problems of the Liberal Studies lecturer, however, do not simply surround the issues of relevance and motivation. Indeed, because Liberal Studies lessons are invariably only one hour in length, he spends his week teaching a host of different classes, so that there is not only a lack of sufficient continuity, but scant opportunity to develop the kinds of relationships which would facilitate better working relations. The sheer number of students with whom he is involved makes it impossible for him even to remember their names. Moreover, the annexe system and the demands it places upon members of the Liberal Studies Department does much to exacerbate an already uneasy relationship with technical staff. The popular image of the Liberal Studies teacher as a dilettante, working in an amorphous subject area, is heightened by the impression that he does not physically 'belong' to the college. In a situation such as that at Western, where even established technical staff willingly confess to a lack of awareness of activities in any department other than their own, the nomadic identity of the Liberal Studies teacher simply exacerbates an atmosphere of disunity. Indeed, many staff are acutely aware of this absence of a common understanding, and some, particularly those in the Liberal Studies Department, suffer feelings of estrangement and anomie. The following comments from one technical lecturer we spoke to epitomises the sense of disunity many staff at Western experience:

'It [the annexe system] makes this a very difficult college to administer and teach in. . . . There's a lack of communication. You don't get the same communication as you would if you were all under the same roof. You don't get the same sort of college atmosphere as you would in a "normal" college. What you tend to get, really, is people building their own little empires up in annexes. We've all become water-tight units, not interested in the progress or problems of the other departments – that is a dreadful thing to say, but it is absolutely true. In fact I believe that there are departments in this college who would take great pleasure in seeing other departments fall down.'

Comments such as these capture something of the problems associated with working in conditions of isolation and competition. Such problems, however, are heightened for the Liberal Studies staff who occupy only three rooms in the main college block, and operate as 'visitors' in the annexes. Such working conditions express the low status of the Liberal Studies Department within the interdepartmental power game. That game, moreover, based upon the need to build and protect points in order to survive, has important consequences for such issues as staffing policy, careers, timetabling, curricular control and working conditions. The Liberal Studies Department, as we have sought to demonstrate, occupies a very vulnerable position *vis-à-vis* such issues within the college departmental hierarchy.

93

The Department and its critics

Over the years, however, the Liberal Studies Department at Western has managed to expand, and its relations with other departments have altered. While the points system and subsequent conditions of competition remain, the department has evolved to the extent that it now occupies a reasonably secure position within the college departmental hierarchy. At the time of writing, the Liberal Studies Department at Western comprises nineteen members of staff, including its principal lecturer. A striking feature of the departmental members, in marked contrast to their technical colleagues, is their academic backgrounds. According to a senior member of the department of some ten years' standing, the department operates a policy of attracting staff from the top end of the educational market. In particular, the Head of Department is keen to appoint teacher-trained graduates whose image is of importance to the status of the department.

The majority of departmental members are specialists in subjects closely associated with the social sciences (sociology, history, geography). A few ex-technical teachers from the old days remain, however, and with this blend, the department seeks to maintain a catholic body of teachers, able to cover a wide range of curricular areas. Members of staff who leave or retire tend to be replaced by younger teachers, so that the average age of the department has dropped by over ten years in the past five years. By building a department of young, academically well qualified teachers, able to cover a wide range of disciplines, the Head of Department and his senior staff have sought to acquire for their department an identity within the college as a young, hard-working body of professional teachers. In this way the department has achieved a stronger position, and has acquired a less vulnerable public face. However, despite the range of teaching possibilities created by this staffing policy, such academic developments within the department have not been without their difficulties.

Initially a tactic to raise the image of the Liberal Studies Department, the policy of recruiting formally trained graduates has attracted considerable criticism from other college bodies. Indeed, in the eyes of many technical staff, graduates simply do not fit into apprenticeship training schemes. Technical staff, on the other hand, are often born, raised and educated in the local area, so that they not only understand the social origins of their students, but share a common industrial experience with them. Such teachers are often of the opinion that the Liberal Studies staff are over-qualified. One such lecturer we interviewed suggested that there were two inhibiting factors working against Liberal Studies teachers: first, in his view, they are too clever, by which he means that they cannot understand the needs of apprentices; and second, their social-class background does not allow them to understand apprentice life-styles and problems. Such a view, moreover, is not an isolated one as we attempted to demonstrate in the ethnographic chapter. Indeed the following comments from a technical lecturer of some seven years' experience would seem to capture the general consensus of opinion among technical staff regarding the image of the Liberal Studies teacher:

'I think, here again, the Liberal Studies teachers fail, in some respects, to communicate with the lads because they haven't got the same common ground we've got. I can relate things to my industrial experience, which is very relevant to what they are doing, and they will listen, because they think – this bloke has done a little bit, he's not just teaching me a load of rubbish that I don't need to know.'

Such a perception of the 'necessary' relationship between apprentice-students and teacher is grounded in shared social and industrial experience, neither of which ingredients the academic has recourse to in his teaching. However it would seem to us that while many technical teachers express considerable empathy with the 'craft lad' they also perceive him to be of low ability and with limited prospects. References to this or that 'class' of student consistently occurred during interviews with technical staff, so that we concluded that their activities in the classroom were based upon their taken-for-granted perceptions of the various ability levels of their students. In our view, there would appear to be something of a contradiction in a situation where lecturers express considerable 'cultural' similarity with their students, but at the same time discredit their abilities and potential.

Thus while technical teachers often refer to such factors as 'empathy' and 'communality' as indicators of their greater success in classroom relations, we would wish to argue that such terms mask a far more subtle method of controlling student behaviour. Such processes of control have been referred to elsewhere as the 'hidden curriculum', a term which denotes the unproblematic transference of the concepts of authority and hierarchy within classroom practice. In this case technical teachers, on the basis of their industrial expertise, simply adopt the hierarchical relations of their industry of origin and bring them to bear upon their teaching relations. In this way control is maintained, and students learn their appropriate place in the industrial process. The Liberal Studies teacher, on the other hand, cannot simply rely on the work ethos in his classroom relations, and his difficulty in establishing a meaningful relationship with his students is perceived as his inability to cope, or 'to face up to' the job of teaching apprentice students. As one technical lecturer put it:

'All you can sort of say, on the outside looking in, is that it's just a relaxation for the student and nothing more than that. . . . There is an unwillingness, on the part of Liberal Studies people, to accept the responsibilities of teaching, and a tendency to want to merely show films and so on. I tend to think they talk a lot . . . about marriage and this sort of thing . . . relationships with the opposite sex. . . . I think they probably overdo this.'

It would seem to us that while the most popular criticism of Liberal Studies staff centres upon their 'inability' to understand the needs of apprentice-students, technical staff are equally critical of the 'freedom' which Liberal Studies appears to afford. They are less willing, however, to voice that criticism and tend to focus primarily upon the more obvious pedagogical difficulties of their Liberal Studies colleagues. Throughout the majority of interviews we held with technical staff on this subject, however, an underlying suspicion of the content of Liberal Studies was apparent. Consider, for example, the following remarks from a lecturer in electrical engineering who perceives the issues of 'freedom' and of 'boundary' as interrelated problems:

'the [Liberal Studies] approach is entirely different. . . . There's no limit to the width or direction. I think the presentation of a syllabus and objectives would mean that everyone would be tied in a way. You see we've got no idea what each teacher in Liberal Studies is doing. . . . A syllabus would give the Liberal Studies Department more coherent aims.'

Here the speaker clearly expresses a preoccupation with precision in terms of set syllabuses and statutory tasks. Thus it is not perhaps surprising that in view of his conception of teaching, Liberal Studies appears in need of structure and direction. Such a perspective upon Liberal Studies content, moreover, is commonly held, so that many technical teachers are of the opinion that the Liberal Studies curriculum should be more geared towards their own departmental interests. The following comments from one technical lecturer we spoke to epitomises the general consensus of opinion among technical staff regarding the 'servicing' role of Liberal Studies:

'I think it would be more useful done in a different way and linked up with us, far better, and helping us a lot. I don't think that they [the apprentices] do enough formal written work in Liberal Studies. . . . They don't get much writing in technical courses . . . because of a national policy to introduce multiple-choice examinations. Now Liberal Studies could help there – technical description, even to the point of taking something into the room and saying "right, describe that".' (See Appendix 3.)

It would seem to us that the eagerness of the lecturer quoted above to redefine the vocational relevance of Liberal Studies reflects the dominance of what we have previously described as the technical ethos at Western. In a college which is geared to the training of young workers, heads of technical departments resent the presence of a non-vocational department whose objectives are not firmly anchored to their own. The rationality behind such resentment arises from the belief that where technical training is the mandate of the institution, technical staff should control all aspects of the education of their students. Thus they believe that Western would be best served if the content of Liberal Studies was inextricably linked to the technical curriculum. Because of this, technical staff tend to be suspicious of the apparent autonomy of the Liberal Studies department. Many fear that the lack of control over that department by the others will be detrimental to the training of the students. One Head of Department we interviewed summed up his relationship with, and indeed suspicion of, the Liberal Studies Department in the following way: 'we have very little control over what they [the Liberal Studies department] do in their classes and, personally, I would prefer it to be a more supportive study. . . .'

Clearly, his opinion is that Liberal Studies attracts no new students, but lives off the students drawn to his department. Consequently, he does not feel that Liberal Studies merits a separate departmental identity. Indeed, technical staff, employers, training board personnel and group training officers, are almost universally agreed that Liberal Studies must have some relevance to the training of a tradesman. In their view, technical education is designed to equip apprentices to undertake a job, and therefore Liberal Studies should subscribe to the same goal. Criticism of those who refute that goal is heated and widespread:

'Talking politics, watching a film, discussing contraceptives: this kind of thing only leads to employers asking "How's this going to help Johnny in his job?" '

'This country can't afford to pay lads to sit and discuss sex, politics or violence for an hour per week.'

There are of course some technical staff who value the contribution of the 'liberal' element. However, they too desire that the relationship between Liberal Studies content and the technical curriculum should be closer and more direct:

'If Liberal Studies was more related to the boys' working environment, it might do a little better. In other words, not Liberal Studies – Industrial Relations – if you want to call it relations, or even Industrial Environment: there's an awful lot you could go into there. . . . Relationships with people and their job, why they are having to do it, why it is necessary, why there's managers, why there's a union.

Basically, you are developing this man around Engineering and that's where all the development should be concentrated.'

Here the speaker sees his task as expressly shaping the vocational identities of his students and, like his more vociferously critical colleagues, he would like Liberal Studies to help him in his task.

Local employers make a similar response to what they perceive to be the educational needs of young workers. Because they invest in FE, they expect a return from that investment in terms of better qualified and more skilled workers. They are interested in how their investment is used, and recognise the immediate returns afforded by technical training and workshop practice. They are sceptical, however, of the contribution of Liberal Studies since it has no apparent relevance to the work situation for which they have sent their apprentices to college to be prepared. Many employers often resent Liberal Studies as a waste of their apprentices' time:

'I have reservations about the work our lads do in Liberal Studies. Liberal Studies is there because educationalists say it should be there. ... If Liberal Studies has got to be done, it should be done in the technical departments ... not somewhere else. ... Quite frankly I think Liberal Studies is a waste of time for our type of student. ... I don't dispute that there's a need to develop students' breadth of knowledge ... but I think that if you're going to have relevant social education it should be dealt with by teachers who are more down-to-earth and who have a knowledge of the lads they are teaching. At present ... and from our standpoint, what goes on is a waste of time and money etc. ... It's very costly. Can an industry really afford a group of people spending an hour and a half doing what? When I look at the syllabus and what goes on in lessons I have grave doubts' (Head of industrial training for a major nationalised industry).

'Take Liberal Studies ... if the Educational Authority, the teachers and so on think Liberal Studies is such a good thing and it's so important, then I think students should learn it at night, in their own time ... not mine' (Managing Director of a local engineering firm).

'there are problems with Further Education. Employers within the group often complain to me that their students are wasting time, or skiving off Liberal Studies. ... They argue that talking about mortgages, rent rebates, civil liberties, Northern Ireland or politics in general is a waste of time' (Group Training Officer for local engineering firms).

With few exceptions, the employers we interviewed identified Liberal Studies as the most problematic area of the technical curriculum.

Contrary to the views expressed by the CBI and other employers' associations in the recent Great Debate, our research indicates that employers are more concerned with the affectual components of the technical curriculum, than with the cognitive. Indeed, there was a general consensus among the employers we spoke to that Liberal Studies knowledge subverts the work ethic. They view Liberal Studies as an unnecessary intrusion into the technical curriculum, imposed by educationalists for its intrinsic worth, but ultimately representing little more than a form of diversion or recreation, which is totally in conflict with their definition of vocational training.

It is not perhaps surprising that employers, seeking the obvious from FE, are sceptical of Liberal Studies, but their attitudes undoubtedly exert a further pressure upon the activities of the Liberal Studies teacher and the content of the curriculum. Although employers and indeed technical staff cannot influence the subject-matter of Liberal Studies through any formal mechanisms of control, they can still exert considerable pressure upon Liberal Studies personnel through the threat of informal sanctions, because of their prominence within a college whose work is essentially technical.

Where formal mechanisms of decision-making and control are practised within the college through the committee structure, employers' representatives and technical staff occupy a far more influential position than Liberal Studies staff. The heavy domination of college work by vocational and technical courses legitimates the more favourable status of the technical departments, which in turn are able to rationalise their work by formulating rigorous syllabuses in order to prepare students for formal examinations.

Because of the greater status and power of the technical staff (they outnumber the Liberal Studies personnel four to one) they carry more weight in the decision-making processes at Western. Moreover, by applying a structure to their work they have reduced their vulnerability to criticism. Thus they are in a position where they can criticise the Liberal Studies Department which shares neither their form of organisation nor objectives. Such criticism, however, is far from reciprocal. Indeed, students are encouraged to express their criticisms of Liberal Studies without being allowed to question the content and teaching methods associated with the technical courses.

Thus examinations and codified syllabuses serve a dual purpose for the technical departments. They endow those subjects not only with common aims, but also with the means to achieve those aims. Such aims, moreover, are legitimated by professional and tradesmen's institutions who recognise the qualifications gained through success in formal examinations. The value of the examination system, therefore, to the technical teacher lies in its psychometric function; that is to say, he is enabled to assess his professional effectiveness through his students' success in public examinations. On the other hand, because there is no formal examination in Liberal Studies, technical lecturers complain that there is no means of assessing the contribution of the Liberal Studies Department or the quality of its work:

> 'You see, we haven't got a measure of success at all, in any shape or form, as to the value of this [Liberal Studies] to these students. This is something which makes it difficult to know what they are doing.'

Comments such as these are a further reflection of the suspicion with which technical staff view the Liberal Studies Department. Without a yardstick of success or tangible means of assessing its worth, there appear to be no limitations upon Liberal Studies and no means by which its work may be monitored.

Another important consequence of the system of formal examinations is that those subjects which are examined become legitimated in the eyes of the students. Indeed, some technical personnel blame the students' lack of motivation in Liberal Studies upon those who resist the introduction of any formal assessment in that subject:

> 'they [the students] know that, at the end of term, or at the end of the year . . . it does not really matter if they've done nothing in that area [Liberal Studies] .'

The instrumental nature of such a view is endorsed by many students, who, as the following comments suggest, believe that the viability of Liberal Studies would be improved if it were formally examined:

Tony: You know you have got to come into this lesson, but you don't have to do anything. You can take no part in the whole thing.
Tim: Yeh . . . but you give the subject an exam, and you're saying this is more important than other subjects, or as important as other subjects. You'd have to do something then, wouldn't you?

It is partly from the weight of such combined pressures, and partly through the influence of the Technician Education Council, whose committees stress the importance of more structured forms of evaluation, that an increasing number of Liberal Studies teachers have lent their support to the introduction of more formal modes of assessment in Liberal Studies. Thus although for many Liberal Studies staff at Western examinations may be in conflict with their definition of Liberal Studies, they clearly address two interrelated problems. First, the introduction of an examination in Liberal Studies would alleviate the criticism that its content is not adequately structured and evaluated; and second, such a process of assessment would provide the Liberal Studies teacher with greater control over his students.

In the section which follows we shall examine how the survival and growth of the Liberal Studies Department at Western depends to a large extent upon its response to its critics. Indeed, it will be argued, the Liberal Studies Department cannot simply be analysed as a separate entity at Western, since it has clearly adopted a number of policies which indicate that its management and rationalisation must be examined in relation to other college bodies.

Growth and response

An important characteristic of the development of the Liberal Studies Department at Western concerns its ability to defend itself against its critics by establishing particular sets of organisational responses. The nature of those responses varies, from attempts to develop close liaison with other departments with regard to the formulation of syllabuses, to explicitly adopting a servicing role in terms of focusing upon vocationally relevant subject-matter, like the teaching of English language and communication skills (see Appendix 3). In addition, the department has sought to make itself indispensable to the social organisation of the college by taking responsibility for student union affairs and social functions. This aspect of the Liberal Studies brief at Western involves departmental members in advising students upon social, personal and welfare matters, as well as in organising various extra-curricular activities such as the sub-aqua and sports clubs, collections for charities, discotheques and so on. By taking responsibility for such activities the Liberal Studies Department has created an essential niche for itself within the institution. Its members have gradually attained important positions within the committee structure of the college, and without their organising abilities, the local branch of their own union (National Association for Teachers in Further and Higher Education) would almost certainly cease to function.

The involvement of the Liberal Studies staff in such activities is a response to an institutional imperative, a college belief that all aspects of the institution should serve a useful purpose. The particular role adopted by the Liberal Studies Department gives it a sense of purpose and some value in the institution as an acting, contributing body. In an introductory talk to a new intake of craft students, the lecturer quoted below outlines some of the ways in which Liberal Studies personnel might be of service to students:

'I think, in so far as it means "the Union", it means the General Studies lecturers . . . if you have any problem . . . things that you can't talk over with anybody else, either because they are of such a nature that you don't want to, or because some people don't have the knowledge, like, for instance, you get done on a criminal charge, or your girl-friend's pregnant, or your father's kicking you out and you want somewhere to live. I'm not saying we can solve that problem, obviously we can't, but we might be able to assist you to seek a solution yourself. . . . We might be able to put you in touch with legal aid . . . or a doctor . . . or advise you on your rights of tenancy, you know, if you want to take up a flat, or whatever. We might have certain knowledge at your disposal, or can put you in touch with how to get hold of it.'

According to the college administration, the varied experience of the Liberal Studies lecturer equips him to handle the emotional and social side of apprenticeship training. Thus he becomes adviser and counsellor to the students, although it is questionable how many students avail themselves of these services, and certainly day-release students, attending college for one compressed day each week, have scant opportunity to take advantage of many of the available facilities. Moreover, with a minority of full-time students, the Union is little more than a nominal body, so that the contribution of the Liberal Studies Department to the pastoral side of college affairs is not thought to render it indispensable.

It is through such involvement, however, that the department has attained a role of some institutional importance, a role, moreover, which other staff are reluctant to adopt. It is through its servicing and liaison work, however, that the department has managed to silence much of the controversy which greeted its introduction. In the following comments, a senior member of the department explains how this has been achieved:

'Through the efforts of the more conscientious staff, we have made quite a good name . . . through liaising with the departments. We have got a certain amount of responsibility to the students, college and employers. . . . We have to recognise that many of the students have exams, which are crucial to them . . . they require support and help in their literacy work.'

By adopting a servicing role and thereby helping with some of the problems of other departments (i.e. literacy), Liberal Studies has managed to consolidate and strengthen its position. In this way it has proved itself valuable in terms of the technological rationale which dominates college affairs. Attitudes towards the Liberal Studies Department, therefore, have mellowed over the years because of its willingness to accommodate the needs of the technical departments. There is considerable readiness on the part of many of the Liberal Studies personnel to acknowledge their critics, and this has been supported by the senior members of the department who strongly favour their subject acting in a servicing role to technical studies:

'Our prime *raison d'être* is as a service department, providing the
General Studies element and physical education opportunities for
students from other departments.'

In the comments quoted above, a senior lecturer in Liberal Studies
acknowledges the point that students do not 'belong' to his department,
but are only temporarily in its charge. The apprentices 'belong' to the
technical departments, and because of this the senior members of the
Liberal Studies Department advocate that the work of their department
should complement that of the technical departments.

It would seem to us that such a *modus vivendi* is not simply a realistic
approach to the problem of survival in highly competitive working conditions, but to a certain extent a reflection of an acceptance of the line
of least resistance. Indeed, from an initial rather *ad hoc* organisation of
its curricular activities, the department has increasingly responded to its
critics, so that over the years it has developed fairly rigorous syllabuses
and curricular guidelines for its personnel to follow. 'Better this', one
lecturer remarked, 'than having them [the technical departments]
doing it for us.' Such a view is endorsed by the majority of the departmental members, one of whom suggested:

'We do need to structure our aims more coherently. . . . But some
departments are never satisfied. . . . they want behavioural objectives
spelt out. . . . it would even make Bloom wince.'

The call for Liberal Studies to structure its content is a reflection of
the philosophy of accountability which governs the work of the technical departments at Western. Such a philosophy is not always appreci-
ated by the Liberal Studies personnel, but a general consensus has
emerged among them, so that where structure *per se* is not considered
unsuitable, the form that structure should take continues to be debated.
Our lecturer we interviewed outlined the gradual shift in departmental
policy over the years in response to criticisms from employers and technical personnel:

'When I first came here, about eight years ago, we used to decide what
sort of things we would teach in an informal meeting. . . . If you had
a pet subject, and you felt it would be worthwhile including it . . .
then it would go into the "syllabus" . . . provided there were no real
objections from any other members of the staff. . . . Now, of course,
everything is much more formal. . . . we talk about "programmes",
and "units" and have to lay down "aims" and "objectives".'

Thus the department has moved towards organising its work in a
more formal manner, partly because of pressures brought to bear by the
technical departments, and partly because of the scepticism of employers

regarding the contribution of Liberal Studies to apprenticeship training schemes. Some departmental members advocate the old approach as the ideal way in which to exploit the strength of Liberal Studies, and see the trend towards more formal syllabuses as a harbinger of the impending demise of their subject area. Others, however, consider that the proposals of such bodies as the Technician Education Council for the introduction of more codified syllabuses in Liberal Studies can only be beneficial to their department:

> 'I'm in favour of a syllabus, I wish we had them for all our courses. This work we've been doing on TEC: I think we've, for the first time, got round to drafting out something that has some kind of logic and consistency of meaning.'

Several departmental members confided, however, that although a departmental syllabus existed, there was no compulsion to adhere to it and no sanctions taken against those who chose not to do so. The introduction of TEC to the department, however, marks a step towards placing some limits upon Liberal Studies knowledge, and hence upon classroom activities. It also indicates a desire at Western to tighten up Liberal Studies work, so that relations will be improved with other college departments.

If one effect of the move towards tightening things up has been to improve the image of the department, another has certainly been that it has created some confusion among departmental members regarding their teaching objectives. This confusion is particularly noticeable in the area of the department's responsibility for servicing the literacy skills of the young apprentice. Although few members of the Liberal Studies Department at Western dispute the importance of teaching the communication skills within their courses, many consider that the technical departments have simply abdicated their responsibilities in this area by dumping basic skill work on to the Liberal Studies staff. It is seen as yet another example of the rather narrow way in which other college bodies redefine the vocational relevance of Liberal Studies knowledge. (We look more deeply at this problem in Appendix 3.)

Controversy within the ranks

We have suggested so far that one important way in which the Department of Liberal Studies has negotiated some institutional credibility at Western is through its adoption of a servicing role to the needs of other departments. In this way, the department has sought to silence its more vociferous critics who question the value of its contribution to the technical curriculum. It would be misleading, however, to give the impression that much of the criticism which is levelled against the Liberal Studies Department is not equally voiced by some of its own members. Indeed, Seymour and Acres (1974) argue that the kinds of criticisms we have outlined so far are not entirely without foundation. They suggest that for many years a large number of Liberal Studies teachers have been culpable of poor teaching and mismanagement of courses. This is not an isolated view, moreover, and is one that is shared by those members of the Liberal Studies Department at Western who favour a more structured approach to the work of their department.

During the course of our field-work, we were able to distinguish a number of distinct groups among the Liberal Studies staff at Western, one of which included a number of lecturers with previous military or industrial experience. Some of that group had been technical teachers themselves, and were generally sceptical of the direction the department had taken, particularly in relation to its policy of recruiting young graduates from the social sciences and humanities. It is not perhaps surprising, therefore, that some tension exists between the various Liberal Studies personnel regarding the aims of the department and the organisation of its work. The following remarks illustrate something of the way in which some more established members of the department perceive the situation:

'We suffer from a lethargy that leaves us wide open to sniping from other departments. . . . it is hard operating within such an amorphous area as Liberal Studies. Some teachers see their job in a free-ranging, open-ended way – not necessarily related to the work situation. I sympathise with this view . . . but, at the same time, we have got a certain amount of responsibility to the students, college and employer.'

Not unlike his technical colleagues, the lecturer quoted above also perceives Liberal Studies as a nebulous area within the technical curriculum, difficult to define and in need of structure. Such problems, moreover, are seen to be compounded for those involved where the department exposes itself to charges of inefficient organisation and mismanagement of departmental affairs. The following comments from one member of the department we interviewed express his anxiety with regard to such matters:

'We need more effective co-ordination, planning and organisation. Without that, we're vulnerable. It's when the technical lecturer talks to the students and they say we've been drawing, doing art work, talking politics, watching a film or discussing contraceptives . . . something that seems way out. . . . A lot of technical lecturers feel that if the lads take this back to work and the boss gets hold of it, then they will be investigated. . . . Technical teachers have to defend the syllabus of the college and resent it if Liberal Studies lecturers attract criticism with the things they teach and the methods they use.'

Such problems, however, as we have previously suggested, cannot be understood in isolation from the wider institutional processes which characterise Western's practice. There is a need, therefore, to examine the ways in which the content of Liberal Studies becomes separated off from other subject areas, a process of separation pursued by many of the Liberal Studies staff themselves. Bernstein (1971) refers to the imposition of boundaries between subject areas as the 'classification of knowledge', and in this section we shall attempt to explain how such boundaries are maintained through the organisation, or as Bernstein (1971) puts it 'framing' of liberal studies knowledge.

Very briefly, the 'framing' of knowledge indicates the degree of control teachers exert over both the content of their field, and the transmission of that content. Principally, we intend to dispel the notion that the framing of Liberal Studies knowledge is non-vocational, or indeed significantly different from that of technical knowledge. We shall also draw upon Esland's (1971) idea that professional knowledge is 'negotiable currency' and that the imposition of departmental boundaries (which we have described as rigidly maintained at Western) promotes competition between those deparments in defence of their separate professional identities. At Western, attempts initiated largely by technical personnel to break down subject boundaries between themselves and the Liberal Studies Department have been resisted by the Liberal Studies staff. In our view, the department seeks to maintain those boundaries in order to defend its discrete identity and to ensure its continued access to 'negotiable currency'. However, although the boundaries or 'classification' of Liberal Studies knowledge have been maintained, it would seem to us that the transmission or 'framing' of that knowledge has splintered into a number of different and sometimes conflictual forms.

First, there are those who approach the teaching of Liberal Studies from a servicing point of view. They liaise clearly with the technical departments and respond to criticisms of their practice. Second, there are those who consider that Liberal Studies offers them an alternative to the restrictions imposed by formal curricula and examinations. They see Liberal Studies as offering an opportunity to teach in a 'critical' way, or as one suggested, 'to raise consciousness'. And third, there are those who maintain that the strength of Liberal Studies lies in the freedom it gives them to do exactly as they please. These separate groups within the Liberal Studies Department will be referred to respectively as 'liberals', 'radicals' and 'cowboys'. Each has a markedly different frame for Liberal Studies teaching, and identifies the other group in such terms.[3]

The 'liberals' in the Liberal Studies Department at Western are characterised largely by their seniority and experience in teaching. This is reflected in their discussions of their work:

> 'Some people are getting Liberal Studies a bad name . . . especially the young members of the staff, who are still in their student days. . . . they still want to set the world on fire. I think, when they've got this out of their system and get down to more serious discussion . . . their own students will appreciate them more. . . . our students aren't radicals.'

The arguments for Liberal Studies as a servicing agent for technical studies are most strongly propagated by these teachers, who represent the dominant ethos of the department. During their many years of teaching, they have not only become aware of the commonest criticisms levelled against their subject, but they have also experienced the problems such criticisms can pose for them. Consequently, they are ready to acknowledge the sensitivity with which both technical personnel and employers perceive work which is not immediately related to vocational studies. Their response has been to accept as valid some of the accusations of irrelevance and to try to answer those accusations by working more closely with the technical departments. Their stated aims and teaching methods, however, may also be seen to be tactics for survival. Indeed, since they do not have sufficient power in a college such as Western to make an autonomous stand, they clearly consider it wiser to liaise and adapt to the technical ethos.

The term 'radicals' has come to be applied to the younger members of the Liberal Studies Department at Western, whose professed aims largely follow those of the lecturer in his first year of full-time teaching quoted below:

> 'General Studies, as it has grown up, is a transmission belt for bourgeois ideas and bourgeois ideology into the working classes. That puts a General Studies teacher, who doesn't accept such an ideology, into a contradictory position.'

Espousing a different philosophy from the dominant ethos of his department which he considers bourgeois, the teacher acquires the reputation of being a radical, and accepts it as an accurate interpretation of his position: 'You can do nothing but take part in that transmission belt – *but* . . . you *are* trying to question it.'

It is this professed critical approach which is rejected by the more conservative members of the Liberal Studies Department, because they believe that such an approach will only jeopardise their position further.

They dissociate themselves from any philosophy which might be interpreted as subverting the training of young workers. Such fears, moreover, as we have previously suggested, are shared not only by technical personnel, but by the majority of employers, one of whom articulated his scepticism in the following manner:

'Radical teachers have been homing in on these courses [Liberal Studies] and putting all sorts of ideas into the heads of lads who would be best suited to learning a trade.'[4]

Such a remark from the boss of an engineering plant is indicative of one of the major constraints imposed upon the Liberal Studies teacher, who clearly is expected to make available to his students only those materials which will help him to assume a useful and indeed passive role within industry. It is a view shared by the Principal of one of Britain's largest technical colleges: 'Unfortunately, there are Lefties who believe that education is the be-all, and that industrial jobs mean working for oppressors.'

Such accounts imply that the 'lefty' Liberal Studies teacher is at liberty to propagate his own ideas. In our view, however, pressures such as those imposed by employers, principals and others exert such heavy restrictions upon the individual teacher that he has little scope to engage in activities which might be interpreted as subversive. The interviews we held with the radicals at Western support this view, and suggest that their position is largely one of compromise, which allows them to raise the consciousness of their students only marginally if at all. One such lecturer describes his work in the following way:

'I'm concerned with suggesting to the lads ways [in which] they might be able to play a part in the wider society. Sticking up for themselves, claiming rights that are formally theirs . . . seeing opportunities that they might not otherwise see and, more generally, to open the wider aspects of culture to them. . . . they are deprived of culture, in terms of knowledge and experience. . . . it's a matter of attempting to broaden these horizons . . . I think that might be called the missionary role.'

While the governing philosophy of such remarks might appear radical, the actual practice of this teacher is heavily tempered by both the college administration and the industry whose needs he is expected to serve. Consequently in class he covers the usual topics – 'earning and taxation', 'taking out a mortgage', 'the political parties', and so forth. Clearly, he must meet the expected definition of what counts as Liberal Studies in order to protect his position. Although the constraints upon his work may only involve informal sanctions, they represent nevertheless significant factors of social control. It is only too easy for the radical teacher to attract criticism of his work at Western and so if he is to remain in employment, he must learn to moderate his radicalism. As the following remarks suggest, although few official sanctions may be imposed, highly efficient forms of control do exist:

'I've seen people drown. . . . they were just left to flounder, and, of course, once they are drowning, the sharks would go for them.'

'no one was willing to help him, and, once he was having trouble . . . the powers that be "put the boot in" rather than providing the help and assistance that the guy needed.'

Thus in practice the radical teacher is not impervious to attack, although the sanctions which may be imposed upon his activities are rarely formal. Such sanctions can take a variety of forms which might include the following: inconvenient timetabling, being given difficult groups to teach, the withdrawal of essential resources, or supervision of teaching duties by a senior colleague. Besides influencing the subject-matter of his classes, such sanctions will also influence his teaching methods. The constant use of films and other visual aids has led to harsh criticism at Western from both within and without the department, that such Liberal Studies classes are not educational and simply entertain the students for an hour. In the same way, the 'discussion group' has been similarly criticised as mere undirected 'talk'. Thus, in order to maintain a respectable public face, radical teachers often emerge in conventional 'chalk and talk' methods. Indeed, from our observations of such classes, the social relations and forms of teaching methods pursued often differ very little from those observed in the workshop.

The kinds of criticisms attracted by radical teachers, however, constitute a major cause of the recent movement towards formalising Liberal Studies within FE. Indeed, many lecturers interpret the structuring influence of TEC as a direct attempt to assert restrictive control over the content and teaching methods associated with Liberal Studies. Attempts to control Liberal Studies in this way, moreover, have important implications for the practice of the third group of Liberal Studies teachers at Western, who are described by their colleagues as 'cowboys'.

While to those outside the department, the radical teacher is seen as a deviant because of his extreme ideological stance, for the actual departmental members the real deviants are the 'cowboys'. It is this third group which does not appear to the others either to shoulder its share of the departmental workload, or to conform to the dominant notion of what should constitute the role of a Liberal Studies lecturer. Indeed, the premise upon which this third group bases its practice is one of freedom in both content and pedagogy, and not one which is primarily concerned with alleviating the pressures brought to bear upon the department because of its delicate political position. Consequently other departmental members are inclined to condemn this approach as too liberal and to interpret the cowboy's rationalisations (no restrictions or impediments) as a mask for selfishness, laziness or a general unwillingness to accept their departmental and teaching responsibilities. However, adherents of this third approach simply reject such stereotyping, and argue that their approach truly reflects the spirit and essence of what should constitute liberal studies: 'Let me say, from the start, that any kind of rigidity is against my idea of "Liberal education" – flexibility is the first requirement of such an education.'

The flexibility this lecturer refers to applies principally to his choice of topics, which may change weekly without apparent regard for structure or continuity. It also involves a full utilisation of visual aids: 'If it moves and it is in colour, it will keep them interested', remarked one lecturer. From such a perspective, the teaching of Liberal Studies becomes a matter of negotiating a lesson with one's students, with the minimum amount of conflict. It is based largely upon an entertainment notion of Liberal Studies teaching, which is reflective of the low expectations such teachers hold of the kinds of students Western attracts. Not all cowboys, however, advocate the entertainment approach, but argue for a pot-pourri of materials which will render Liberal Studies an open field, in which both teachers and students may pursue their own interests. It is this latter approach, however, which elicits almost universal hostility within the college. Nevertheless, those who adhere to it are no less committed to their philosophy than the liberal or the radical, and consider the enforced structuring of liberal studies through TEC as inevitably leading to the demise of their subject.

As in most institutional contexts, however, no matter how many groups co-exist, one tends to dominate. At Western it is the liberals, whose seniority and greater numbers, allied with the reluctant support of the radicals, allows them to maintain an overall balance of control. Such control, as we have previously suggested, is rooted in the avoidance of controversy, and maintained through the expressed public concern for vocational relevance. Nevertheless, employers and technical personnel, sensing that this control is precarious, continue to exert their influence upon the department by actively supporting its servicing ideology. In such circumstances, it is not perhaps surprising that the senior members of the department welcome such support, despite its instrumentality, since it represents an acknowledgment of their positive contribution towards the worth of the college.

In this way the department seeks to present a unified public face, and is seen to be in control of its 'dissidents'. However, despite that public façade, it is not perhaps surprising that the definitions the various departmental groups give of their roles are fraught with defensive and justificatory rhetoric. There remains, moreover, a further if not more compelling feature of control which prevents *all* Liberal Studies personnel at Western from pressing their particular ideals too far, and that is firmly rooted in the realities of *practice*.

During the course of our field-work, it became apparent that the various characterisations of the Liberal Studies teacher outlined above are indistinguishable within the classroom. Indeed, in our view the terms 'liberal', 'radical' and 'cowboy' are simply political positions adopted by the various Liberal Studies personnel to identify themselves and others at the institutional level. We would wish to argue that those terms reflect the response of those involved to the technical rationality of the college, in the sense that they indicate the degree to which teachers either associate or dissociate themselves from the determining influences of the technical curriculum. In our view, therefore, such characterisations bear little relation to teaching methods, but reflect the attempts of those involved to express their 'theories of survival' within working conditions which might well be described as repressive. In other words, such typifications or 'vocabularies of motive' (Mills, 1963) represent the various responses of those involved to the marginality of their professional status.

Within the frustrating conditions of classroom life, moreover, to which we have already made brief mention, Liberal Studies teachers confront a further perhaps more compelling impediment to the implementation of their theoretical ideals. Indeed, our observations suggest that within the closed conditions of the vocational day, the classroom activities of Liberal Studies personnel do not conform to any one self-professed typification of their practice. On the contrary, confronted with disillusioned and poorly motivated students, the Liberal Studies teacher must adopt a variety of strategies in order to survive. Indeed, our observations suggest that the Liberal Studies teacher *has* very little autonomy or control over his own practice or conditions of teaching. The frustrating reality of classroom life would seem to explain why such teachers tend to describe themselves in theoretical or idealised terms as opposed to those drawn from the realm of practice which might well indicate a painful recognition of their own impotence.

In conclusion, therefore, we have attempted to argue that the process through which liberal studies staff both criticise and typify the practice of others is not based upon their knowledge of one another's classroom activities. Such a process rather is a response at an institutional level to both alienating working conditions and the policy their department has been forced to adopt in order to maintain a 'respectable' public face. In addition, we have sought to explain that such a response to the marginal status of the Liberal Studies personnel is firmly rooted within the technical rationality which determines social relations at Western College. It is our contention, therefore, that Liberal Studies knowledge does not exist in vacuum, but can only be understood in relation to those external contingencies of institutional life which constrain both expression and action. Thus while the Liberal Studies teacher might appear free to do as he pleases, his activities are heavily tempered by forces both within and without the classroom. And finally, we would wish to contend that the conditions of educational practice, such as those at Western, render the nature of Liberal Studies vocational in orientation.

In order fully to comprehend why this should be, however, there is a need to investigate in greater depth the wider theoretical issues which impinge upon the structural relations between college and industry. It would be misleading to assume that the problems to which we have so far referred might be resolved by enlightened reform, new curricula, greater resources or better teachers. Indeed in the chapters both on Mining and on Liberal Studies we have attempted to explain how the departmental response is largely influenced by conditions which exist outside the institution. In the chapter which follows, we return to some of the theoretical problems raised at the outset of the study and, in particular, to the question of the 'fit' (or synchronisation) between education and industry. In so doing, our analysis explores some of the weaknesses of both functionalistic and economistic explanations of the structural relations between education, economy and society.

Chapter 6

On the 'fit' between Further Education and industry

So far in this study we have sought to examine at a number of levels the relationship between technical education and the economic infrastructure. We have sought to argue our case from an investigation of 'practice', as manifested within one institution, Western College. In this section, we shall attempt to enlarge upon some of the empirical examples we have recorded, and to offer a more conceptual explanation of the functioning of FE within the social system. In so doing, we shall address a number of issues arising from one central problematic, namely the question of the relative autonomy of the institution from the economic infrastructure it serves. Our focus of attention, therefore, returns to some of the theoretical problems raised at the outset of this study, and centres more specifically upon some of the weaknesses of both functionalistic and economistic explanations of the relations between education, economy and society.

We do not wish to repeat at length many of the criticisms of such analyses which have been made elsewhere. None the less, it seems important to preface our chapter with a number of introductory remarks. We do not consider, for example, that much will be gained by adopting the recently favoured argument that functionalism tends to reify the connections between education, stratification and the social structure. Indeed, it seems to us that such a line of argument often suffers from very similar faults of over-simplification to those associated with the position it seeks to attack. Moreover, we would not necessarily agree that functionalistic theory is predicated upon an over-simplified explanation of such social relations. In our view, the most important failing of both functionalistic and economistic conceptions of education in general is their shared tendency to obscure, within their various rationalisations of the relationship between education and the economy, the real mechanisms through which existing social and economic forms maintain their hegemony. It would seem to us that such forms of analysis reduce important social relations to mere technical connections, inputs and outputs, so that institutions like Western College are seen as *mechanically* responding to an external demand for trained labour, whereas our experience within the field has demonstrated that the inner workings of institutions like Western are far from mechanical, and indeed highly complex in character.

Thus we shall look in some detail at the problematic concept of institutional autonomy. That concept is of importance here, not only because it brings to light a number of contradictions within the system of FE itself, but because it provides an alternative conception of the fit between education and the economy. We shall focus more specifically upon the current debate about the competing aims of education and training within the sphere of FE. It is not our intention to give detailed definitions of those terms, but rather to suggest that their usage within current debate has often served to mystify some of the more essential functions of FE in terms of its contribution to the process of production. Before considering those important issues, however, some preliminary observations are required.

General observations

It is not uncommon within both political and philosophical debate that confusion over conceptual terms and their precise meanings can sometimes lead to an impasse in their powers of explanation. This tendency would seem to be particularly pertinent to both past and present attempts to understand the workings of the educational system. Indeed, at one extreme of current debate education is seen to be no more than an agent of the capitalist State, reproducing the pre-conditions of capitalist modes of production; whereas, at the other, a position favoured by more liberal theorists, education is seen to be independent of the economic infrastructure, and possessing the potential for transcending both the actions and understandings of social actors. It would seem to us, however, that both positions lack a *fundamental* understanding of the actual practices upon which such theoretical formulations are predicated. In other words, both perspectives are based upon different but equally over-simplified models of what, at the empirical level, is a highly complex and dynamic set of social processes.

Indeed, our own initial assumptions at the outset of this study were clearly influenced by such broad viewpoints. Initially, we were concerned to examine the assertion that there exists, or could exist, some *clear-cut* connection between technical education and the work situation. The convenience of reducing teacher/apprentice relations to some assumed need of the economy was, to say the least, appealing, and would have saved us a great deal of hard work and soul-searching. Moreover, we could have extrapolated some radical new theory out of that truism and completed our study on page 1.

Our immediate experience of Western College, however, despite its apparent dependence upon the local industrial environment, made such a crude correspondence between technical education and industry impossible to sustain. Indeed, since its inception the college has not only established an identity of its own, but generated an institutional dimension which, although strongly influenced by the proximity of local industry, is not *overdetermined* by it. Thus the focus of our analysis became the complex nature of that relationship, and more specifically, the 'social space' in which the institution negotiates the terms of its autonomy. The focus of interest, however, proved highly contradictory since it could be described in terms of relative autonomy as well as in terms of economic determinism. Hence Althusser (1971) contends that the autonomy of educational and superstructural processes is a necessary feature of their function of legitimation in a capitalist society, where the underlying functional interconnection with production is only made manifest in the last instance. It would seem to us, however, that such a neat explanation fails to spell out how that apparent autonomy actually occurs, and suggests that in the last instance the structural parameters of college life actually *determine* the conditions of teachers' work. In this way, autonomy is relegated to a mere manifestation of false consciousness in a social setting where capital holds an *independent* and *causal* control over both the perceptions and activities of participants.

In our view, therefore, the last instance thesis often serves as a mere safety mechanism whereby the theorist can save the baby no matter how much bath water has been thrown away. So that by abstracting the analysis from a total examination of underlying social relations, everything can be reduced to an oversimplified explanation. It would seem to us that this criticism might well be brought to bear upon many contemporary economic analyses of production. Indeed, both Keynesian and Marxist economists alike use such terms as 'the economy', 'demand', 'capital' and 'training', as if they were objective concepts divorced from the social relations of which they are a part.

Recent developments in the use of Marxist perspectives in the study of education, for example, may also be seen to objectify such concepts. Indeed, while they have undoubtedly contributed to our understanding of the relationship between schooling and the State, they have done little to elucidate the social relations which characterise that relationship. It has become commonplace to describe schools as state apparatuses, cultural reproducers, ideological agents, and servants of monopoly capitalism, but the use of such global terms, accurate or not, does little to enhance our understanding of the empirical and practical connections which exemplify the relationship between education and the social structure.

It is, we believe, inaccurate to perceive such concepts as the economy, capital, and the needs of industry in reified or purely instrumental terms, for the important point such terms ignore is that the relative autonomy of those concepts, in relation to each other, must be spelt out empirically, if it is to be understood. Despite all the methodological and empirical risks that such a task involves, we would wish to argue that only a thorough-going examination of the character of interpersonal relations within the empirical setting will reveal the complex impact of the use of capital upon human forms.

Our focus in this chapter, therefore, is to examine the key manifestation of that problem, within FE, namely the rhetoric which surrounds the concepts of *education* and *training*. For it would appear that the confusion which characterises the use of those terms, among those who seek to explain the processes of FE, gives rise to the most pertinent discourse *vis-à-vis* the nature of practice within that important area of educational provision.

Education and training

The assumption is often made that the sole purpose of education is *not* to service industry, and that not only should education possess some autonomy, but that it should contain some potential for developing a consciousness which is independent of the needs of the labour process. If we were to present such a view, however, to the vast majority of technical teachers who are concerned with educating young workers to become competent members of the production process, there would almost certainly arise considerable opposition to such an assertion. Indeed, in our experience, most technical teachers not only perceive their primary objective as the provision of appropriately trained industrial personnel, but consider any deviation from that objective as rendering the activity of *instruction* an impossible task. Moreover, apprentice-students themselves find any form in instruction, which is not immediately relevant to their work, not only a waste of time, but an unnecessary intrusion into what they *need to know*.

Such instrumentality tends to be frowned upon by many educationalists who fail to understand the 'culture of technicism' from which such views emanate (Gorz, 1977), and which not only shapes work roles but also the expectations and life-styles of those who adhere to it: that is to say, employers, workers, indeed many teachers within the sphere of technical education.[1] In other words, what we are suggesting is that as educationalists we should not be surprised when technical teachers look in disbelief at our criticism of their instrumentality for, given the culture of technicism, how could their practice be reformed by the application of more liberal philosophies of education (Holly, 1977)?

On the other hand, it would be mistaken to assume that such teachers are incapable of adopting educational structures which appear to strengthen their position as technical personnel.

The development of TEC courses serves as a case in point in this respect. A considerable number of the technical staff we interviewed at Western expressed an initial enthusiasm for the TEC proposals. However, while we have no evidence of the practical outcome of such proposals at Western we have a large amount of documentary evidence which indicates how technical personnel thought TEC would influence their work. Consider the following remarks from two separate technical lecturers:

'From what I have seen of the new syllabuses I think they are a real improvement. They are more specific about the areas that have to be taught. . . . The present syllabuses are too open-ended . . . anything and everything seems to be included. . . . they're too open in standard as well. . . . you don't know quite how far to go with a particular section. With the TEC syllabuses you have more guidelines about exactly what to cover . . . this is a big advantage.'

'I'm very enthusiastic about TEC. I see TEC doing an awful lot of good for two main reasons. . . . The first is that it puts a national standard on you. . . . this is important since we do need national standards of comparison. At present there are real disparities between colleges and between regions. . . . Second, TEC syllabuses specify very clearly the depth that you should go to and the level of comprehension that you can expect. . . . I certainly welcome TEC from this point of view alone. The feeling here is that these syllabuses have been thought out . . . there's a link between local and national policy if you like.'

Such remarks suggest that TEC will support and strengthen the work of existing departments. Indeed, the TEC proposals appear to promise that existing syllabuses will be legitimated to a far wider audience. Yet the remarks quoted above fail to recognise that TEC may also give rise to a re-questioning of existing practice. It would seem to us that such an omission is of considerable importance, for while it might *appear* that TEC will strengthen the autonomous development of centralised aims and objectives, and thereby support technical teachers in their day-to-day activities, it is also the case that such teachers have simply interpreted the TEC proposals as necessarily supportive of their own particular conception of what constitutes FE.

In our view what is of interest about such an interpretation of TEC is the continual search for rational arguments which will support both the theory of FE as well as the specific relations and forms of training which make up its practice. It would seem to us that that search for rationalisation marks an interesting contradiction, which not only characterises the *modus vivendi* of many technical teachers, but also serves to mask both the logic of the production process and the part played by FE in its reproduction. So that by taking the development of autonomous aims through TEC as part of that rationalisation, the technical teacher is enabled to legitimate both his authority within the process of FE, as well as his subservience to the industrial infrastructure. Moreover, since the centralisation of aims and objectives through TEC is construed as a fairly *ad hoc* process, it becomes a way of strengthening the mechanisms of control available to the technical teacher when dealing with critical students. It is our contention, therefore, that such a process of rationalisation allows the technical teacher to adopt educational arguments to legitimate his practice, which is largely one of training young workers for the labour market. In other words, we would wish to argue that for the technical teacher the competing interests of education and training become synonymous, a point previously made by Keddie (1971) with regard to teachers adopting educationalist's arguments as rationalisations of their practice.

However, we would wish to go further, and to suggest that the process of rationalisation discussed above which allows the concepts of education and training to appear synonymous is merely a mask for a far more important aspect of the role of FE within the wider social system: that is, its function as a qualifying mechanism *vis-à-vis* the social differentiation and distribution of labour within a free market. In other words, it is our contention that the whole debate about education and training merely serves to support an autonomous image of the FE system, which in turn legitimates the allocative function of FE in terms of providing trained labour for the industrial infrastructure. Colleges such as Western, therefore, are seen to be legitimate because of their role in providing vocational training and the necessary qualifications for entry into the production process. Moreover, it is through this apparent legitimacy that apprentice-students are initiated into certain forms of technical and pedagogical relations which are essential for the acquisition of their 'ticket' and subsequent entry into the world of work.

Ticket and control

It is important at this point to stress that the FE system, through its teaching function, acts to legitimate existing apprenticeship training schemes. Without some form of FE, it is impossible for the young worker to become qualified 'out of his time'. FE performs this role under the auspices of professional examination boards, and specifically prepares apprentice-students for statutory examinations and practicals. While syllabuses tend to be constructed outside, in collaboration with professional associations, employers and unions, it is the colleges themselves which actually furnish the appropriate professional training in order to 'pass' the examination. We shall explain how this process enhances rather than restricts college autonomy later, but for the moment it is sufficient to recognise that the young worker is seen to be qualified not because his employer or union judge him to be, but because he has obtained his 'ticket' by passing the necessary college examination.

The college is the crucial mechanism of mediation in this process. Thus it would seem to us that the college in that capacity exercises a high degree of control over both the learning and earning prospects of apprentice-students.

While it might be argued that the college administration alone does not wholly decide who should or should not qualify, it is that body which possesses the expertise to channel students along the necessary route towards those important qualifications. We have attempted to exemplify that process of channelling in our examination of the Department of Mining at Western. We argued that student identities were shaped to those deemed appropriate by industry, through the syllabus and kinds of teaching relations they experienced at college. Moreover, since there is no other route through which apprentices can achieve professional status, that process of channelling would seem to denote a considerable degree of control which is vested in the lecturer's status. Consequently, technical lecturers enjoy a high degree of flexibility with regard to the kinds of teaching methods they adopt, and the ways in which they interpret their responsibilities within the bounds set by the examination boards. However, in our view, that flexibility with regard to the content and pacing of curricular knowledge becomes subject, during the course of practice, to various taken-for-granted assumptions about the labour process and the kinds of personnel who are considered suitable for entry into that process. The justification of such a process of rationalisation is that the lecturer must reach a balance between syllabus constraints, what he *knows* about industry, and what he *knows* about the kinds of students he is dealing with.

The learning situation, however, is often more problematic for the student, since syllabuses often reflect the jostling and competing interests of employers, unions, government and examiners. Thus it is not perhaps surprising that for the apprentice-student, if not sometimes for the teacher, the relevance of the curriculum to the work-place is often far from clear. In such circumstances the student becomes almost totally dependent upon the lecturer to interpret the syllabus for him, and this dependence strengthens the lecturer's position further, since it is he who holds the keys to the apprenticeship door. Thus the autonomy of the institution may be seen to be enhanced on two counts: first because, contrary to popular belief, unions, professional associations and examination boards allow the individual colleges to organise their own teaching programmes within certain guidelines; and second, because of the dependence of apprentice-students upon the college administration to make sense of oversubscribed and often outmoded syllabuses.

In our view it is virtually impossible for a technical syllabus to satisfy all the competing interests outlined above, and therefore individual colleges must negotiate their most appropriate path. Thus technical education becomes the province of the expert, financed as it is from rates and tax relief, rather than from the pockets of employers and unions whom it supposedly serves. It is not perhaps surprising, therefore, that college administrations are often 'sensitive' about their autonomy, choosing to negotiate diplomatically between those opposing interests. As we argued in our analysis of the organisation of Western College, such a process of negotiation gives rise to a whole rhetoric of legitimation, through which *all* appear to be satisfied, but in practice *none* is completely satisfied.

'Off the job' training, therefore, is cost-effective, since the educational institution rather than industry carries the responsibility for training labour and 'getting it through' the appropriate examinations. Thus because the apprentice is being trained elsewhere, it does not matter if at work he only cleans up and makes tea, as was the fate of some apprentice-student we interviewed. Ultimately, the assessment of successful apprenticeships, in terms of the acquisition of qualifications, is carried out outside the workplace, so that the young worker who is engaged at work in low-grade manual work finds it difficult at college to generate the necessary enthusiasm for more demanding theoretical and practical tasks, which appear to bear little relevance to his day-to-day work experience. Indeed, we interviewed a large number of craft apprentices, who despite reservations about the low levels of skill required by their work, expressed considerable scepticism about the kinds of tasks they were required to perform at college. Thus the relative autonomy of the technical lecturer does not necessarily carry weight in the practical world of the craft apprentice. As the following remarks suggest, compulsion plays a decisive part in both the work and college experience of apprentice-students.

'It's boring. . . . it's like work really. . . . 'cept you sit in lessons and takes notes down all day.'

'I don't know why we come here. . . . no one's told us why yet . . . we just come.'

'You have to come. . . . they make you. . . . if you miss too much college they can sack you.'

'I told them I didn't want to go to college . . . but they said I had to . . . it's as simple as that.'

'It's a day off at least . . . a bit of a skive . . . you can relax a bit. . . . at least it's a break . . . something different. . . .'

'Trouble is you need to come and pass the exams . . . your money's all tied up with it.'

'I'd rather be at work. . . . it's a waste of time. I think they look down on us here.'

'I get tired being lectured at all day . . . but if you miss a couple of weeks you've had it . . . you'll never catch up.'

The comments quoted above suggest a general agreement among apprentice-students about a disturbing degree of compulsion which is brought to bear upon the recipients of day-release education. It would seem to us that this element of compulsion raises a number of question-marks *vis-à-vis* the supposed benefits which are normally associated with FE, since those in receipt of day-release training tend to experience it as oppressive as opposed to liberating. Why then do young workers continue their studies? One answer would be that they have very little choice, since the qualifications acquired through day-release training are very closely associated with improved working conditions and promotion. Thus, not only are such workers caught in the cheap-labour trap facilitated by apprenticeship training schemes, but they have little option but to support it since qualifications and higher wages cannot be acquired through any other means. Moreover, in areas where youth unemployment figures are high, alternative forms of employment simply do not exist.

However, the greatest resentment apprentice-students bear against college concerns the disjunctures which are seen to exist between training schemes and the actual world of work. We outlined that problem in some depth in our chapter on the Department of Mining at Western. We argued that many mine managers were critical of the broadly based training their apprentices received at college, and were in favour of day-release students receiving direct instruction for specific job requirements. At a superficial level, this criticism from industry gave rise to some degree of contention between the college department and Coal Board officials. It would seem to us, however, that within engineering generally many of the traditional aspects of craft work have changed as technological developments at the plant level have taken over. The apprentice-training schemes associated with craft work, however, have changed very little over the years, so that despite innovations like day-release, exam reform and shorter apprenticeships, young workers today follow much the same courses as their teachers did many years ago. It is not perhaps surprising, therefore, that the frustrations the apprentice in training experiences are very closely associated with the ever-increasing disparities between theory (education), training (institution) and work (industrial practice).

The frustrations experienced by the apprentice-student stem from his belief that college over-trains him for the requirements of the work situation, while at the same time providing him with inadequate preparation for dealing with the social and technical problems associated with the world of work. It is our contention, however, that while the apprentice may *not* receive the necessary job skills for his activities within a changing industry, he does acquire through his college course 'appropriate' attitudes and work habits, since those are not subject to technological change. In other words, unions and employers continue to support outmoded college courses *not* because of the skills they impart, but because of the kinds of work habits and forms of social relations they serve to initiate apprentice-students into. On the one hand, therefore, such courses ensure that particular craft skills are conserved, no matter how outmoded they may be in terms of production, and despite the conflict that may arise between union and employer; while on the other, such courses ensure the supply and demand for a particular category of worker, for despite the fact that his skills may be outmoded, they still serve to denote certain pay-differentials and conditions of work which, contrary to the machinations of the media, may well serve the interests of both union and employer. Thus the apprentice training system acts as a screening device for both sides of industry, at one level regulating the supply and control of labour, and at another, ensuring that labour is socialised into the appropriate trade traditions. As Hussain (1977) points out:

'The implication is that educational requirements for entry into occupations need not bear any direct relation to what is technically necessary to perform the work in question. Instead, their function may just be to place the occupation with respect to others.'

It would seem to us, therefore, that no real cognitive fit or rational correspondence exists between training and the world of work. Moreover, in our view arguments which support a definite fit between training and industry merely serve to cloud the forms of social relations within which apprentice-students move. The craft-apprentice may be well aware of the disparities between training and the world of work, but his ignorance of the wider structural forces which facilitate them, allows him little option but to support existing forms of training, since once successfully completed, they will, it is hoped, bring promotion and higher wages. More importantly, within the very process of receiving specific job skills, his view of those wider structural forces will become even less clear and more fragmented. It is not perhaps surprising, therefore, that many of the apprentice-students we have quoted in this volume express considerable frustration with their lot, as well as a grudging acceptance of existing forms of apprenticeship training.

We have suggested that this frustration is rooted in the recognition that college not only expects *too much* of them, but that the standards of expertise they are required to reach bear little relation to the work they perform. In addition, they confront the paradox that while their teachers express reservations about theory and pride themselves upon their first-hand knowledge of industry, the apprentices themselves often experience the training they provide as esoteric and obscure.

It is our contention that this latter paradox serves as yet a further example of the way in which professional appearances serve to mask the real nature of the social relations which underpin them. Yet the autonomy of those appearances allows the underlying relations to continue unheeded. In the section which follows, we shall seek to understand how and why this process occurs by considering the nature of this apparent autonomy.

Autonomy

We have attempted so far to examine the mystification inherent in much of the rhetoric which surrounds the education and training debate. It is our contention that inasmuch as that rhetoric is employed by *both* theorists and practitioners for their separate ends, we are blinded as to the exact nature of those concepts and the practices they denote. More importantly, it would seem to us that such debate serves to mask the crucial allocative function of FE within the labour process. Moreover, while many apprentice-students recognise a fundamental contradiction between work and college, they continue to support existing training schemes because of the material benefits they undoubtedly lead to.

It could of course be argued that industry in collusion with the college administration is empowered with monetary sanctions which render failure to attend college virtually impossible. While such an argument brings into the open certain of the less public links between college and industry, it serves to suggest that coercion represents the major *raison d'être* why apprentice-students continue to support existing training schemes. What we wish to argue, however, is that ultimately the autonomy of the college as an educational institution gains the support of the student through the mythology of deferred gratification. In other words, the college celebrates its autonomy by suggesting that far from supplying the student with a 'ticket' which will simply gain for him higher wages and promotion, that 'ticket', which can only be acquired through success at college, also represents the key to greater social mobility and improved life chances. It is that autonomy which is abstracted from the real and which projects the ideal. In our view, such a process serves to legitimate existing social relations of production by both assisting in their development and inverting their real nature. Thus, it would seem to us that because FE both divides and controls its recipients, it cannot be separated off from the social relations of production. Indeed, we have sought to argue that a major function of FE is to invest students with the appropriate attitudes and habits for entry into those social relations.

For the apprentice-student, the shop floor represents the *real* basis of his material existence. College represents an escape route, a ladder to potential promotion and higher wages. It is also seen to be a 'perk', a day off from industrial reality. If it were to become part of the industrial world, by the incorporation of training schemes into the workplace, it would cease to possess that potential and become part of the humdrum. In our view, it would also become dysfunctional in terms of its part in the reproduction of the labour force, simply because it would no longer possess the promise of possible escape. Thus the apprentice-student *believes* that he has entered his apprenticeship freely, believes that he has *chosen* to commit himself to day-release, and believes that he has *chosen* to become qualified. Moreover, in our view it is not the firm or industry which creates that illusion, but the college ethos which appears to be independent of the world of work.

The paradox, however, lies in the fact that while FE legitimates existing and sometimes outmoded apprenticeship training schemes to those who receive them, it also caters for the needs of the production process, inasmuch as that process requires a flexible and changing labour force. However, that process is not seen to determine supply and demand, simply because colleges of FE appear to be independent of the economic infrastructure. Thus, in terms of the logic of capitalism, it is not contradictory that apprentices are instructed in outmoded skills, for as long as a flexible level of skilled manpower is provided, the process of production actually benefits by appearing to be *dissociated* from training. Clearly, although the apprentice must receive training, the attitudes he learns in the course of that training are *more* important than the actual skills he acquires, so that when his skills are found to be inappropriate, the production process itself cannot be seen to be at fault. Thus the system receives what it requires in terms of a *flexible* labour force, but avoids involvement in any public recrimination which may subsequently occur; a feature of capitalism which has been clearly

exemplified in our recent Great Educational Debate, where our industrial problems were blamed to a large extent upon poor schooling and
inadequate training.

In our view the autonomy of the FE system represents a crucial
juncture in the relationship between industry and education. It provides
a classic example of the way in which the real function of a social
institution, in terms of its contribution to the capitalist system, becomes
masked or hidden to those who participate in it. In other words, industry requires from FE certain fundamental factors, i.e. a steady supply
of skilled labour with appropriate attitudes and work habits for entry
into the production process. However, in the course of training, that
initial demand and the relationship it gives rise to between college and
industry becomes inverted, so that those who enter the production
process assume that they have done so voluntarily and without any
compulsion from wider structural forces.

The apparent autonomy of the college, moreover, is supported by
the position of technical teachers within the FE system. As we have
already suggested, a large number of them have been recruited from
industry because of their industrial expertise, but are no longer ostensibly part of their industry of origin. Thus they are able to translate
what they feel the apprentice should know about the world of work
(i.e. the culture of technicism) into the context of a seemingly *laisser-
faire* college course. In other words, they are no longer dependent upon
the logic of the production process, the profit and loss of the shop floor,
but yet a large number of them fundamentally adhere to that process
within their new career as teacher. Thus it often seems that if the
apprentice-student doesn't want to learn, he doesn't have to. However,
it would seem to us that once again reality is not as it might appear.
Indeed, the illusion of autonomy from the production process which
seems to characterise the work of the college administration, renders
the apprentice-student increasingly dependent not only upon his
teachers, but upon the whole underlying industrial process which
provides, albeit in a complex and mystificatory form, the *raison d'être*
of apprenticeship training.

It is this hidden link between college and industry which, we wish to
argue, provides the nub of the relationship between FE and industry,
and in terms of which the autonomy of colleges of further education as
educational institutions, can only be assessed. Indeed, it would seem to
us that if any progressive changes are to occur in the sphere of FE, then
that complex and unclear relationship must be demystified and clearly
stated.

In this chapter we have attempted a difficult, and some might say
almost an impossible, task: that is, to examine an apparent phenomenon.
In our view that apparent phenomenon, i.e. the autonomy of the college,

is apparent only in its complex role of obscuring the problematic relationship between FE and industry. In other words, the apparent autonomy of colleges of further education from the production process masks the mechanisms by which the natural relationship between training and production is realised in practice. It would seem to us that only by demystifying that relationship can one begin to understand the problems which confront FE today. However, before taking up the challenge of such remarks, we shall first examine those aspects of methodology which have shaped our investigations so far. Such a chapter, we believe, provides an important bridge between the ideas discussed here and those advanced in our final conclusions.

Chapter 7

A note on methodology

Towards the end of most empirical studies, the writer(s) usually attempt to explain the theoretical foundations of their methodological procedures. In a study of a macro-orientation, such an attempt might take the form of some pre-emptive explanation of the design and various research instruments employed during the course of the study. At another level, however, particularly in studies of an interactional character, such an attempt might tend towards an 'apologetic' glimpse at the various sources of information, or at the particular observational theme carried out.

The basis of our process of legitimation, however, lies in the necessary justification of our initial epistemological stance *vis-à-vis* the world and our object of study. Indeed, without such a justification, it would seem to us that social science might aptly be described as mere speculative philosophy. Such a position, however, has of course been recently challenged by those seeking to provide a structural rather than empirical analysis of society. Such analysis, usually associated in some way with the work of Althusser (1969 and 1971), seeks to question the whole basis of empiricism, arguing that whatever form such analysis takes, it represents little more than a kind of idealism, as opposed to the real search for scientific understandings of the social world.

The attempt to explain our methodological procedures, therefore, must take into account not only our research activities, but also those arguments which challenge their validity. The problem being that methodological pluralism or 'anarchy' as Feyerabend (1975) has recently described it, tends to give rise to a kind of research purity which is totally inconsistent with its data. Indeed, as Bernstein (1974) points out:

'Every new approach becomes a social movement or sect which immediately defines the nature of the subject by redefining what is to be admitted or what is beyond the pale, so that with every new approach the subject starts almost from scratch.

127

In effect what Bernstein is suggesting is that so much time is spent in debating the various possible approaches, that insufficient attention is given to the object of study. To paraphrase Bernstein, one might say that it is not 'news' about 'news' which is important, but the 'condition' of news production which dominates the arguments.

What we shall argue in this chapter is that while the condition of news is undoubtedly important, it neither precedes nor follows the news itself. Thus a static deliberation of methodological choices not only ignores the very nature of *creating* knowledge, but also ignores the nature of the social world, namely its dynamic, processional character. Producing news, therefore, involves a set of active practices that are both complex and insecure. In our view, any analysis which ignores those features is merely myopic utopianism.

Because of the complex nature of any methodology, many of the arguments we shall advance will overlap and interrelate. Thus, in order to provide clarity, we shall divide our materials into a number of specific areas: first, the pre-emptive issues, or the problems related to carrying out an empirical study; second, a consideration of the way in which we developed our particular methodological course; third, the relationship of that methodology to our specific empirical situation; fourth, the problematic nature of writing up empirical data; and finally, some conclusions upon the methodological procedures adopted.

Our concern in this chapter, therefore, is to highlight and provide insights into the process of doing research.[1] We shall in no way suggest that our particular research activities represent a definitive text upon methodological procedures. What we would wish to argue is that they offer a commentary to our arguments and conclusions, which will allow the reader some insight into our usage of empirical materials. Before proceeding to the specifics of our procedures, however, some issues of prior theoretical importance would seem to require further consideration.

Pre-emptive issues

Until quite recently it was commonly believed that any researcher entering the field had at his disposal a variety of tried and tested formulae to choose between. Indeed, traditions as diverse as documentary investigations, experiments and ethnographic observations provided the researcher with a ready-made list of viable procedures. For the most part, the choice of any method was pre-empted by two related factors; first, the nature of the object of study (populations, small groups or individuals), and second, the particular theoretical orientation espoused by the researcher. An interesting observation upon such choice is that rather than being of a positive nature, the result of logical argument about a set of assumptions related to the researcher and his object of study, they tended to be negative in character, researched by the rejection of inappropriate alternatives. Examples of this process of rejection may be found in the preambles to numerous small-scale studies of a participant-observational nature, particularly those inspired by the phenomenologically oriented sociology of the early 1970s. Many such researchers, while rejecting the scientism of the natural sciences, failed to fully articulate the logic of their own particular methodological assumptions. More importantly, the process of rejection often resulted in inconsistencies at a number of levels within the studies themselves. This in turn led to the well-founded accusation that they were merely 'speculative', and failed to contribute to the rational advancement of the social sciences.

Although the wide division between scientific and interpretative modes of analysis has been at the heart of much recent debate upon methodology, the basic premise of that debate has undoubtedly been founded upon a general belief in the value of empirical work. Thus two important and highly divergent texts, Cicourel's (1964) *Method and Measurement in Sociology*, and Moser and Kalton's (1971) *Survey Methods in Social Investigation*, at least agree upon their object of interest and fundamental principles of social research, which necessitates entering the field to gain information. Disagreement occurs at a much higher epistemological level, namely the question of the validity of research observations regarding the *real* nature of the phenomena under analysis. However, with the recent resurgence of interest in Marxism within British sociology, a new variable has entered the equation. Indeed, structuralism suggests that all forms of empiricism, as a means of gathering information, are of secondary importance to the process of prior theorisation. One exponent of this position, Saussure (1960), perhaps summarises it best when he argues: 'Far from it being the object that antidates the viewpoint, it would seem that it is the viewpoint that creates the object.'

In other words, theoretical deliberation must *guide* research activities, rather than issue from them. The debate about how a subject knows an object which has constituted the major point of contention within empiricism, is thereby submerged within the assertion that the object of study becomes *known* through theoretical deliberation. Although the proponents of such a view would undoubtedly disagree, this assertion clearly echoes Schutz's concern that problems of understanding arise from pre-emptive suppositions on the part of the researcher regarding his object of interest (Schutz, 1972). Thus the process of raising such a notion from everyday life to the level of theory would seem ultimately to represent little more than a complex play of semantics.

While there exist strong arguments which affirm the similarity[2] of those apparently opposing perspectives, certain basic epistemological differences clearly cannot be denied. Generally speaking, such differences arise from the problem of consciousness and its relation to the construction of the *Liebenswelt*. Within *verstehen* analysis, consciousness becomes the prime focus of consideration while, within more structurally oriented analysis, consciousness is merely an epi-phenomenon, determined by the underlying structural relations of the participants involved. Thus from such apparently divergent perspectives, methodological premises may be based entirely upon *perception*, or at another level, be founded upon issues of *structure*. In the latter case, perception is considered to be determined by structural forces which constitute the real focus of investigation.

This incompatibility suggests that theoretical deliberation generates from within a clearly bounded set of assumptions. More importantly, such incompatibility requires that certain positive decisions should be carried out in order to avoid a state of methodological anomie. Clearly, one way forward might involve the adoption of a synthesis model, thereby producing some grand new methodological insight. However, such a course often represents little more than a new search for the elusive pot of gold at the rainbow's end, so that what one ends up with has proceeded from such contradictory premises that it ultimately satisfies none of them.

Such courses of action, however, although theoretically interesting, lack one very important ingredient. In other words, they are guilty of abstracting the development of methodological procedures from the underlying processes of the research itself. So that ultimately it is of little importance what was decided before entering the field, because it is the actual activities of the researcher within the field which determine his success or failure. Thus, it is of little value to involve oneself in problems of an epistemological nature too early within the course of a study. What is of prime importance is to recognise those tensions and contradictions as they occur, so that they become part of the justificatory foundation of the study.

The compromise, therefore, is not between one theory and another, but between theory and practice. The researcher must examine as closely as possible the assumptions made about his object of analysis, how those assumptions informed his initial methodological stance, and how in the course of the study they became modified. One does not start, therefore, from what *should* be done, but from what *was* done. It is the relationship between the two which is vital, and it is to the consideration of that relationship, with regard to our own study, that we now turn.

Developing methodology

Our initial concern, as outlined in the introduction to this study, was to locate the nature and form of social relations within FE. In addition, we were concerned to highlight the possible relationship of those social relations to the industrial infra-structure. Such concerns suggested to us that it was necessary to proceed from an initial understanding of the structural relations between the participants within our object of study, Western College. Clearly, one way of examining such relations would have been to undertake a morphology of the institution, without carrying out any form of empirical investigation. However, in our view, such a course of action represented little more than an illusionary game. Indeed, such explanation is based upon the notion that the social world can be understood *totally* independently from its material practices. While such explanation might appear coherent, its definition of terms within the area of discourse ultimately represents little more than an idealised and speculative model of the social system, which in our view is over-deterministic in the extreme. What such structural explanation fails to address is how the form of the structure relates to the existential activities of its members. In particular, it ignores how similar structural forces often give rise to dissimilar and sometimes contradictory formations at the empirical level.

It seemed to us that if our understanding of the structure of Western College was to mean anything, then some discussion of the material practices which characterised that structure was desirable, if not essential. In our view, the structure itself cannot be understood without some examination of the ways in which its participants relate to the material conditions of their world. Only then can the researcher develop an understanding of the ideological and potentially mystificatory nature of social reality. To construct a morphology of the institution, therefore, seemed to us to relegate those involved to mere puppets operating in a reified dynamic, and unable to transcend their own reality. Such a course of action, moreover, rests on the assumption that the understanding of the theorist is superior to that of the participant.

What we would wish to argue, therefore, is that the explanation of the social world is neither dependent upon nor independent of the object of study. In our view, it is the linkage between theory and its objects which is vital and needs articulation. Thus it was necessary for us to reach a rigorous understanding of both the activities and the perceptions of the actors involved. Such perceptions, however, were not simply to be accepted as a definitive explanation of material practice, but were to be linked to the underlying 'structural dynamic' we sought to articulate. Thus we proceeded to gather information about how those involved perceived the day-to-day organisation of college affairs, the relationship between their work and local industry, and the material and ideological constraints imposed upon their practice. Such perceptions did not represent topics in their own right, but provided a focus around which theoretical discussion and deliberation might take place.

As a result of our initial methodological course, based upon the relationship between theory and the empirical, three problems of specific importance came to light.

First, there was the question of validity. Without wishing to ignore the initial question of 'validity to whom', and a highly theoretical discussion of its specific definition, we chose to adopt a purely pragmatic approach in this respect. In our view, validity can only really be assessed in terms of the particular theoretical position of the proponents. To appeal to some independent and objective principles, which deny the complex links between theory and practice, would seem to us to be simply contradictory. More importantly, such an appeal would elevate highly problematic scientific practices to a position far beyond any proven justification.

In our case, and within the scope of our own particular assumptions, two types of criteria were adopted as a measure of validity. First, our structural explanations were required to be rational and coherent; and second, substantive and coherent links were seen to be an essential feature of the mediation between our descriptive and analytical categories. Very simply, at each stage of our argument, we sought to explain how our particular descriptions of social reality related to our specific theoretical frame. How, for instance, the practices of departmental members within a competitive and institutional structure bore relation to the wider demand for trained labour. We sought, moreover, not only to demonstrate that relationship, but to reduce the possibility of any alternative explanations. For the less likely the validity of any such alternative explanation, the more coherence our explanation assumed, not only in terms of our own criteria, but also in those of others.

The second problem that we confronted was that of bias. Many of the arguments we have advanced in relation to the problem of validity are also of relevance to this area. Traditionally, the question of bias has been related to the process of data selection *vis-à-vis* the argument one seeks to advance. If the researcher adopts a model based upon the premise that the social world is *independent* of its method of discovery, then the question of bias becomes highly contentious.[3] Our particular model of social explanation, however, rests on the assertion that the basis of such explanation resides in the vital links between theory and material practice. It is within those vital links, however, that bias may potentially occur. In our view, the major mechanism through which such bias may be avoided involves a scrupulous attendance to the criteria adopted in order to assess validity, namely that the vital links between theory and material practice should be both rational and coherent. Within our model of explanation, therefore, bias may be said to occur where the relationship between analytical and descriptive categories is insufficiently substantiated, for instance, where some aspect of classroom practice might be described as a feature of capitalism, without a thorough exemplification of that conclusion. In other words, our model seeks to avoid the simplistic choice of data to *fit* theory, and requires that the links made between theory and data should be fully substantiated.

The third immediate problem which arose on entering the field, concerned the nature of the information gathered. While we have tended to concentrate so far upon issues of a theoretical nature, it is the problematic question of the relationship between theory and practical methods which so often gives rise to the most important difficulties. A large number of methodologies contain within themselves a number of intractable propositions with regard to the collection of data. In our case, however, we experienced no such hypothetical imperative. Indeed, our major concern was to examine practice and the descriptions of practitioners in relation to the theory which sought to explain that practice. More importantly, the ontological status or validity of those descriptions did not pose for us a central issue, since our conclusions were not entirely dependent upon their truth. On the other hand, we could not ignore the fact that there are limits to what is available and what can be accepted within any social scene one seeks to understand. In particular, the sheer complexity of any institution, both hierarchical and bureaucratic, renders the collection of 'sensitive' information extremely difficult. Indeed, the complex character of any institution tends to constitute its own rationality, which must be brought to bear upon the statements of participants and their potential use. In the section which follows, we shall look more closely at such problems.

Entering the field – or where the 'talking' stops

Prior to entering any particular field of discourse for the purpose of collecting data, the researcher must act upon a number of specific decisions regarding the relationship of his theoretical position *vis-à-vis* the practical course he proposes to adopt. As indicated in the previous section, however, we experienced no specific imperative in this respect, which many alternative methodologies undoubtedly impose. Indeed, a large number of paradigmatic persuasions share a common failing in their separate attempts to eliminate bias on the part of the observer. Thus, given our assumptions about the nature of theory, the idea of the social world as being independent of its theoretical articulation simply did not pose a problem. Indeed our expressed purpose was not merely to observe, but rather to explore certain interests, ideas and theories. Therefore our immediate concern was to gather what might be described as 'focused information'. In other words, we sought to explore that information in terms of its relevance to the structural parameters of educational practice we were attempting to understand.

On entering the field, however, our major assumption was immediately challenged. Indeed, we had expected to find at Western College a relatively close fit between its practices, both cognitive and affectual, and the workings of the immediate industrial environment it expressly sought to serve. Such a close correspondence, however, was far from the case. Indeed very few of our observations of college practice appeared to bear immediate relation to the local industrial world. Thus we concluded that at this stage we were seeking to *prove* a correspondence between theory and practice, rather than to examine the two as interrelated aspects of the same process. Having arrived at that initial conclusion, we then ceased to be so dogmatic about what we were looking for.

From our modified premise, therefore, information had no greater significance than its face value. It might derive from a variety of sources, at many levels, and through a complex number of means. However, hearsay gleaned perhaps from an informal discussion over coffee could not be attributed lesser significance than say a pre-meditated question asked of the Principal during a formal interview, since that would be to assume a level of validity inappropriate to our model.

This level of generality, however, with regard to what should count as data, was complicated by a number of problems associated with time, since not only does the institution change over a period of time, but also the information the researcher collects regarding the workings of that institution. For example, when we commenced our field-work, the development of TEC courses was being carried out, and we were able to observe to some extent the course of that development. However, our field-work came to an end before the college administration had modified those courses in terms of their relative success or failure after one year. That meant that we were unable to fully follow up our observations of course development with regard to TEC.

A second problem we immediately confronted centred upon the degree of confidence we, as researchers, were able to establish with those we sought to observe. Indeed, the level and kind of information gained from a first interview differed significantly from that acquired from subsequent ones. However, to suggest that the data gained from later interviews is any nearer the truth than that acquired from initial ones is to assume that truth does *in fact* exist. Thus, we chose to view both forms of information as expressions of separate aspects of the social relations of the institution, so that the use of any account did not depend upon its degree of confidentiality, but upon the explanatory power it bore in relation to our theory.

In line with our particular assumptions, therefore, our model of data collection became no more than a process of gathering information. More specifically, the major means we adopted of acquiring that information was through verbal contact with members of the college staff. Thus we might involve ourselves in informal discussions with departmental members, or, alternatively, in more formalised interviews of an exploratory nature, or, indeed, in semi-structured interviews which were to be recorded on tape. We also sought to include any written records of college activities that we were allowed access to.

We were also aware of a further important problem, which is intrinsic to a large number of research methodologies,[4] namely that of *no* apparent information with regard to a particular aspect of the object of study. The priority of many interpretative forms of research often gives rise to the assumption that if it has not been said, then it cannot be articulated. In our view, however, such an assumption simply accepts the dominance of verbal access to understanding, which far exceeds its capability of describing much that is of interest in the social world. Moreover, it would seem to us that in certain areas of social life there exist a number of aspects of social relationships which are 'closed'[5] even to the participants themselves, and which for the researcher are very difficult to gain access to. In such circumstances, the researcher can only make inference from what is available.

In the preceding sections we have attempted to set out the logic of our particular theoretical position, together with some problems related to its translation into practical formulations. However, the purely practical process of collecting data, and the further complications that this gave rise to, clearly warrants careful documentation, and in the section which follows we shall attempt to highlight some of the difficulties we confronted in the course of that fundamental task.

Collecting data

It would not be an exaggeration to say that many people regard social scientists with considerable scepticism. Indeed, the image of the social researcher as an interfering, uncomprehending theorist is often justified, particularly when one reads certain obscure forms of analysis which have been carried out in the name of social science. Many studies of a 'macro' orientation, for example, which have utilised highly sophisticated forms of survey methodologies, can be well understood to be seen by participants as yet more statistics for the DES computer.[6] Alternatively, it is easy to understand why many of the in-depth studies of classroom practice have been interpreted by participants as mere 'teaching-bashing' programmes. Thus, the most important initial problem that the researcher must deal with on entering the field concerns the image he presents to those he is attempting to understand. Indeed, one cannot expect to find out about the world, if one denies the world knowledge of oneself. Yet that very attempt at mutual contact involves numerous unavoidable and sometimes disagreeable consequences. Indeed, the 'presentation of self' usually determines whether or not further avenues of potential understanding will remain closed. Thus, in his initial negotiations, the researcher must take into account that the teacher who is questioned about his procedures of assessment, may well interpret those questions as a blatant attack upon his practice. Moreover, the Head of Department, who is approached about the process of decision-making within his department, is usually only too well aware of the political significance of those questions. Thus a clumsy beginning can often close many doors for ever for the researcher. On the other hand, an over-indulgent attitude towards the interviewee can often make of one's research little more than an exercise in psychotherapy.

However, establishing oneself in the research context and building a relationship with participants only serves to designate the parameters within which a number of initial and rather pragmatic decisions will be made, and from which the study will hopefully develop. For example, one of our most important initial decisions concerned which aspect of the institution was most favourable *vis-à-vis* the observation of our interests. Here our choice was guided by two important assumptions: first, since our major concern was to examine the relationship between FE and industry, we needed to locate our study within a college whose major task was to prepare students for their future industrial roles; and second, we needed to narrow that focus to an institutional setting where little else other than vocational courses were carried out. In other words, we assumed that given such a 'manifest' setting, it would be easier to explore the 'fit' between FE and industry, and to assess the validity of our theory of that relationship in terms of our observations of practice.

Having made those initial rather *ad hoc* decisions, we then had to deal with the problem of access. Through a variety of informal negotiations, it became possible for us to locate our study within a number of colleges within the area. However, we finally opted for Western College, because the institution seemed the most appropriate setting within which to examine the practical manifestation of our research interests.

However, our initial contact with the staff at Western only allowed us access to *one* particular department, and since our research interests were such that we needed far wider access to the processes of the institution, we again confronted a serious obstacle. Indeed, as we soon discovered, initial access to one aspect of any institution often impedes entry to others. In particular, our original contact felt considerable responsibility for our actions. Thus our movements were often restricted until we had gained official consent through various bureaucratic channels. In the meantime, we attempted to establish a number of informal contacts among a range of college staff. Inevitably, however, having arranged an informal meeting with a member of another department, which had not been officially cleared by our original contact, we found ourselves called to a meeting and reprimanded for not going through official channels. This demonstrated to us the very precarious control the researcher is able to exert over his sources of information. This limited control was further exemplified a few weeks later, when having gained official permission from a Head of Department to approach his staff, we were presented with a list of pre-arranged interviews. In other words, we had no control over the selection and context of those interviews. Thus it was very difficult to gain access to the views of departmental members regarding the social relations of the department, because we were so clearly identified with the authority structure of the department.

Throughout the course of our field-work we continually found that as a new channel of information opened, another closed: the problem being that when one is seen to be close to a particular person or group of persons, relationships with others became problematic. Indeed, we found on the one hand that simply being seen in an accidental conversation with, say, a Head of Department often pre-empted any further discussion with certain college staff. On the other, we also became aware that our research was not enhanced if we were seen to be in close relations with those members of the college staff who were identified by their colleagues as in any way 'deviant'. In addition to such problems, we had to deal with the further complication of establishing fruitful links with both students, employers and other outside agencies, so that our initial activities within the field had to be tempered with considerable discretion.

Our pragmatic decision with regard to the kinds of problems outlined above was to adopt what we referred to as a 'spiral technique' of contacts. That is to say, we sought to begin our relations with the various college personnel at an informal level. We simply discussed FE in general in the hope that we would gain both their confidence and some useful perspectives upon their activities. When and if we had gained sufficient information in this way, we adopted a different course of action. For those sources who were prepared to discuss their work in greater depth, we sought to arrange more formal interviews and to tape-record any useful information. Records of other discussion were simply recorded in our field notes.

We did not, however, carry out this 'spiral technique' in our dealings with the organisational hierarchy of the college. We felt that a more formal approach was more appropriate in such circumstances. Here our questions were prepared, but the situations were usually unstructured.

It is important to mention at this point that we did not rely entirely upon information gained through interviews. Indeed, two of the research team acquired some part-time teaching at the college and were thus enabled to gain more first-hand knowledge of both staff and students. We also observed numerous lessons within various college departments. Indeed such classroom observations proved invaluable in guiding the direction of subsequent interviews with college personnel. It is as well to point out here, however, that such a form of data collection is extremely difficult to negotiate, and often antagonises those under observation. Thus we provide few examples drawn from our observations of classroom practice.

In addition to our examination of activities within college, we considered that substantial contact should be made with those external bodies who were also concerned with the structures and processes of FE. Thus we sought to interview a range of employers, training officers, employment officers, trade unionists and school staff, specially those engaged in link courses with the college. Again our activities had to be tempered with considerable tact, particularly when the question of limited time posed innumerable problems of technique. Our solution was to engage in guided discussions which would allow the participants to express their views on the process of FE in general.

In this section, we have attempted to elaborate the specific procedures we adopted in order to gain useful information from the participants we sought to understand. In effect, the role of the researcher is lonely, difficult and often boring. He spends the greater part of his time building up to 'doing' something, rather than actually doing it. Not only do contacts have to be made, re-made and sustained, but more importantly, dissolved, when the researcher wants to move on to other areas. Information must be checked and re-checked, ideas sounded out and procedures re-evaluated. Thus we often found at our research meetings that we had spent several hours discussing the problem with very little to show for our efforts. Very often the person we had arranged to interview had been called away, or didn't turn up, or simply didn't want us in his classroom.

Our greatest enemy, however, was undoubtedly 'time'. We 'wasted' innumerable hours collecting information which simply did not make sense or relate in any useful way to our theoretical frame. Moreover, we continually rejected materials which had appeared eighteen months before to be crucial but which now with the knowledge of hindsight were totally irrelevant to our major concerns. And finally, we had to continually re-charge our initial enthusiasm since it was so easy to lose sight of our original idea, and indeed during the course of our field-work that idea often appeared irrelevant to the day-to-day practicalities of FE.

Our major means of controlling the course of our work at this time was through regular meetings of the research team, where we simply discussed our observations and gave some on-going impetus to the fulfilment of our initial objectives. However, those meetings only provided minimal support during a period of potential alientation. Indeed, we still faced the difficulty of condensing our materials and structuring them into a rigorous, well-founded report. In the section which follows we shall outline some of the problems associated with writing up research observations.

Writing up

The problems discussed above in relation to data collection become infinitesimal when compared with those associated with writing up. At best the structuring of research materials can only be described as an exercise in reducing a whole range of dynamic social relations to mere words upon a page. Indeed, it is extremely difficult to avoid reproducing an artificial description of human forms. The problem is that social scientists have few tried and tested formulae to guide them. Traditional forms of research have largely relied upon the process of abstracting an argument from ever reducing materials.[7] Our theoretical position, however, did not allow us to adopt such a procedure. Indeed, rather than being concerned with abstracting a theory from data, we had set ourselves the task of exemplifying our theory through the materials which were available. In other words, our methodology required that we should convince an audience that our observations of the empirical related coherently to the assumptions we had made about the nature of the structural.

Our major objective, therefore, was to construct an interpretation of practice which was more plausible than any alternative explanation. Inasmuch as we would not wish to deny the possibility of alternative interpretations, however, it is equally the case that we seek to avoid the trap of relativism. For to adopt a relativistic stance would be to support the view that reality has a transient nature, and to deny the significance of those material practices which underpin it. In our view, therefore, the validity of alternative interpretations must be assessed according to their ability to explain their own particular structural assumptions in terms of the accounts used to exemplify them.

An area of difficulty which is highly relevant to our methodology lies in the problem of empathy with regard to the accounts of participants. Moreover, since our major concern was to exemplify the structural in terms of the empirical, the practices we sought to describe could not always be treated as commonsensical accounts. Indeed they often appeared to be extremely critical, yet it was never our intention to attack those we sought to understand. We were concerned simply to explore the conditions of practice, rather than the reactions of participants to those conditions. Those reactions, however, served as a means of gaining greater understanding of the social relations under observation.

In other words, rather than concentrating upon the account of participants, which might well be undervalued or indeed overvalued, we focused upon the relationship between those various accounts and our specific theoretical assumptions. Our major difficulty, however, was that the relationship could never be totally and reflexively monitored. Thus we were involved in a process of trying and re-trying particular explanations, which changed both over the course of time and as we received new information. Consider, for example, the following comments from Terry, a third-year craft apprentice, which would appear on face value to be a plausible criticism of much technical teaching. Indeed, his remarks echo the commonsense view held by many students that teachers are out of touch with present-day industrial reality:

'The trouble with him [i.e. the teacher] is that he's been away from the job so long that he's out of touch. . . . things have changed since he did his apprenticeship. . . . I know he means well. . . . in fact he's a good bloke . . . and can teach . . . but he gets us making things, using equipment and methods that must have gone out with the Ark. I know he's a craftsman . . . but you see craft has changed. . . . blokes like him aren't needed any more. . . . Yet he gets us making bits and pieces of machinery, parts and the like . . . the kind of machinery that either isn't used any more or that at work you simply send down to the stores for. It seems that so much of what we learn, even in the workshop, doesn't relate to what we do at work. . . . the blokes at work tell us not to pay too much attention. . . . You don't know where you are.'

Clearly, from accounts such as this, the researcher might achieve considerable 'mileage' with regard to the similarity of Terry's account with the corresponding problems outlined in the recent Great Educational Debate, namely that of the lack of fit between education and the occupational structure. Yet we were not entirely convinced by the apparent correspondence between such remarks and much that had recently been stated in public debate. For it seemed to us too simple an explanation of our industrial problems, and implied that if teaching could be up-dated, then all would be well. Moreover, such an explanation clearly begs the whole question of how teachers themselves view their contribution to industry. Indeed, when one juxtaposes Terry's account with that of his teacher, a very different version emerges, which while recognising the lack of fit, views the teaching difficulties from a very different angle:

'Yes . . . of course he's right, but it does depend on how you look at it. I'm sure apprentices don't need to know a good deal of the stuff we have to teach them . . . the City and Guilds and the Professional Institutes have a lot to answer for on that one. On the other hand, just because the lads can get parts from the stores, does that mean they shouldn't know more about those parts; how they're made, what they're made from . . . even how to make them? Yes, I often get my lads making things, learning manual skills and using measuring procedures that they won't use at work. . . . I also get them to strip machinery down, demonstrate its principles . . . get them to know how it works. But just because they're never likely to do all this at work, it doesn't mean to say it's irrelevant. . . . He's right, people like me aren't needed any more . . . technology has turned craft into a process of fitting, replacements . . . that sort of thing . . . the skill element has largely gone. But these lads are still on craft apprenticeships and I'm not just concerned with teaching them to fit and replace spare parts as if they were robots. . . .they're already like that, some of them. I think they need to know what's behind the technology . . . even if they aren't called on to work on it . . . though they might want to get involved in that side of things one day. . . . but it they haven't a clue, how can they? So, if everything I teach doesn't relate to the routine humdrum of everyday work you can say that what I was doing was irrelevant. But it depends how you see things.'

The comments quoted above provide an alternative to Terry's explanation of the problem of relevance. Clearly the lecturer is operating with a critical perspective of changing work patterns, and recognises the implications of craft de-skilling for teaching and training. Indeed, his account suggests that he sees his role as providing more than a simple introduction to the limited demands of work, so that he would seem to demonstrate a more comprehensive understanding of the requirements of modern technology than Terry would give him credit for. Indeed, although he recognises that 'people like me aren't needed any more', he avoids the temptation to treat his students like robots, thus exercising some power of intervention in the process of training.[8]

Having considered both accounts of the problem of correspondence between industry and training, we were able to reach an alternative viewpoint *vis-à-vis* that problem. For, from their different viewpoints, both accounts argue that training can be irrelevant to the work situation. Moreover, that overlapping of views suggests that participants perceived education to be to some extent autonomous of the economic base. However, what was of interest to us was that both actors, while recognising a lack of fit, continued to support existing practice. Thus, having located that initial contradiction, we attempted to arrive at some plausible explanations of it, and in this way the process of elaboration continued. Clearly, we had no power to set limits upon empirical possibilities, only the motivation to propose limited theoretical alternatives.

However, that process of developing links between theory and empirical reality can never be adequately realised, for it requires a continual re-negotiation of accounts at both the theoretical and empirical levels. Thus the researcher must also explore the views of participants with regard to each other's accounts, not to triangulate some assumed reality, but simply to generate alternative conceptions which will shed greater light upon his own theoretical elaborations.

Finally, we are aware that in articulating our methodological procedures, we are speaking to a small audience, and that a large number of that audience will be more interested in criticising the 'conditions' of news that in examining the 'news' itself. Indeed, given our particular perspective, such a response is to be expected. However, our concern is not entirely with such readers. Indeed, the practical involvement of social scientists in any situation requires a high degree of empathy with those they seek to understand. We wish to make it clear, therefore, that our major purpose in this section has been to develop an explanation of how (in the widest sense) we constructed our argument.

As social scientists, we attempt to look beyond the obvious, yet in doing so we cannot ignore the social relations we find and the world to which we speak. Thus, we hope that our readers will appreciate that our primary concern has been simply to locate and exemplify the opaqueness and contradictions of everyday life. If we have in any way succeeded in locating those contradictions, we will have at least provided some food for thought for those who wish to gain some control over them.

We have attempted to argue that methodological procedures are at best idealistic, and at worst simply *ad hoc* pragmatism. The researcher can do no more, however, than set out his combination of ideas and practice as they develop, so that they will provide a basis through which his study may be examined. In our view, it is not the question of methodological purity which is important, but whether we have justified our own assumptions, and arrived at some plausible explanations of the process of FE.

Clearly, one could produce a volume devoted entirely to the issue of methodology, but as the proverb suggests, 'the proof of the pudding is in the eating'. Thus we have provided minimal insight into our procedures, and leave it to the reader to judge their appropriateness. It is our contention, moreover, that the reader can only do this when the researchers have made public their specific theories, assumptions and prejudices. In the chapter which follows, we shall attempt a brief review of some of the possible points of consideration which arise from our analysis so far.

Chapter 8

Conclusions

Any 'micro'-orientated study of this type can only ever be partial in its conclusions. However, its contribution to wider debate concerning the connections between education, economy and culture, depends largely upon its level of success in locating the relationship between the particular and the general. Our aim here has been to identify a number of crucial if not contentious issues associated with the theory and practice of FE. At the outset, and against the background of conventional wisdom, we sought to examine what it was like for young workers and their teachers to operate within the sphere of FE. As we explained in the previous chapter, we chose the case-study approach in order to elucidate some of the complexities involved at the level of practice. However, since many of our observations reach beyond the local level, it is our intention by way of conclusion to draw together a number of strands arising from our study of a *particular* technical college, which may have some importance for our understanding of the process of FE in *general*.

In the preceding chapters we have attempted to examine a number of theoretical and practical issues at a variety of levels of analysis. For example, we have sought on the one hand to consider the theoretical rhetoric associated with the development of FE, while on the other we have attempted to understand apprentices within the day-to-day routine of college affairs. Indeed, the major problematic of our research involves this juxtaposition of issues drawn from both the theory and practice of FE. However, our investigation has not rested there: indeed, one of our major concerns has been to challenge the view that apprentice-students represent no more than passive commodities processed by means of FE to meet the changing needs of the economic infrastructure. In addition, we have sought to challenge the view that the FE system itself is solely determined by external forces beyond its influence or control.

However, in addressing such questions, we were brought face to face with a major theoretical problem associated with empirical research, namely that of *explaining how* the educational system 'double-functions', so as to represent both a mechanism of autonomy and of control (Althusser, 1971). It is perhaps for this reason that we have devoted an important section of this volume to the problem of the 'fit' between education and the economic infrastructure (see chapter 6). Moreover, our attempt to provide some methodological accountability clearly describes how our initial deterministic assumptions were soon undermined by our observations of college practice (see chapter 7). Indeed, at the outset of this study we imagined that the internal workings of a college like Western would be heavily influenced if not controlled by the dictates of its local industrial environment. However, our experiences within the field soon proved the college/industry relationship to be far less explicit than we had imagined. While clearly bounded by local industry, Western was seen to negotiate its role rather than simply serve its master. Thus it became an important focus of our study to indicate those areas of autonomy as well as of control through which the institution ensures its continued existence.

Theoretical insights into such phenomena may of course be found in the work of various critical theorists. In particular, Althusser (1971) insists upon the 'relative autonomy' of superstructural processes from the material base. Yet despite the significance of such arguments, our knowledge of what actually *happens* at the empirical level remains unchanged, and our understanding of *how*, within the existing conditions of institutional life, socialisation and cultural reproduction take place, is not really deepened. The impetus of empirical research, therefore, tends to be theoretical in orientation, but its task is not simply one of explaining *how* and *why* social institutions operate, but perhaps more importantly of explaining their operative functioning in relation to the material base.

We attempted to address this complex task by analysing the organisational ethos of one particular college. However, it soon became clear to us that no matter what aspect of institutional life we focused upon, one major factor dominated: namely, the way in which college practice seeks to legitimate the wider social relations and conditions of work which characterise industrial life. It has been our contention, moreover, that the relative autonomy of the institution from its local industrial environment gives rise to a whole range of expectations and values well beyond those of which the participants are aware. Thus it seemed to us that the relative autonomy of the institution from local industry actually served to facilitate the maintenance of existing social structures, simply by obscuring their more obvious processes. In other words, by allowing an element of autonomy, processes which might otherwise appear imperative, take on an appearance of being natural or

145

indeed chosen. In such a light, therefore, FE may be seen to represent a means of legitimising existing industrial processes, and as constituting a neutral mechanism for rationalising the education and training of young workers (see chapter 6).

Yet at the level of college practice, the suggestion that FE provision constitutes a visible or even unitary mechanism of control is misleading. Indeed, such control is operated through a variety of symbolic mechanisms, some of which are far from obvious. At the organisational level, for example, it finds expression in the independence the college administration has acquired to manage its own affairs. It is reflected, moreover, in the way in which the college negotiates its own particular character and internal order with regard to such matters as departmental strife, scarce resources, discipline and so on. Indeed, despite the apparent flexibility of Western's institutional make-up, its internal structures are inextricably linked with certain economic boundaries, most notably those associated with its reciprocal relations with local industry. However, since the nature of those relations are non-controversial, there being no overt disharmony between college and industry, the forms of interaction which take place do not *appear* conflictual.

Western is an FE college which has established an important connection with local industry, and which over time has built a reputation upon that connection. As we have described in previous chapters, the growth of Western has followed a largely entrepreneurial pattern, through which an appropriate self-image has been transmitted to industry. The college administration has achieved its status by 'coming up with the goods'; that is, by training and qualifying large numbers of engineers. Thus, most local employers consider the contribution of Western to local industry as not only a 'good' thing, but generally speaking, beyond question. We, however, would wish to pose an alternative perspective upon that 'reality'. Indeed, the conclusions we have drawn from our observations of both apprentice-students and their teachers would suggest an alternative viewpoint, which we would argue is of considerable importance to our general understanding of the workings of FE.

An alternative viewpoint

It is our contention that FE does little more than reify the existing social relations of production. Most technical courses prepare apprentice-students to 'fit in with' rather than challenge the existing order of things. Indeed, to do otherwise would not only transgress the 'reality' of many technical teachers, but simply would *not* be tolerated by most college administrations. Thus few students are encouraged to criticise or examine the social, political or economic changes which occur within our society, and fewer still are allowed to question the influences which affect the conditions of their work. The consequences of such an approach towards technical education are clearly demonstrated within this study, reflected for example in instrumental student/staff relations, or in the forms of grudging acceptance commonly associated with apprentice-students. Indeed, far from receiving a challenging preparation for industry which might open up new horizons, all most apprentice-students receive is a narrow form of instruction which does little to stretch their understanding of the relationship between theory and practice, not to mention other important matters of a non-vocational nature. It would seem to us, therefore, that FE neither encourages young workers to 'find their way in the world', nor helps them to realise personal ambitions through some 'alternative route' (Crowther, 1959). The fact is that for many apprentice-students, FE represents little more than a short cut to a dead end. If this is the case, however, why then does FE constitute an increasingly important area of educational provision?

We would argue that the liberal façade which has come to legitimise FE has also acted to obscure the real patterns of socialisation which characterise the training process. We have suggested that this blinkering of reality occurs through a commonly accepted emphasis upon the joint returns which supposedly accrue to both the individual and society through planned investment in technical education (see chapter 1). It is our contention, moreover, that this popular belief in shared returns from common investment and effort represents little more than an ideological illusion, which masks the fact that there can be no equable distribution of rewards within a system where returns *from* labour rather than *to* labour constitute a crucial source of capital accumulation. The problematic relationship between apprentice and employer is thus obscured by the FE process. It is obscured because apprentice and employer are presented as co-existing in some common endeavour, in order to pursue certain shared interests. It would seem to us, however, that such an image of the apprentice/employer relationship clearly overlooks the crucial distinction between wages and profits.

There are of course numerous contradictions within this theory of vocational education, and we have tried to outline some of the more important ones during the course of the study. It is not simply that the 'human capital' school of thought does not actually *work* in practice, or even that it legitimises exploitative social relations, but rather that it totally mystifies our understanding of the relationship between qualifications, work and wages. Thus it would seem to us that the policy which has guided the development of FE, in recent years, legitimated as it is by such rationale, has proved a useful tool in disguising the more

147

exploitative features of capitalism. It is our contention that FE has assisted the ideological dominance of industrial structures by presenting their modes of industrial practice as natural through the supposedly interlocking imperatives of education, training and the world of work.

A central feature of this study, however, suggests that education and training are not necessarily guided by distinct ideologies, but constitute separate aspects of the *same* mechanism of control. In this respect education may be seen to function by translating industrial imperatives into professional rhetoric. Thus the term Further Education becomes a misnomer which acts to legitimise the training process through which young workers are instructed in the cognitive and affectual skills deemed appropriate to their position within the industrial hierarchy. Not only does this process rationalise the rites of passage associated with the acquisition of the apprenticeship ticket, but it also reconciles young workers to the realities of industrial life, including deferred gratification.

At a more explicit level, the pay and differentials incentive constitutes an incessant reminder of the need for apprentices to complete their studies, although in recent years that incentive has lost a great deal of its initial compulsion. The contradiction of which many apprentice students are increasingly aware is that their socialisation into particular skills at college bears little relation to their actual experience of the world of work. Indeed, industrial de-skilling in recent years has led to a growing complaint that FE actually over-trains apprentice students, so that many of them experience college as not only alienating but distinctly boring. Concerning this disjuncture between college curricula and actual industrial practice, we have argued that employers and unions alike tolerate such a situation because FE actually reconciles students to such contradictions by reinforcing the importance of the relationship between qualifications, differentials and cash. In other words, both employers and unions, those uneasy industrial bedfellows, share certain less obvious interests, in particular those associated with differentials and pay. In this respect, FE performs a crucial service by differentiating industrial workers in line with those differentials through the examination system, even though those qualifications may bear little relation to actual job requirements (see chapter 6).

From such a perspective it is sometimes difficult to understand why apprentice-students constitute a privileged minority within the educational system. Students on day- or block-release attend college for only a small part of their working lives, but although the reasons for their attendance are often expressed in a highly persuasive manner, they are rarely recognised by the students themselves. For them, the reality of FE is one of compulsion rather than choice – 'it's part of the job'. Indeed, the reality *is* that they are at the bottom of a highly competitive technological hierarchy over which they have little control. Moreover, they are dependent upon the goodwill of others (unions, employers, college staff) to guide them through the industrial maze. It might of course be argued that apprentice-students are well aware of the structures and contradictions of which they are a part, and indeed our observations suggest that they are. However, it would be mistaken to assume that they are in a position to act upon that awareness in any *positive* manner. Indeed, dropping-out or voting with one's feet offers only limited radical potential (Lipshitz, 1972). The stark reality for most apprentice-students is that they are lads in training for a man's world, which means that they are not only of low status but that they lack any alternative forms of occupational choice. As we have already pointed out, the choice of a career in engineering is seldom positive, and is often the result of an aversion to the other forms of available work. Moreover, since few alternatives exist either within the industry or FE for such students, any discussion of possible future change remains unlikely. Despite such a bleak outlook, however, we shall attempt in the section which follows to indicate some alternative directions in which technical education might proceed.

Directions forward

It would seem to us that one of the major problems of FE, which affects its relations with both government, industry and apprentice-students, concerns its similarity to a treadmill. By that we mean that despite efforts to negotiate and respond to the various industrial convolutions as they have arisen, curricular reform within the sphere of FE remains little more than the re-packaging of an old and time-weary product. It has not been our intention to illustrate the pedagogical limitations of Western College as a prime impediment to alternative practice. Indeed, we have attempted simply to present an accurate account of that college in its daily affairs, without advancing simplistic recommendations about improving its organisational and curricular structures. In addition, it has been our concern to provide a wider perspective upon the way in which FE interacts with industry, so that a more thorough-going understanding of the relationship between work and education might be reached. Thus we have tried during the course of this study to identify those areas both within and without the FE system upon which pressure for chance might fruitfully be brought to bear. It is clear that the contradictions associated with the further education of young workers cannot be improved simply by the action of radical teachers operating within those 'spaces' which are presently afforded by existing relations between college and industry. Indeed, a more fundamental reappraisal of the overall connections between technical education, government and industry is clearly required. A major factor which brings us to that conclusion concerns the fact that as the conditions of production change, FE experiences increasing difficulty in legitimising its practice. For example, it is becoming increasingly difficult to convince apprentice-students that they will become an integral part of an industrial aristocracy as a result of further education. Indeed, most young workers are only too painfully aware of the problems which currently threaten industrial harmony – de-skilling, the erosion of differentials and impending unemployment, to name but a few. Moreover, the major justification of vocationally orientated courses for the unemployed school-leaver is commonly recognised as residing more in the maintenance of good work habits, than in preparation for any future industrial enterprise (Holland, 1977). At that level, it seems, all pretence has been abandoned, but young workers are still required to turn a blind eye to the underlying problematic which may render them unemployed or unemployable even after the benefits of FE.

In the absence of any clear policy guidelines, therefore, it would seem important to outline certain premises from which change might be realistically mounted. It is not our intention, however, to provide answers to problems which arise from social divisions outside the sphere of education. We would wish to focus rather upon those dimensions of autonomy with regard to educational institutions which, contrary to current economic debate, may hold important implications for change. In so far as we have emphasised the *active* rather than passive role of Western College *vis-à-vis* its local industrial environment, we would go so far as to suggest that the key to possible alternative practice is contained within the very *flexibility* of college life. We have suggested that the institution together with its internal arrangements is organised in terms of certain premises established by the wider social structure. However, since those premises clearly *do not* constitute official dictates, they remain challengeable. In other words, if the conditions of teaching and learning within FE are bounded by the logic of industrial practice, and the format of the curriculum supports that practice, then change can only take place when the logic itself is examined and reformulated. It is important to emphasise, therefore, that a major focus of our concluding comments concerns this overriding need to question the policy which has guided the development of FE in recent years. Indeed, it would seem to us that no realistic impetus for change can be achieved without this fundamental examination of the objectives we have hitherto taken for granted.

Clearly, there exists at present a crucial need for the hidden nature of the production process to be laid bare. Indeed, the recommendations we have advanced so far for initial changes at the level of practice cannot be carried out in isolation from the institutional climate. Moreover, that institutional climate and the overall competitive nature of the FE system in general is heavily tempered by the combined influences of employers, unions and professional bodies. It would seem to us, there-fore, that the many and various connections between colleges like Western and their local environments should be re-examined, so as to establish more mutually fruitful relations between FE and the wider social structure.

However, perhaps most problematic of all, remains the whole question of the apprentice-system itself, an archaic and often exploit-ative mechanism which results in passivity in the learning situation (Webb, 1898).[1] Even where unions support existing apprenticeship schemes as a means of defending their members against sharp industrial practice, the actual conditions and means whereby young workers receive their education tend to be overlooked.[2] At present, the over-emphasised connection between wages, differentials and training schemes makes this aspect of FE one of the most explicitly pernicious forms of educational control. For in so far as employers release labour for training, their expectations of that activity centre largely upon profits and returns, both of which dimensions tend to reduce apprentices to commodities rather than active learners in a critical process.

It would seem to us that this *questionable* connection between industrial expectations and the FE of the young worker has over time been so successfully institutionalised, that we no longer recognise it as a major contradiction among our overall educational objectives. Any alternative approach to the further education of young workers would clearly depend upon the questioning of the legitimacy of such rational-isations. Ultimately, what we are suggesting is that the life experience of apprentice-students should be of greater significance in the construc-tion of vocationally oriented courses. Indeed, it would seem to us that where the production process actually governs what should count as education, there is very little chance of counter-argument or alter-native action. In such circumstances, pragmatism becomes the only sensible path. Thus it would seem to us that if alternative strategies within FE are to be achieved, we must start by questioning the taken-for-granted nature of the industrial world, for at present FE does little more than reinforce its main assumptions.

At the explicit level the competitive aspect of FE, supported by the points system, acts against the interests of the vast majority of young people whose economic value renders them unsuited for FE. Indeed the worth of both students and teachers, as measured by the commodity value of courses (advanced and non-advanced) has been detrimental to both groups. Not only has this led to the shelving of lower status courses and the arbitrary up-grading of others, but it has also tended to devalue the contribution of those who teach craft or generally vocational courses.

151

As a consequence, the diversification of FE to which we refer in chapter 1 has involved the separation of advanced from non-advanced courses, and in many cases not only the shelving of non-advanced work, but the simple dumping of it. Indeed, many colleges have actively run down low grade courses as a means of enhancing their status and of improving career opportunities for their staff (Tipton, 1973). For those dealing with the education of the unemployed, the illiterate, the less able or 'craft', few opportunities for promotion exist beyond the basic lecturer scale. Moreover, such lecturers and their students tend to suffer increasing alienation from the wider developments of FE. If this then is the plight of the low status groups *already* in FE, what hope exists for the 53 per cent of the 16–19 age group presently outside, who will inevitably be drawn into FE as a result of government policy? It would be complacent to imagine that the activities of the Manpower Services Commission will, through its short-term objectives, rectify such inequalities in FE.

In our view, the long-term answer to the 16–19 problem cannot simply be seen in terms of extending forms of FE provision to meet the needs of *all*, nor in the specific funding of short-term courses for the disadvantaged. A more comprehensive policy is required which would not only end the present connection between points, grades and numbers but which would also place FE within a more democratic framework. Such a course of action would inevitably require a thorough-going analysis of what should *count* as FE provision, including a careful examination of the frustrating disjunctures which presently exist between college courses and industrial practice. We have argued throughout the course of this study that we need to define more accurately what is meant by education and what is meant by training. Indeed, without wishing to repeat discussion which may be found elsewhere in this volume, it would seem to us that in practice the FE of apprentice-students is characterised by a form of control which shares more in common with certain forms of instruction or induction, than with any of the principles of education or training discussed in chapter 1. From our observations of practice, it would seem to us that many of the widely-espoused educational objectives that we as educationalists take for granted as properly guiding practice, ultimately represents little more than a means of legitimising quite pragmatic forms of industrial socialisation when applied to the FE of craft apprentices. It is not our intention in this conclusion to extend the discussion of the political or ideological significance of that process for young people, but simply to point out that one of the unintentional consequences of their experience of FE may involve a distortion of their understanding of the industrial world.

It would seem imperative that trade unions and other interested bodies (DES, Teacher Associations, Training and Examination Boards and so forth) should be more actively involved in both the construction of apprenticeship training schemes, and in the ordering of the FE of their younger members. In recent years the principal concern of the engineering unions has been with securing a higher-status social image for the engineer through such means as the extension of training provision. As usual, however, they have paid little attention to the FE route their members must travel in order to acquire their qualifications, and even less to the sociological consequences of that process. The same criticism, moreover, applies to NATFHE (National Association of Teachers in Further and Higher Education), whose policy for the universalising of FE for all 16- to 19-year-olds (NATFHE, 1977; Mansell, 1977) would seem to ignore a serious critical examination of what constitutes current FE provision, particularly in relation to the experiences of low-status students and their teachers.

Our message is therefore clear; the opening up of FE as a right for all within existing conditions of FE practice will do little to challenge the sometimes short-sighted influences which have so far guided its direction. Policy initiatives, in other words, must first of all recognise the nature of those often obscure problems which exist at the grass-roots level. What we are suggesting is that in an age of rapid industrialisation and economic change what constitutes the further education of young workers must be constantly reappraised. This reappraisal will necessarily imply changes both *within* and *without* the classroom. At the level of practice we would stress the need to establish frameworks within which young workers and their teachers are encouraged to think more critically about themselves in relation to both college and the world of work. Professional identities should no longer be moulded by the narrow and often outmoded requirements of industrial life. In other words, FE should represent a critical means of broadening both professional and industrial horizons, so that the young worker might acquire a more realistic picture of the social and economic world of which he is a part. It has been an argument of this book that the *flexibility* of college life itself provides one important framework from which initial strategies for change may be mounted.

Further Education should, we believe, constitute a challenge to the existing forms of pedagogy which have hitherto influenced its practice. Thus, our final comment suggests that FE may become less concerned with differentiating the production process, and more with developing in students both interpretative and integrative skills which will allow them to participate more *positively* within the production process. Such a reforming of the objectives of FE would, we believe, counteract the potential cynicism of young workers by encouraging a realistic understanding of the facts of individual life, together with some critical

153

awareness of the consequences of changing skills within society, as well as their social distribution. Our study, however, in no way provides answers to the numerous questions we have raised, and is intended only as an exploratory document. Nevertheless, by concerning ourselves with the FE of young workers in the conditions of modern capitalism, we have attempted to contribute to a wider debate about the channels through which young workers are socialised into industry and society. We can only hope that some of the observations we have outlined here will stimulate others in their analysis of the processes which underpin FE.

Appendix 1

Patterns of advancement

City and Guilds

The vast majority of apprentice-students at Western follow part-time City and Guilds Craft courses. Figure 1 illustrates a typical pattern of advancement in technical education via City and Guilds.

For further discussion of the relationship between City and Guilds scheme and FE see *City and Guilds Broadsheet No. 84 October 1978*. For more detailed analysis of the range of courses currently being offered in the 'Non Advanced Sector of Further Education' see DES Report no. 94, December 1978: *Non Advanced Further Education*.

(b) Mining

Figure 2 shows the method of entry into *mining courses* and the method of progression through the various courses offered within a typical mining department.

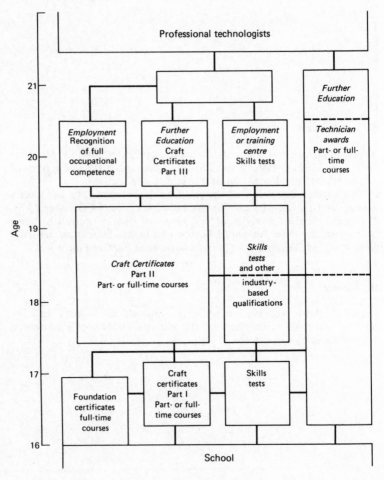

Figure 1

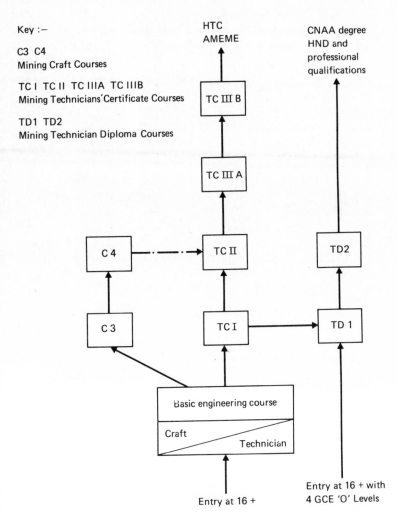

Key :—

C3 C4
Mining Craft Courses

TC I TC II TC IIIA TC IIIB
Mining Technicians' Certificate Courses

TD1 TD2
Mining Technician Diploma Courses

HTC
AMEME

CNAA degree
HND and
professional
qualifications

TC III B

TC III A

C 4

TC II

TD2

C 3

TC I

TD 1

Basic engineering course

Craft

Technician

Entry at 16 +

Entry at 16 + with
4 GCE 'O' Levels

Figure 2

157

Appendix 2

Craftsmen and technicians

Craftsmen and technicians – social differentiation in apprenticeship

In this section we wish to argue that 'definitions' in FE are less than helpful for analysing the social distinctions which characterise college practice. The use of definitions which, for example, seek to differentiate the craft apprentice from his technician counterpart often tend to trivialise a number of underlying tensions in the nature of apprentice relations. Here we explore some of the practical distinctions which influence the *streaming* process in FE, and which separate off young apprentices from one another at both the work and the college level. But first we turn our attention to the kind of arguments used in the literature to identify the apprentices' general characteristics.

The craft apprentice

The craft apprentice is normally selected by the company for apprenticeship training. He is expected to possess a minimum number of passes at CSE, in Maths, Physics and English. However, in recent years tight employment conditions have meant that companies are increasingly able to recruit apprentices with 'good CSEs and 'O' Levels'. Those apprentices recruited by the larger companies spend the initial year of their apprenticeship beween work, the company school and the college. Not only do they acquire some experience of work and college during this period, but they are also observed and assessed for their suitability in particular areas of production. Apprentices recruited to the smaller employers, particularly those not involved in a group training scheme, tend to find their initiation into the work situation more abrupt. In both cases, once the apprentices have become indentured into a particular craft skill, opportunities for transfer from one skill to another, or into technician training, remain minimal. Final completion of apprenticeship is dependent upon a number of interrelated factors, for example, satisfying the conditions laid down by the Engineering Industry

Training Board, performance at work and success in college exams. Mode of study is usually by day release.

The technician apprentice

The technician apprentice is normally selected by the company and is generally seen to be of a higher academic calibre than the craft apprentice. The school leaver is expected to have a minimum of four grade 1 CSEs or 'O' Levels in Maths, English, Physics and one other subject. Not unlike the craft apprentice the technician apprentice spends much of his initial time between work, training-school and college and, at the end of his first year, is allocated to a particular area of technician training. In theory, both the craft and the technician apprentice student have some choice about the area of production in which they are to work, but in practice the prevailing conditions of employment and production limit the exercise of that choice. In some cases, technician apprentices who do not perform well in their initial year are reclassified for craft training. One reason why the technician apprentice is often considered to be of a higher calibre than his craft apprentice counterpart, is that his work is not specifically geared to one practical application of production. In other words, his work and training is not simply concerned with manual dexterity, but also with the wider theoretical problems of technology, design and management. Final completion of the apprenticeship is dependent upon satisfying the conditions laid down by the Technician Education Council, performance at work and passing the necessary college examinations. Unlike the craft apprenticeship, facilities now exist within the structures of TEC for students to transfer to higher-level courses in technology on completion of their technician training. Mode of study varies between day and block release.

The problem with such rather bland descriptions of craft and technician apprentices is that they obscure a number of other important distinctions in college practice.[1] Though both groups of apprentices are often employed by the same firms, share similar social-class backgrounds and enjoy common leisure activities, the similarities tend to stop there. The mechanisms by which school leavers are selected and differentiated have a marked bearing on the streaming process at college. The distinctions which characterise craftsmen from technicians in practice generate tension in their social relations, and not only separate off young workers from one another, but also maintain hostility and antagonism between them. The intention of this section is to explore the underlying basis of such tension and also to provide some insight from apprentice-teacher accounts of its origins.

Despite the fact that the vast majority of apprentices at Western are craft oriented, the existence of a small but growing number of technician apprentices is gradually undermining their status. This new breed of apprentice, associated as he is with education, school success and ability, is seen by the craft student as stuck up and phoney. The feeling that the technician 'looks down on them' is a perspective which recurringly appears in this study and has been noted elsewhere (Simon, 1977). Simon's report of a large Midlands factory points to the tendency for technicians to describe craft apprentices as 'nothing more than skilled operatives, (and) ... as being a "rough lot", "not interested in work", and "out for a good time" '. However, there is also a tendency for sociologists to indulge in such typing of the craft apprentice too. Venables (1967) for example, in her study 'The Young Worker at College' argues as follows:

> Viewed sociologically as a male group they were muscular, non-verbal, non-anxious and extravert ... they were rooted in the family, following in their father's footsteps, and looking for only modest improvement in social status ... their social attitude was authoritarian. ... With such compliant students the college is not faced with major disciplinary problems – they are moulded by the system and self-selected for it.

From our interviews with employers, teachers and technicians such general stereotypes would seem to hold true. In the following account, a third-year apprentice technician talks about the prospects of craft and technician work:

> *Andy*:   Well, we've been told by the GPO ... whether it's true or not I don't know ... that when we've done our apprenticeship we can go into different jobs, if we want ... computers, management, training ... that sort of thing. If we've followed all these different courses then we have the background to take up these jobs ... even go on to transfer to degrees, so they tell us anyway. That's why I say Yes and No. ... it's very frustrating following a good many courses that don't connect up with the job you're doing at a point in time ... but there are other long-term benefits, aren't there? ... I mean I don't want to be a telecoms man for the rest of my life. ... I'd like to move into management or go on to further study ... a technician's course gives you more scope. ...
> *Interviewer*:   More scope ... a technician's course gives you more scope than ... what ... you mean a craft course?
> *Andy*:   I wouldn't get the same opportunities off a craft course would I? ... craft work is too limited. ... there aren't opportunities to do really skilled work. Nowadays, most craft jobs are boring ... repetitive work on machinery ... where you don't use your brain. I wouldn't do a craft course. ... if you do, you're stuck. ... you haven't got the same chances or choices, have you? You've only got to look around this place. ... Most of the craft lads aren't interested in their work or college. ... they didn't do so well at school to get on to a technician's course. ... they're stuck. ... they haven't got a future outside craft work. If I couldn't get a job as a technician ... or something like it ... I certainly wouldn't take craft work.

At this juncture it is not our intention to question Andy's illusions about the avenues open to him or his perceptions about craft practice. Rather, we suggest that such an account tends to be typical of the arguments through which technicians differentiate themselves from craftsmen.

At Western, technician apprentices tend to be defensive about their status, reacting strongly towards the craft apprentices' insinuations that they are 'wankers', 'poofs', 'girls', and so forth. In these circumstances, the technician apprentices tend to keep to themselves, often referring to the craft apprentices as 'yobos', 'thickos' and 'morons'. In the following remarks a final-year maintenance fitter, employed by a large foreign company, identifies one source of this tension from a craft perspective:

'Our job is bascially maintaining a section of machinery . . . really maintenance engineers. . . . Sometimes, the machinery breaks down and it's our job to fix it. . . . But before that there's procedures to go through. . . . The technicians have to look at the machinery first. . . . they look at what's wrong and give instructions about what to do . . . not that we need any telling. . . . Sometimes they work with us . . . but not often. The thing is we are left hanging around waiting for them to come. . . . They arrive in their white coats . . . collars and ties . . . pens sticking out everywhere . . . and then give us a bollocking for letting the breakdown happen. They look down on us . . . they think we're rough . . . you know as if we don't know the job . . . not really skilled blokes, if you know what I mean.'

Again, it is not our intention here to take sides on an account which is equally defensive. However, the question does ultimately arise, how does one explain the underlying nature of such friction? One explanation is that change in plant and technology bring the two types of worker into closer contact, and into relationships which are often fleeting and conflictual. On the shop floor, for example, each brings different skills to bear but the relative 'newcomer', the technician, is often viewed with suspicion by the industrial craft worker (Gorz, 1977). 'White coats', 'collars and ties', 'pens' and so forth are often seen as the symbols of a 'marginal man', who belongs neither to the world of the shop floor nor to the world of the management. In other respects, the craft worker may also associate the technician with the forms of modern technology which are gradually eroding his status, employment and differentials.

The nature of the craft apprentices' paranoia about educated people 'looking down on them' is compounded by another issue. There would seem to be some concensus of opinion in official reports (Haslegrave, 1969) and amongst professional bodies (the Technician Education Council) that the technician is, and should be, of a higher calibre than his craft counterpart. Whilst, in some areas, there remains a demand for craft training, there is little doubt that the technician is a relatively faster growing category of trained worker. According to Haslegrave (1969) industry increasingly requires workers trained less in the principles of manual dexterity and more in the broader skills associated with the application of science and technology at plant level.

However, the actual nature of such new skills is yet to be clearly defined either by industry or by the professional interests that currently comprise the Technician Education Council Reading between the lines, it would seem that technician work is generally perceived to be less specific than industrial craft work, and less dependent upon outmoded forms of division of labour and union practice (Haslegrave, 1969). It is also seen to be more concerned with 'diagnosis', 'testing' and 'supervisory' work. Consequently, in recent years numerous moves have been made, particularly through the influence of TEC, to raise the training and entry requirements for technician students. Few corresponding curricular changes have been initiated, however, for the majority of day-release craft students.

In recent years, therefore, it is not surprising to observe a rapid increase in the number of technician courses offered in FE. Not only have the proportions of technician apprentices grown *vis-à-vis* other groups, but also the colleges have been able to recruit better qualified apprentices than those traditionally associated with the craft intake.

At Western, for example, these developments are welcomed by many lecturers who associate such recruitment with the more able and motivated student.

As the following comments from two lecturers would seem to indicate, such policy is not without its advantages:

'They grasp things much quicker than the craft lads . . . no disrespect to these lads of course, but they are limited. The Technician student is more literate and numerate . . . he seems to take an interest in his work, and seems, somehow, more in tune with what's going on around him. Of course he's got a lot going for him . . . he can take his studies on to degree level . . . and if he wants to, can transfer into management . . . that kind of thing. You can see it in the classroom . . . compared to some of the craft lads they're a joy to teach . . . their behaviour is different for a start . . . less inclined to extremes of boredom or misbehaviour. . . . They're more stimulating to teach. . . . This may sound bad I know . . . but as a teacher it's imporant to feel that your students at least want to be there.'

Similarly:

'Some of the craft lads . . . though by no means all . . . are lacking in interest and involvement, both here and at work. It's hard to stimulate them when you know that some can't read or write properly . . . or that others are very bright but bored with college and work. It's more likely your craft lad who has to be pushed, shoved and cajoled all the way. . . . the truth is that he really doesn't want to be here . . . but he does come either because he wants his ticket or the employer forces him. We're expected to teach kids in these circumstances and get them through the exams. So there's that kind of pressure on us too.'

Clearly, such remarks contain within them quite 'deficit' assumptions about the relative abilities of craft apprentices. It is ironic that technical teachers also express empathy towards these students, often arguing that they were once apprentices themselves. However, despite the fact that an increasing number of craft apprentices achieve similar school qualifications to those of their technician counterparts, teacher expectations of 'the craft lad' remain low.

But on what criteria are these stereotypes founded? It may be the case, for example, that the technician apprentice *appears* to be more motivated and able in his college studies, but to what extent are such characteristics related to the actual work conditions in which he performs his tasks? This kind of argument equally applies to the craft apprentice. In other words, to what extent are teacher stereotypes based upon *actual knowledge* of the apprentices work on the job, or are they solely linked with behavioural assumptions associated with scholastic achievement and academic ability? It may be the case, for example, that the technician's propensity to absorb education at college bears little relation to his ability to perform well at work. Similarly, the craft apprentice's apparent ambivalence towards academic study should not be confused with his propensity to learn and perform well on the job.

Yet the rapid expansion of technician education, and the corresponding raising of educational requirements, has widened the gulf between the craft and the technician apprentice. The process of credentialism has done much to reinforce the belief that technician skills and training are necessarily more sophisticated and complex than those associated with craft work. On the shop floor, however, there is little to support such an assumption, wherein the distinctions between craft and technician work are often difficult to identify. Though training institutions may perpetuate such educational distinctions, the actual distribution and proportion of work skills in the occupational structure varies in relation to other factors, namely production, plant and jobs *available*. Whilst, of course, much may be achieved by workers, unions and employers in dispute over job definitions, pay differentials and status, there is little to be achieved in trying to separate out the actual categories, 'craftsman' and 'technician', in a rigid manner.[2] Indeed, despite the fact that many employers, training officers and union officials remain often notoriously ignorant about such definitional matters, it does not prevent them from spending time and energy in testing school-leavers and apprentices for 'craft' and 'technician' skills. Until recently CSEs and 'O' Levels provided a crucial rule-of-thumb guide, but youth unemployment has changed that situation drastically.

Today employers have more choice. How they select and differentiate school-leavers with similar exam passes involves them in testing for other criteria than simply the number of 'O' Levels passed. Careers records, school reports, interview style, attitude and aptitude test performance constitute important aspects in the process of recruitment. There is a tendency for the FE college environment to reinforce these behavioural characteristics, wherein student ability is judged according to a range of observable criteria such as interest, motivation, ambition, and so forth. Our argument here is that once stereotyped and indentured within the interlocking processes of work, training and education the craft apprentice cannot aspire to re-categorisation. The fact that many school leavers are ignorant about such processes suggests that the streaming mechanism will continue to act in favour of the college and the firm's manpower projections. It is difficult to understand how improved selection procedures, testing and counselling services will overcome such a deep-rooted problem. In the circumstances, therefore, it is not clear how FE, or the apprenticeship system, benefits the school-leaver since such divisive conditions both exploit his ignorance and encourage his future discontent. One is reminded here of Berg's (1973) assertion that contemporary developments in education would seem to bear little correspondence to either economic or rational argument:

> Economic evidence indicates no clear contributions of education to economic development, beyond the provision of mass literacy. . . . Education is often irrelevant to on the job productivity and is sometimes counter productive; specifically vocational training seems to be derived more from work experience than from formal training. . . . Education needs to be informed . . . by striking a balance between 'too much' for some and 'not enough' for others. The tendency on the part of employers to raise educational standards *without careful assessment of their needs, in both the long and the short run**, can benefit neither managers nor the system they extol. . . . This purposeless credential consciousness further handicaps education . . . in the pursuit of its promise to liberate people and to help preserve for society its better traditions and commitments (*Berg's emphasis).

However, it is now almost a truism to suggest that skill requirements in industrial society change in relation to capital investment and technological innovation. One assumption made by functionalist theorists of stratification (and by the theorists of the 'human capital' school in economics) is that a need exists to raise educational requirements to accommodate the demand made by the proportional increase in the number of skilled workers in the economy. This perspective suggests that an expanding occupational structure demands a more highly trained labour force able to cope with the new range of complex skills made available. Education, it is argued, should respond to such demands and needs, and should thus constitute an important area of investment. In the post-war era this perspective has been influential, not only in rationalising the extension of mass schooling and technical education, but also in fostering the myth that the proportion of unskilled work in the economy is diminishing (Braverman, 1974). One side effect of the ensuing expansionist policy of the 1960s has been the 'semi-professionalising' of a vast new range of occupations (Wilensky, 1964). It is our argument here that this process has been influential in the 'semi-professionalising' of technician education.

165

As this pattern has grown it has not only obscured the problematic connection between the apprenticeship system and work, but it has also mystified the process of education and training which sustain it. As FE has responded by raising its educational requirements (i.e. developed higher-level courses) relatively low-status groups in society, the craft apprentice, the unemployed, women and blacks have become alienated from its ranks. Lee (1975), for example, notes that the overriding concern with qualifications in FE has led to a scant regard for education itself.

> At the present time . . . this educational concern is growing daily
> weaker – not least because the tech is expected to be a kind of
> second-rate finishing school, dispensing qualifications for second-rate
> citizens. The capacity, even the desire, to confront the problems of
> its students in its own way as an institution of vocational is made to
> appear thoroughly unrealistic. . . . How far does the system challenge,
> or instead go along with the progressive obsolescence of the skill
> structure in a community? Secondly, what does the college do about
> the problems of disadvantaged youth, whether it be through un-
> employment, or type of employment or discrimination against colour
> or sex?

Certainly, it is unlikely that the introduction of a curriculum for 'life skills', compulsory day 'release' or short courses for the 'young unemployed' will change the situation much. It would also appear that craft apprenticeships will be allowed to run down in areas where demand is low. This partly explains why many colleges are anxious to shelve lower-level courses in favour of higher-status students. In this respect FE may be seen to be playing a double game with Crowther's ghost. On the one hand, it actively reinforces the de-skilling process, whilst on the other it professes some public commitment to 'help young workers find their way in the world'. In these circumstances, and within the existing languid conditions of day-release education, FE both misleads apprentices (through the streaming process) about their *real* prospects and also encourages unrealistic conceptions about the nature of skilled work. As Liepmann (1960) has noted,

> the increased degree of automaticity of machines, the greater
> standardisation of materials, and the introduction of scientific tests
> of quality (for both raw materials and final products) have rendered
> obsolete some of the craftsman's specialised knowledge, his physical
> sensitivity and his intuitive 'feel' for machines and materials. . . .
> Thus increasing mechanisation and specialisation have led to the de-
> skilling of many traditional crafts; except for a minority of workers,
> trades are narrowly specialised.

In these circumstances it is not surprising to observe dispiritedness and disinterest on the part of craft apprentices to their studies. Their hostility and contempt for people who are seen to look down on them is to be understood within the differentiation mechanisms associated with the two apprenticeships. However, the situation for the technician apprentice is not necessarily more advantageous. Whilst FE is seen to challenge and extend his academic talents (there is some doubt about this), he may also find that his involvement in the apprenticeship system, and skilled work, leaves much to be desired. It is equally understandable why such students also display defensive and exclusive attitudes toward their craft colleagues. They too are often apprehensive about the actual pay-offs associated with extended training. The final realisation by some that they might also be caught in the same trap as the craft apprentice may be too much for them to handle. And, paradoxically, such shared frustrations, usually articulated in terms of the lack of connection between education, training and work, may actually fan the flames of tension between the two groups. In such circumstances FE may be seen to sustain rather than challenge the social relations which separate off young workers from one another.

Appendix 3

Basic skills in the technical curriculum

One aspect of the Liberal Studies Department's policy of making itself indispensable, as noted in chapter 5, is to neutralise its critics by appearing to take notice of them. Indeed, in some areas of its work this has involved the department in serving sectional needs and interests. However, despite such manoeuvring heated controversy remains over responsibility for teaching the basic skills. The aims and objectives of teaching literacy skills in FE has, for many years, been a bone of contention. It has its roots in the days when technical teachers argued strongly that whilst they were prepared to 'repair' some of the numeracy deficiencies of their apprentices, the responsibility for teaching literacy skills should rest elsewhere. It was argued then, as it is today, that liberal studies should accommodate such work and, whilst the definitions may have changed from 'technical report writing' to 'Communication Studies', the dimensions of the problem remain the same. The problem has, as the following comments from a Ministry of Education White Paper (1962) suggest, much to do with perceptions of the apprentice.

> [Through] the development of communcation skills . . . they [the apprentices] must be able to make themselves understood in speech and writing, and through listening and reading, to understand others . . . English should be taught, in a context, . . . a body of material involving discussion and written work can be used.

Similarly, the City and Guilds Institute allocates English a specific role in their Liberal Studies programme (1970), a role associated with: 'The Expansion of the linguistic resources of the student, which are basic to his personal growth and effective social behaviour.'

More recently, the Technician Education Council has attempted to develop such aims by redefining them within a set of structured guidelines specifically geared to future curriculum development. However, to avoid the controversy traditionally associated with the use of such terms as 'basic skills', 'English in Liberal Studies', 'numeracy and literacy', and so forth, the Council has replaced them with the new terminology, 'Communication Studies.'

Effectively, such redefinition formalises the place of numeracy and literacy skills in the technical curriculum and, as has been noted elsewhere (Pearce, 1978) locates 'English' and 'Maths' teaching in a highly vocational and technicist manner. In this form innovation may not, at college level, constitute any great advance upon the traditional practice of 'report writing'. However, at Western, Liberal Studies teachers are less concerned about the ideological implications involved in the 'bastardising' of English teaching, and more about what they interpret as outsiders meddling in their work.

Though few members of the Liberal Studies Department at Western dispute the importance of teaching 'English', there exists some resistance to what is seen to be the technical departments' policy of dumping such a responsibility onto them. The apprehension and suspicion which this generates between the departments accounts for continued conflict over the aims of Liberal Studies teaching. However, at Western, English has always had a strong claim to a place within the Liberal Studies Department. In keeping with its explicit servicing role it readily inherited the task of alleviating the burden from technical departments for teaching 'report writing' and 'basic skills'. Indeed a college such as Western, with its emphasis upon apprenticeship training, places great importance on the teaching of such skills since failure and wastage rates are seen to be closely associated with poor performance in this area. Consequently the genesis of the argument about what constitutes English is quite specific and relates to the institution's perceptions of the cultural levels of its apprentices. The issue of teaching English within Liberal Studies at Western is, despite the progressive rhetoric of contemporary literature, a matter of transmitting basic levels of skill. One technical lecturer, for example, expresses frustration at the low level of ability of his students: 'I get lads in my classes and, quite honestly, I wonder what they've been doing for the previous eleven years in primary and secondary education. Lads who can barely add up and spell.'

Such teachers face the problem of teaching apprentices whose basic education is inadequate. They look at the dense demanding syllabus of their technical courses and realise it is not feasible for them to undertake the teaching of literacy and numeracy as well. Logically, to them, the role of the Liberal Studies teacher is to help in this area and redress the problems caused by poor elementary education. This is endorsed by a Head of Department: 'One of the weaknesses of my students is the lack of ability to communicate and I would rather them spend far more time learning communicative skills than learning about Greek mythology. . . .' Whilst we did not, however, observe lessons in Greek mythology, such remarks would seem to suggest that some technical teachers at Western remain far from satisfied about the progress made by the Liberal Studies Department in servicing their interests. These and other comments (see chapter 5) affirm a dominant concern among technical teachers to make Liberal Studies assume a greater vocational relevance. It is a position summed up by one technical lecturer who feels that his Liberal Studies colleagues do not take 'notice' or 'listen':

'Liberal Studies could be a little more helpful to these lads . . .
because they do have problems in general with the old three "R's". It
would be a great benefit to us if they . . . the Liberal Studies people
. . . would pay less attention to such issues as "the police", "crime",
"sex", "politics" and that sort of thing, and more on helping these
kids with their real problems. It would be of great benefit to us, but
very few Liberal Studies people will take any notice, or even listen
to us.'

Here the technical teacher laments the fact that he is unable to divert
some Liberal Studies teachers into the area which he considers important. But as the following counter-claim from a member of the Liberal
Studies Department would seem to indicate, there remains some considerable doubt about what constitutes 'important':

'I have nothing to do with that approach [i.e. teaching English] . . .
equipping them to be better writers of memorandums and reports. I
wouldn't necessarily see that as my job. Any way, if such aims are
important why shouldn't all staff be involved?'

The defensive nature of such remarks capture something of the frustration and ambiguity associated with how Liberal Studies teachers
define their responsibilities. Whilst many, if not most, recognise the
importance of basic skill work in their teaching, there is the general
feeling that such work is largely dumped on them. This often leads to
feelings of apprehension and alienation wherein the policy of servicing threatens to remove any semblance of autonomy from the Liberal
Studies teachers' domain. As one probationary teacher notes:

'There always seems to be someone looking over your shoulder in
this place . . . someone always telling you what *you* should be doing.
. . . Other departments wouldn't tolerate such interference for one
minute. . . . It puts you on your guard . . . wary if you know what I
mean.'

It is not surprising to observe a bewildering array of approaches to
Liberal Studies emanating from within such 'relative' conditions. Its
elusive subject-matter is, however, only partly the problem; another is
that confusion rather than clarification is maintained through the influence of external bodies such as the City and Guilds, TEC, BEC[1] the
unions and government. Indeed, controversy over the place of 'English'
within Liberal Studies may be only the tip of a much deeper-rooted
problem, namely that associated with the contradictory social relations
which exist between education, training and work (see chapter 6). It
may be the case that, until a concensus is reached on whether or not
'English' is included and assessed in Western's Liberal Studies syllabuses,
no one will teach it. But, as the following remarks indicate, some
teachers have adopted and maintained firm stand points:

'General Studies affords me the best opportunity to teach ideas with
a minimal number of restrictions. I am *not* an English teacher – if

these apprentices have reached this far in the system, without an adequate grasp of English, then the system has failed.'

Whilst this teacher would seem to adopt an extreme position others, though sympathetic with such a viewpoint, choose to express themselves more cautiously. In the first place, for example, they recognise that the gradual emergence of TEC courses not only necessitates the formulation of set syllabuses but also their formal evaluation. Second, senior members of the department argue, for example, that the expression of extreme viewpoints could adversely rock the boat with the other departments. They maintain, for example, that apparent non-co-operation with their technical colleagues may be interpreted as yet another indication of the departments' reluctance to accept responsibility for the imperatives set by the technical curriculum. In such circumstances, radical stances on autonomy may lead to a reinforcement of the prevailing belief that the department possesses only marginal relevance to the life of the college.

Such confusion of opinion over the inclusion of English and Communication Studies is, therefore, only a surface manifestation of a number of deeper problems (see chapter 5). However, despite developments towards the establishment of more structured syllabuses at Western (developments considerably influenced by the impact of TEC) controversy and conflict concerning the aims and objectives of Liberal Studies teaching remain. Indeed, the splits and factions would seem to proliferate as the organisation expands and, as we have argued in chapter 3, these may well reflect the particular attempts by the staff to maintain, at least in theory, some semblance of their own dignity and sense of purpose. Indeed in these circumstances it becomes only too apparent that it is not only the apprentices whose control over the conditions of their education, training and work is in question.

Notes

1 Background to the study

1 Whilst stricly speaking 'The Great Debate' focused upon *schools*, it should not be simply taken as a school-related phenomenon. Its concern with 'progressivism' and the nature of applied scientific and technical knowledge has for long been a political issue. The principal interest of 'synchronising' the relations between education and industry is rooted within recurring historical and economic debate, particularly that associated with national growth, unemployment, inflation and so forth. 'The Great Debate', therefore, should be understood within wider structural parameters and assessed as part of an ongoing discussion of the relations between education, economy and society (Halsey, Floud and Anderson, 1960; Karabel and Halsey, 1977). In relation to FE, for example, Venables (1974) assesses the 'facts of industrial life' associated with such discussion in the following matter:

> The reality is that we all – individuals as well as corporations – act in ways which produce a pay off. Individuals are often content with an emotional reward without thought of material gain but for industrial concerns an emotional pay off must come, if at all, after commercial success, not before. How could it be otherwise? Why do we, and particularly those of us in the education industry, go on imagining that this reified concept 'industry' can be cajoled or 'encouraged' into accepting responsibility for the broader education of work people if the economic pay off is not existent.

Since the 1950s there have been numerous reports, documents and texts which have, with recurring predictability, pre-empted those issues raised in Callaghan's (1976) speech. Indeed, the arguments concerning 'investment in training', 'the importance of technological and applied manpower', 'National Progress', and so forth, are not 'new'. See, for example, Crosland (1956); Zuckerman (1956);

172

Ministry of Education (1956, 1957, 1961, 1962); Williams (1957);
Cotgrove (1958); Crowther (1959); Henniker Heaton (1964); Musgrave (1967); Vaizey and Sheehan (1968). For more up-to-date discussion of the need for 'synchronisation' see Training Services
Agency (TSA) (1976); Holland (1977); National Association of
Teachers in Further and Higher Education (NATFHE) (1977);
Roberts (1977); Mansell (1977); Stanton (1978); Further Education Curriculum Review Unit (FEU) (1978). There are, of course,
less policy-oriented perspectives which do however analyse the
same theoretical issues associated with 'synchronisation'. These, for
example, focus upon the sociological and ideological dimensions.
See Marcuse (1964); Althusser (1971); Habermas (1972); Bowles
and Gintis (1976); Gorz (1977); Karabel and Halsey (1977).

2   This argument relates to the 'square pegs in round holes' notion
exemplified in Callaghan's speech (1976). The speech itself opti-
mistically assumes that youth unemployment, for example, is a
cyclical phenomenon, and that its resolution rests largely in the
education system's ability to respond to changing skill requirements
in society. This argument would seem to suggest that if young
people are more adequately trained in those skills where national
demand is greatest, unemployment will decline. Subsequent to the
Great Debate there has been much discussion on the need for
parents, teachers, counsellors and others to channel young people
along the appropriate path, e.g. into technical work, applied subjects and training. Progressive education is thus now seen to be
antagonistic to such interests, and it is perhaps no historical accident that the Great Debate has initiated the closure (at both the
financial and the pedagogical levels) of certain liberal initiatives.

3   There remains some confusion about the term 'alternative route'.
What, for example, is it an alternative *to*? Raffe (1979) suggests
that one should be clear about the meaning of the term, particularly
when assessing social mobility through FE. He distinguishes two
dimensions, the 'educational' and the 'social', i.e. 'part-time education has provided an alternative route in the educational sense
because its association with occupational achievement was greatest
among those with the lowest school attainments; it provided an
alternative route in the social sense because this association was
greatest among those from the lowest status background'. Furthermore, he suggests that for the middle-class student, with negligible
school qualifications, FE remains a second choice rather than an
alternative route. It is not our intention here to dispute the thrust
of such argument, but it is important to note that for the growing
numbers of middle-class students taking 'O' and 'A' Levels, FE
does represent a second chance. To what extent Raffe's analysis
(based as it is upon a small sample of men) points to *significant*
trends in social mobility of large sections of the working class
remains open to question. Hordley and Lee (1970), for example,
analyse the increasing bias of FE courses and resources towards a

middle-class (full-time) intake. At another level the corresponding connection between FE, apprenticeship and the occupational structure ensures a tight control over the sponsorship of a highly select section of the educationally successful working class (Carter, 1975). Other factors such as de-skilling, unemployment, regional decline, redundancy, and so forth, need to be taken into account when analysing the incidence of social mobility through FE. For discussion of those who do not qualify for access to FE see Lee (1975) and Roberts (1977).

4 It is not our intention here to become bogged down in the political and organisational dimensions of FE policy. Part of the motivation for researching the area of FE *practice* is to avoid the descriptive 'org and admin' (organisation and administration) tradition of FE research which largely ignores questioning the *criteria* of provision. The division of responsibilities between the DES and the DEP over 'education' and 'training' not only constitutes a wasteful duplication of resources but also obscures what actually occurs within FE practice. Official definitions of the terms 'education' and 'training' are therefore unreliable, since they both reflect the competing interests of separate dimensions of state control and project simplistic definitions of FE practice. To assume, for example, that 'training' and 'instruction' do not form part of the ideological mechanism of Further 'education', or that 'education' is unrelated to training or instruction, is clearly absurd. However, it would be misleading to assume that current provision is made up of an integration of both concepts, for if that were the case we should have some conception of what that 'coalition' looks like. At present we know little about what actually underpins FE practice (though see Venables, 1967, 1974; Tipton, 1973). At the policy level little co-operation presently exists between the DES and the DEP. For further discussion of the ways in which such agencies perceive the problems associated with vocational education see DEP (1972); TSA (1975); TSA/MSC (1975); DEP/MSC (1976); TSA (1976); MSC (1977); Holland (1977); DES (1974); DES (1976); FEU (1978); Stanton (1978). Also see Roberts (1977); NATFHE (1977); Mansell (1977). For a wider assessment of the sociological and ideological implications of the relations between 'education' and 'training' see chapter six, particularly pages 116–18.

5 Here we emphasise the point that the FE college does not simply respond to external demand. Rather, it is seen to *interact* with external forces. This constitutes a recurring theme in this study, which stresses the *active* nature of the relations between college and industry.

6 For further discussion of the type and level of courses within the non-advanced sector of FE see DES (1978, Report no. 94, December).

7 The 'Points system' is the term used to describe the means by which staffing formulas, resources and so forth are calculated. Staffing

levels, ratios of junior to senior staff, departmental allocations and college development is dependent upon 'healthy student numbers. In FE the numbers game is crucial for survival, since the FE college has ostensibly no compulsory student population. Not only must the college sell its courses to Commerce, Industry and so forth (to attract numbers) but it must also attract sufficient students to higher grade courses in order to sustain a career structure for its staff. This voluntaristic process is not simply a matter of 'horses for courses' but is part of a wider process described by Tipton (1973) as the rat race associated with career patterns in FE. Furthermore, this entrepreneurial aspect of FE not only generates wasteful competition *between* FE colleges (i.e. duplicating courses and so forth) but it also encourages inter-departmental competition *within* them (see chapters 3, 4 and 5). Unlike school, for example, the FE college is in closer proximity to the immediate contingencies of supply and demand. It is largely dependent upon 'earning a living' through part-time students, and is thus ultimately affected by the fortunes of the industries from which its students are recruited. Essentially, there exists a cash and careers nexus built around the points system, i.e. in its relations with student numbers and the range/status of courses (high to low) on offer. If, for example, a college or particular department within it is able to attract students to higher grade courses, then this will increase its claim for a greater share of resources. On the points system craft or operative courses possess less value than technician or technology courses. Indeed, if one compares part-time or overtime payments to those who teach on such courses there exist marked differences in financial remuneration. In institutions where there is a greater population of higher grade work available the opportunities for career advancement beyond the basic lecturer scale (e.g. to Lecturer II or Senior Lecturer level) is greater than in institutions where low grade work predominates (craft, operative, the unemployed, the disadvantaged, and so forth).

8   Figures collated from DES (1978, Report no. 94) and Roberts (1978).

9   In August 1977 over 700,000 young people under twenty-five were registered as unemployed. Of these 250,000 (approximately) were school leavers. This figure represents about one-third of all school leavers. The remaining 450,000 had either been unemployed for long periods at a time or having found employment soon left it. (See DES, 1974; Holland Report, 1977; and the DEP Gazette, 1977, for further discussion of these figures. However these figures only record those who are registered as unemployed and clearly understate the full extent of youth unemployment. See Phillips, (1973.) Watts (1978) argues that 'the number of school leavers is currently shooting up: present projections indicate that whereas there were 816,000 school leavers in 1975/6, there will be over 900,000 in 1980/81 (though the final figure will decline thereafter).

It seems unlikely, therefore, that the problem of school leaver unemployment will diminish significantly over the next few years,
however successful Britain's economic policies may be: a more
likely possibility is that it will assume even longer dimensions.' The
British Youth Council (1977) and the Holland Report (1977) have
both commented on the social costs apparent in such rising figures
(alienation, boredom, delinquency, racial conflict and so forth).
But for a more enlightened discussion of the effects of unemployment see Marsden (1975) and Orwell (1962).

2   Western College: an ethnographic description

1   Western College was established in 1968/9 and, by the time
this research took place, had fast developed into an institution
comprising five main departments, Production and Fabrication;
Mining Engineering; Electrical and Electronic Engineering; Mechanical Engineering; Liberal and General Studies. Approximately
3,150 students attend the college, of whom less than 200 are
enrolled on full-time courses. The majority of Western's students
are craft apprentices drawn mainly from local industry. The pre-
dominance of apprentices illustrates the college's main concern,
which is the training of young workers for industry. Dominant
industries include engineering, mining and ceramics, and these
provide the major source of employment throughout the
region. The students mainly follow City and Guilds courses (see
Appendix 1).

In addition to the Principal and Vice-Principal, the college is
staffed by 145 full-time lecturers. Of these, five are Head of
Departments; two are Principal Lecturers, twelve are Senior Lecturers and approximately twelve are Lecturers Grade II. The majority, therefore, are Lecturers on the Grade I scale.

Teaching covers a broad range of courses, most of which are
'vocationally orientated'. At the time of our research Western
offered 1 sandwich course, 13 full-time courses, 16 block-release
courses and 17 evening courses. The lion's share of the work, however, is part-time day release (over 40 courses in all, mainly craft
but with a gradually increasing technician commitment).

The college is described by one of its staff in the following
way:

A new campus was built in Barton but from the outset it was
totally inadequate for the student population and, thus, all seven
Dickensian Institutes were retained as annexes. The College has
five departments – Mining, Engineering, Fabrication/Welding/
Production Engineering, Radio/TV/Electrical Engineering, Motor
Vehicle/Foundry/Mechanical Engineering and the General
Studies Department. Thus in its lack of Commerce, Business

Studies, Domestic Science, Nursing, Law, Art or 'O' and 'A' Level courses, the College retained many features of the Mechanics Institute, with little to act as a counterbalance. This situation remains today and, with a student population of 3,150 (approx.), almost entirely male, the college provides craft, technician and ONC/OND level courses across the entire engineering spectrum.

This description of Western College is quoted from a university diploma thesis presented by one of the lecturers at the college (1975/76). It is interesting to contrast this description of the Mechanics Institute with that of Engels, who described its forms of education as 'tame, flabby, subservient to the ruling politics and religion, so that, for the working man, it is merely a constant sermon upon quiet obedience, passivity and resignation to his fate' (Engels, 1892 p. 239. Also see Shapin and Barnes, 1976).

2 Apprentices in the early part of their training often identify with their trade, but many soon tire of their work and training, particularly those aspects which maintain their status as 'lads in training'. One recurring criticism of college life is that it is not unlike school (see Carter, 1962, 1969; Lee, 1964; Maizels, 1970; Weatherell, 1974; Brown, 1975; Ashton and Field 1976).

3 We are aware, for example, that there exists evidence to suggest that craftsmen identify with, and are interested in, their work (Blauner, 1964; Goldthorpe *et al.*, 1968; and Wedderburn and Crompton, 1972.) But the craftsman's commitment varies by trade, industry and region. Within engineering, for example, there exists a variety of craft skills, motor vehicle, foundry, fabrication, welding, electrical and so forth. However, rapid changes in technology have eroded many traditional craft skills which have resulted in general de-skilling (Braverman, 1974). Though much of the craft work remains categorised as skilled by unions and managements alike, it has become, *in practice*, semi-skilled. It is our argument here that to romanticise about the commitment of young apprentices to their chosen trade would be misleading. (For an 'anti-romantic' perspective of industrial craft work see Beynon, 1973; Blackburn 1972.) Also see Liepmann's (1960) and Williams's (1957) critiques of apprenticeship.

4 Here we refer to the distinctions between the practical and the academic man (see Snow, 1959; Williams, 1958; and Young, 1971).

5 Despite the sense of communality or shared work experience, students and staff tend not to mix at break times. Indeed, many technical staff prefer to brew their own tea on the job, favouring the precincts of their own workshops to the canteen or staff room. Consequently, the division not only between staff and students, but also between departments, is heightened. It would seem to us that such insularity derives largely from the technical teacher's

image of himself as 'an engineer in teaching', the former identity, as Venables (1967) suggested, taking precedence over the latter.

6 The technician Education Council (TEC) was established in March 1973. It is a response to the recommendations made by the Haslegrave Committee (1969). The Council's terms of reference are summarised in its policy statement as follows:

> The Council will be concerned in the development of policies for schemes of technical education for persons at all levels of technician occupations in industry and elsewhere. To this end, it will, as proposed in the Haslegrave Report, plan, administer and keep under review the development of a unified national system of courses . . . and will devise or approve suitable courses, establish and assess standards of performance and award certificates and diplomas as appropriate.

However, there remains a tension between TEC's concern with establishing a unified national system and its shared aim of encouraging college-based curricular initiatives.

3   Organisational framework

1 For further discussion of the methodological problems involved see chapter 7.
2 New Directions refers to the phenomenological influence, in the late 1960s and early 1970s, on sociology and the sociology of education. See M.F.D. Young (1971).
3 Rather than simply to be seen as a determined relationship.
4 A phrase borrowed from C.W. Mills (1970).
5 For a review of a variety of approaches to Organisational Studies see D. Silverman (1970).
6 See G. Mardle and M. Walker in S.J. Eggleston (1979).
7 Secretarial assistance, laboratory technicians, caretakers, cleaners, canteen workers and so forth.
8 Where students fail to meet expectations the cause of the failure is seen to rest within the individual himself. Lack of motivation, interest, or articulation, for example, are often used to explain high wastage rates. Consequently it is not surprising that the role of counselling is increasingly being seen as important in FE.
9 Thus not only producing flexible factors of production but also justifying the equality of opportunity myth. The two are seen as mutually reinforcing.
10 The Technician Education Council is a case in point. It is not surprising that given the process we describe here, a failure to produce a more flexible work force has often led to repeated demands by Government for a more centralised curriculum. TEC (following Haslegrave, 1969) and BEC (Business Education Council), may be seen to be two recent initiatives in this direction. Yet both claim to be concerned with supporting college-based innovations.

11 Inasmuch as the particular climate of an organisation will give
rise to variations in the degree of involvement and commitment
of its staff. For further discussion of such analysis see Etzioni
(1961).

12 The only committee with any *internal* executive power was that
known as the 'Head of Department's Committee' which advised
on college policy.

13 An example of this may be found in the Mining chapter (chapter
4) with reference to the coalition between that department and
others in times of crisis, i.e. declining student numbers.

14 This term derives from the work of March and Simon (1958) to
whom reference has been made earlier in the chapter.

4 The Department of Mining

1 Previously work organised and taught at the local College of
Advanced Technology.

2 Only a very small minority of lecturers in the deparment did not
have experience in the mining industry.

3 Approximately 25 per cent of Western's entire staff are teacher-
trained. The majority of those trained tend to teach in the General
Studies Department.

4 This argument is taken up in more detail in Appendix 2.

5 The Department of Liberal Studies

1 Arnold's concern with liberal education is to be found throughout his writings. See, for example, *Culture and Anarchy* (1935);
Reports on Elementary Schools, 1852–1882 (1808). For further
discussion of his views see Williams (1958).

2 Here we refer to the distinctions between the 'practical' and the
'academic' man (see Snow, 1959; Williams, 1958 and 1961; Young,
1971).

3 The different factions referred to here as 'liberals', 'radicals' and
'cowboys' are parts of a typology *not* constructed by the writers.
They represent the terms by which different groups identified and
described one another.

4 Both comments have been extracted from an article entitled 'Van-
ishing Apprentices' which appeared in the *Daily Mail* 17 September
1975.

6 On the 'fit' between Further Education and industry

1 By 'culture of technicism' we refer to the translation of industrial
social relations into the professional rhetoric and practice of

179

technical education. The instrumentality associated with this
process is bounded by historical traditions (F. Engels, 1892) which
strongly influence the present narrow conceptions of vocationalism
within the FE curriculum. See Gorz (1977), Holly (1977), Habermas (1972), Marcuse (1964) for a wider analysis of instrumentalism
and technical control.

7 A note on methodology

1 It is our purpose in this chapter to provide a basic rationale to the
theoretical and practical activities adopted in the study. Field-work
was carried out between September 1975 and June 1977. During
that period the three researchers, between them, spent an average
of three days per week in the field. The team held a formal meeting
each fortnight. Autumn 1977 to summer 1978 constituted the
main writing-up period.
2 Of particular interest is the way in which both depend on a coherence theory of truth.
3 As, for instance, in survey methods.
4 This problem remains more often than not at the implicit level.
5 For example, power and decision-making processes.
6 A point expressed a number of times by the participants themselves.
7 This applies to both qualitative and quantitative modes of research.
8 However, we would want to maintain that such a teacher remains
far from typical.

8 Conclusions

1 Sidney and Beatrice Webb (1898) describe the apprenticeship
system in the following manner: 'Over by far the largest part of the
limited field in which apprenticeship once prevailed, the system has
gone practically out of use. Undemocratic in its scope, unscientific
in its educational methods, and funamentally unsound in its financial aspects, the apprenticeship system, in spite of all the practical
arguments in its favour is not likely to be deliberately revived in
modern democracy' (quoted in Ryrie and Weir, 1978). See also
Williams (1957) and Liepmann (1960).
2 It is too cynical to assume that craft unions, in the face of rapid
technological change, act in elitist self-interest to preserve outmoded apprenticeship systems. It is our argument however that in
attempting to protect their members against employers' sharp
practices, they have tended to ignore the processes by which young
workers are initiated into their trades. In this respect the role of FE
has largely been ignored by the unions. It is also the case that employer sponsorship and maintenance of the apprenticeship system

and its links with the FE system has also been overlooked. It should be remembered that in engineering it is also the employers who enforce day-release attendance on apprentices. Failure to attend may meet with dismissal. FE is thus seen to be part of the job. For further discussion of trade unions under collective bargaining see Aldridge (1976), Clegg (1976) and Collins (1977).

Appendix 2

1   For discussion of the claustrophobic relations concerning selection within FE see Brook (1971) and Erben (1974).
2   The 1978 dispute amongst the tool-room workers at British Leyland over pay differentials provides an interesting, if not limited, example of the tensions which exist between workers possessing different levels of craft skill.

Appendix 3

1   BEC stands for Business Education Council. For further discussion of English under BEC see Pearce (1978).

Bibliography

Aldridge, A. (1976), *Power, Authority and Restrictive Practices*, Blackwell.

Althusser, L. (1969), *For Marx*, Allen Lane The Penguin Press.

Althusser, L. (1971), 'Ideology and Ideological State Apparatuses. Notes towards an investigation', in his *Lenin and Philosophy and other Essays*, New Left Books.

Argles, M. (1964), *South Kensington to Robbins – An Account of English Technical and Scientific Education since 1851*, Longman.

Arnold, M. (1908), *Reports on Elementary Schools, 1852–1882*, HMSO.

Arnold, M. (1935), *Culture and Anarchy*, Cambridge University Press.

Ashton, D.N., and Field, D. (1976), *Young Workers*, Hutchinson.

Bane, M.J. and Jencks, C. (1977), 'Five Myths About your IQ', in N. Block, and G. Dworkin (eds) (1977), *The IQ Controversy*, Quartet Books.

Benn, A.W. (1974), *Speeches*, Spokesman Books.

Berg, I. (1973), *Education and Jobs: The Great Training Robbery*, Penguin.

Berger, P.L. (1971), *A Rumour of Angels*, Penguin.

Bernstein, B. (1971), 'Classification and Framing of Educational Knowledge', in M.F.D. Young (ed.) (1971).

Beynon, H. (1973), *Working for Ford*, Penguin.

Blackburn, R.M. *et al.* (1972), *Perceptions of Work*, Cambridge University Press.

Blackman, C. *et al.* (1962), *Liberal Studies 1*, Cassell.

Blackman, C. *et al.* (1964), *Liberal Studies 2*, Cassell.

Blackman, C. *et al.* (1967), *Liberal Studies 3*, Cassell.

Blaug, M. (1976), *An Introduction to the Economics of Education*, Allen Lane The Penguin Press.

Blauner, R. (1964), *Alienation and Freedom*, University of Chicago Press.

Bourdieu, P. (1971), 'Systems of Education and Systems of Thought', in M.F.D. Young (ed.) (1971).

Bourdieu, P., and Boltanski, L. (1978), 'Changes in Social Structure and

Changes in the Demand for Education', in S. Giner, and M.S. Archer, (eds), *Contemporary Europe*, Routledge & Kegan Paul.

Bowles, S., and Gintis, H. (1976), *Schooling in Capitalist America*, Routledge & Kegan Paul.

Bratchell, D. (1968), *The Aims and Organisation of Further Education*, Pergamon Press.

Braverman, H. (1974), *Labor and Monopoly Capital*, Monthly Review Press, New York.

Bristow, A.J. (1976), *Inside the College of Further Education*, HMSO (1st edn 1970).

British Youth Council (1977), *Youth Unemployment: Causes and Cures*.

Brook, L. (1971), 'Further What?', in D. Rubinstein and C. Stoneman (eds), *Education for Democracy*, Penguin.

Brown, R. (1975), 'The Attitudes to Work, Expectations and Social Perspectives of Shipbuilding Apprentices', in T. Leggatt (ed.), *Sociological Theory and Survey Research*, Sage.

Callaghan, J. (1976), 'Ruskin Speech', (18 October).

Cantor, L., and Roberts, I. (1974), *Futher Education in England and Wales*, Routledge & Kegan Paul.

Carr Report (1957), *Recruitment and Training of Young Workers in Industry*, National Joint Advisory Council, HMSO.

Carter, M.P. (1962), *Home, School and Work*, Pergamon Press.

Carter, M.P. (1969), *Into Work*, Penguin.

Carter, M.P. (1975), 'Teenage Workers: a second chance at 18?', in Brannen, P. (ed.), *Entering the World of Work: Some sociological perspectives*, HMSO.

Catchpole, G. (1971), *Assessing Liberal Studies*, The Association for Liberal Education.

Central Training Council (1966), *Industrial Training and Further Education – a Further Statement*.

Cicourel, A.V. (1964), *Method and Measurement in Sociology*, Free Press, New York.

City and Guilds Institute (1970), *General Studies*.

City and Guilds Institute (1978), *City and Guilds Broadsheet No. 84*, October.

Clegg, H.A. (1976), *Trade Unions Under Collective Bargaining*, Blackwell.

Collins, R. (1977), 'Functional and Conflict Theories of Educational Stratification', in J. Karabel and A.H. Halsey (1977) (eds).

Cosin, B.R. (1972), *Education, Structure and Society*, Penguin.

Cotgrove, S. (1958), *Technical Education and Social Change*, Allen & Unwin.

Crosland, A. (1956), *The Future of Socialism*, Cape.

Crosland, A. (1974), *Socialism Now and other Essays*, Cape.

Crowther Report (1959), *Fifteen to Eighteen: A Report of the Central Advisory Council*, vol. 1, HMSO.

Davies, W.B. (1973), 'On the Contribution of Organisational Analysis to the Study of Educational Institutions', in R.F. Brown (ed.), *Knowledge, Education and Cultural Change*, Tavistock.

Dean, J., and Choppin, B. (1977), *Educational Provision 16–19*, NFER.

Dennis, N., Henriques, F., and Slaughter, C. (1969), *Coal is Our Life*, Tavistock.

Department of Education and Science (1974), *Unqualified, Untrained and Unemployed*, HMSO.

Department of Education and Science (1976), *Unified Vocational Preparation: A Pilot Approach*, HMSO.

Department of Education and Science (1978), *Non Advanced Further Education*, HMSO.

Department of Employment (1972), *Training for the Future: A Plan for Discussion*.

Department of Employment (with Manpower Services Commission) (1976), *Training for Vital Skills: A Consultative Document*.

Department of Employment Gazette (1977), Statistical Series, vol. 85, no. 8, August.

Dore, R. (1976), *The Diploma Disease*, Allen & Unwin.

Eggleston, S.J. (ed.) (1979), *Teacher Decision Making in the Classroom*, Routledge & Kegan Paul.

Engels, F. (1892), *Conditions of the Working Class in England* (Preface), Sonnenschein.

Erben, M. (1974), 'Teachers' Views of the Role of Liberal Studies in a Technical College', *Research in Education*, No. 11, May.

Erben, M. (1977), 'Socio-Historical Background to Developments in Further Education', unpublished mimeo, Garnett College of Education (Technical), London.

Erben, M., and Gleeson, D. (1977), 'Education as Reproduction: A Critical Examination of some aspects of the work of Louis Althusser', in M.F.D. Young and G. Whitty (eds) (1977).

Esland, G. (1971), 'Teaching and Learning as the Organisation of Knowledge', in M.F.D. Young (ed.) (1971).

Etzioni, A. (1961), *A Comparative Analysis of Complex Organisations*, Free Press, New York.

Feyerabend, P. (1975), 'Against Science', *Radical Philosophy*, no. 11.

Further Education Curriculum Review Unit (1978), *Annual Report*, DES, HMSO.

Gleeson, D. (ed.) (1971), *Identity and Structure. Issues in the Sociology of Education*, Nafferton Books, York.

Goldthorpe, J.H. *et al.* (1964), *The Affluent Worker: Industrial Attitudes and Behaviour*, Cambridge University Press.

Gorringe, R. (1977), 'Furthering Education?', *Radical Education*, no. 9.

Gorz, A. (1977), 'Technical Intelligence and the Capitalist Division of Labour', in M.F.D. Young and G. Whitty (eds) (1977).

Gregory, D.L. and Smyth, R.L. (1971), 'The School Leaver and the British Pottery Industry', *North Staffordshire Journal of Field Studies*, vol. 11.

Habermas, J. (1972), *Knowledge and Human Interest*, Heinemann.

Halsey, A.H., Floud, J., and Anderson, C.A. (eds) (1960), *Education, Economy and Society* (Introduction), Free Press, New York.

Harding, B. (1969), *Ten Years of General Studies*, A collection of lectures on Liberal Studies in Further Education, The Association for Liberal Education.

Haslegrave Report (1969), *Report of the Committee on Technician Courses and Examinations*, HMSO.

Henniker Heaton Report (1964), *Report of a Special Committee of the Minister of Education on Day Release*, HMSO.

Holland Report (1977), *Young People and Work: Report of a Working Party on the Feasibility of a new Programme for Unemployed School Leavers*, Manpower Services Commission.

Holly, D. (ed.) (1974), *Education or Domination?*, Arrow Books.

Holly, D. (1977), 'Education and the Social Relations of a Capitalist Society', in M.F.D. Young, and G. Whitty, (eds) (1977).

Hordley, I., and Lee, D.J. (1970), 'The Alternative Route – Social Change and Opportunity in Technical Education', *Sociology*, vol. 4, pp. 23–50.

Hoyle, E. (1973), 'The study of schools as organisations', in H.S. Butcher and H.B. Pont (eds), *Educational Research in Britain 3*, University of London Press.

Hunter, L.C., and Robertson, D.J. (1969), *The Economics of Wage Labour*, Macmillian.

Hussain, A. (1977) 'The Relationship between Educational Qualifications and the Occupational Structure: A Re-Examination', in D. Gleeson (ed.) (1977).

Jackson, Willis (1964), 'Foreword' to the Symposium on Liberal Studies, British Association for Commercial and Industrial Education.

Jencks, C. (1972), *Inequality – A Reassessment of the effect of Family and Schooling in America*, Basic Books, New York.

Kaneti-Barry, S.M. (1974), *Engineering Craft Studies and Monitoring a New Syllabus*, NFER.

Karabel, J., and Halsey, A.H. (eds) (1977), *Power and Ideology in Education*, Oxford University Press.

Keddie, N. (1971), 'Classroom Knowledge', in M.F.D. Young, (ed.) (1971).

Lee, D.J. (1964), 'A Study of Apprentice Training and its effects upon the attitudes and achievements of students at a local technical college' (unpublished PhD Thesis, University of Birmingham).

Lee, D.J. (1975), 'Neglected Territory: The Regional Factor in Further Education', in W. Van der Eyken, *Learning and Earning*, NFER.

Liepmann, K. (1960), *Apprenticeship: An Enquiry into its Adequacy under Modern Conditions*, Routledge & Kegan Paul.

Lipshitz, S. (1972), *Wastage Among Craft Apprentices*, Hutchinson Educational.

McCourt, J. (1979), 'The Social Context of Liberal Studies – A Case Study of a local FE College' (unpublished MA Dissertation, University of Keele).

Maizels, J. (1970), *Adolescent needs and the Transition from School to Work*, Athlone Press.

Manpower Services Commission (1976), *Towards a Comprehensive Manpower Policy*.

Manpower Services Commission (1977), *The New Special Programmes for Unemployed People. The Next Step*.

Mansell, J. (1977), '16–19: Pride or Prejudice', *Technical Journal*, February and October.

March, J.G., and Simon, H.A. (1958), *Organisations*, John Wiley.

Marcuse, H. (1964), *One-Dimensional Man: Studies in the Ideology of Advanced Industrial Society*, Routledge & Kegan Paul.

Mardle, G., and Walker, M. (1979), 'Autonomy and Organisation', in S.J. Eggleston, (ed.) (1979).

Marsden, D. (1975), *Workless*, Penguin.

Mills, C.W. (1963), 'Situated Actions and Vocabularies of Motive', in I.L. Horowitz, (ed.), *Power, Politics and People: The Collected Essays of C. Wright Mills*, Oxford University Press, New York.

Mills, C.W. (1970), *The Sociological Imagination*, Penguin.

Ministry of Education (1956), *Technical Education*, HMSO.

Ministry of Education (1957), *Liberal Education in Technical Colleges*, circular 323 HMSO.

Ministry of Education (1961), *Better Opportunities in Technical Education*, HMSO.

Ministry of Education (1962), *General Studies in Technical Colleges*, HMSO.

Moser, C.A. and Kalton, G. (1971), *Survey Methods in Social Investigation*, Heinemann.

Musgrave, P.M. (1967), *Technical Change, the Labour Force and Education*, Oxford University Press.

National Association of Teachers in Further and Higher Education (1977), *The Education, Training and Employment of the 16–19 Age Group*.

National Institution of Adult Education (1955), *Liberal Education in a Technical Age*, Parrish.

Orwell, G. (1962), *The Road to Wigan Pier*, Penguin.

Pearce, I. (1978), 'The Death of Essay: English under BEC', *Journal of Further and Higher Education*, vol. 2, no. 1, Spring.

Peters, A.J. (1967), *British Further Education: a Critical Textbook*, Pergamon Press.

Phillips, D. (1973), 'Young and Unemployed in a Northern City', in D. Weir (ed.), *Men and Work in Modern Britain*, Fontana.

Raffe, D. (1979), 'The Alternative Route Reconsidered', *Sociology*, vol. 13, January.

Roberts, I. (1977), '16–19 The Vital Age Group in FE', *Education and Training*, May.

Roberts, I. (1978), *School and Further Education*, Working Paper no. 3, NUT.

Robinson, E. (1968), *The New Polytechnics – a Radical Policy for Higher Education*, Penguin.

Robinson, P. (1977), *Poverty and Education*, Methuen.

Ryrie, A.C., and Weir, A.D. (1978), *Getting a Trade*, Hodder & Stoughton.

Saussure, R. (1960), *Course in General Linguistics*, Peter Owen.

Schutz, A. (1972), *The Phenomenology of the Social World*, Heinemann.

Seymour, R., and Acres, D. (1974), *General and Liberal Studies – A Teachers' Handbook*, Darton, Longman & Todd.

Shapin, S., and Barnes, B. (1976), 'Science, Nature and Control: Interpreting Mechanics' Institutes', in R. Dale *et al.* (eds), *Schooling and Capitalism: A Sociological Reader*, Routledge & Kegan Paul.

Sharp, R., and Green, A. (1975), *Education and Social Control*, Routledge & Kegan Paul.

Shipman, M. (1974), *Inside a Curriculum Project*, Methuen.

Silverman, D. (1970), *The Theory of Organisations*, Heinemann.

Simon, M. (1977), 'Youth into Industry. A Study of Young People's Attitudes to Work in a large Midlands Factory', National Youth Bureau.

Singer, E.J., and MacDonald, D. (1970), 'Is Apprenticeship Outdated?', Institute of Personnel Management.

Snow, C.P. (1959), *The Two Cultures: A Second Look*, Cambridge University Press.

Stanton, G. (1978), *Experience, Reflection, Learning,* Futher Education Curriculum Review Unit, DES.

Thompson, E.P. (1967), 'Time, Work Discipline and Industrial Capitalists', in *Past and Present*, no. 38, December.

Tipton, B. (1973), *Conflict and Change in a Technical College*, Brunel Further Education Monographs, No. 6, Hutchinson Educational.

Training Services Agency (1975), *Grouping of Skills*.

Training Services Agency (1976), *The Vocational Preparation of Young People: A Discussion Paper*.

Training Services Agency (with Manpower Services Commission) (1975), *Vocational Preparation for Young People*.

Tyler, W. (1977), *The Sociology of Educational Inequality*, Methuen.

Vaizey, J. (1967), *The Political Economy of Education*, Duckworth.

Vaizey, J. (1975), *Education in the Modern World*, Weidenfeld & Nicolson.

Vaizey, J., and Sheehan, J. (1968), *Resources for Education*, Allen & Unwin.

Venables, E. (1967), *The Young Worker at College. A Study of a Local Tech.*, Faber & Faber.

Venables, E. (1974), *Apprentices Out of Their Time: A Follow-up Study*, Faber & Faber.

Venables, P.F.R. *et al.* (1955), *Technical Education: its aims, organisation and future development*, Bell.

Warnock, M. *et al.* (1978) *Special Educational Needs: Report of the Committee of enquiry into the education of handicapped children and young people* (Warnock Report, Cmnd 7212), HMSO.

Watts, A.G. (1978), 'The implications of school leaver unemployment for careers education in schools', *Journal of Curriculum Studies*, vol. 10, no. 3, September.

Weatherell, T. (1974), *Looking Forward to Work*, HMSO.

Webb, B. (1948), *Our Partnership* (ed. B. Drake and M.I. Cole), Cambridge University Press (first published by London School of Economics).

Webb, S. (1948), *Fabian Essays*, Cambridge University Press (in association with LSE).

Webb, S. and B. (1898), *Industrial Democracy*. London School of Economics.

Wedderburn, D., and Crompton, R. (1972), *Workers' Attitudes to Technical Change*, Cambridge University Press.

Westoby, A. (1974), 'Economics and Human Capital', in D. Holly (ed.) (1974).

Wilensky, H. (1964), 'The Professionalisation of Everyone', *American Journal of Sociology*, May.

Williams, G. (1957), *Recruitment to Skilled Trades*, Routledge & Kegan Paul.

Williams, R. (1958), *Culture and Society 1780-1950*, Chatto & Windus.

Williams, R. (1961), *The Long Revolution*, Chatto & Windus.

Young, M.F.D. (ed.) (1971), *Knowledge and Control*, Collier-Macmillan.

Young, M.F.D., and Whitty, G. (eds) (1977), *Society, State and Schooling*, Falmer Press.

Zuckerman Report (1956), *Scientific Manpower in Great Britain*, Advisory Council on Scientific Policy and Ministry of Labour, HMSO.

Index